GarageBand

THE MISSING MANUAL

*The book that
should have been
in the box*

GarageBand
THE MISSING MANUAL

David Pogue

POGUE PRESS™
O'REILLY®

Beijing • Cambridge • Farnham • Köln • Paris • Sebastopol • Taipei • Tokyo

GarageBand: The Missing Manual
by David Pogue

Published by O'Reilly Media, Inc., 1005 Gravenstein Highway North,
Sebastopol, CA 95472.

O'Reilly Media books maybe purchased for educational, business, or sales
promotional use. Online editions are also available for most titles: *safari@oreilly.
com*. For more information, contract our corporate/institutional sales department:
(800) 998-9938 or *corporate@oreilly.com*.

June 2004:   First Edition.

 This book uses RepKover™, a durable and flexible lay-flat binding.

ISBN: 0-596-00695-0

Table of Contents

The Missing Credits

About the Author

 **David Pogue** is the weekly computer columnist for the *New York Times,* technology correspondent for *CBS News Sunday Morning,* and the creator of the Missing Manual series. He's the author or co-author of 30 books, including ten in this series and six in the "For Dummies" line (including *Macs, Magic, Opera,* and *Classical Music*). In his other life, David is a former Broadway show conductor, a magician, and an incorrigible pianist (photos await at *www.davidpogue.com*).

He welcomes feedback about his Missing Manual titles by email at *david@pogueman. com.* (If you're seeking technical help, however, please refer to the help sources listed in Chapter 12.)

About the Creative Team

Nan Barber (copy editor) co-authored *Office X for the Macintosh: The Missing Manual* and *Office 2001 for Macintosh: The Missing Manual.* She's the principal copy editor for the Missing Manual series, having edited the Missing Manual titles on Mac OS X, Mac OS 9, AppleWorks, iMovie, Dreamweaver, Windows XP, and Mac OS X Hints. Email: *nanbarber@mac.com.*

Rose Cassano (cover illustration) has worked as an independent designer and illustrator for 20 years. Assignments have spanned everything from the nonprofit sector to corporate clientele. She lives in beautiful Southern Oregon, grateful for the miracles of modern technology that make living and working there a reality. Email: *cassano@cdsnet.net.* Web: *www.rosecassano.com.*

Phil Simpson (design and layout) works out of his office in Stamford, Connecticut, where he has had his graphic design business since 1982. He is experienced in many facets of graphic design, including corporate identity, publication design, and corporate and medical communications. Email: *pmsimpson@earthlink.net.*

Acknowledgements

The Missing Manual series is a joint venture between Pogue Press (the dream team introduced on these pages) and O'Reilly Media, Inc. (a dream publishing partner). I'm indebted, as always, to Tim O'Reilly, Mark Brokering, Glenn Bisignani, and the rest of the gang.

I was particularly fortunate to hook up with several members of Apple's iLife team, who proved to be gifted communicators, software visionaries, and really great guys. Product managers Fred Johnson and Xander Soren provided an articulate and enthusiastic entree to GarageBand—and they introduced me to Gary Drenan. Gary may have authored GarageBand's online help, but the help he gave *me* online—by serving as technical reviewer for this book—was absolutely incredible. Apple is lucky to have him, but I was luckier.

Thanks are due, too, to agent David Rogelberg; proofreaders Danny Marcus and Stephanie English; copy editor John Cacciatore; Steve Alper, who created the sheet-music examples in Appendix A; Dave McFarland, who wrote the tutorial song in Chapter 3 (on his first attempt at GarageBand, no less!); and, above all, to Jennifer, Kelly, and Tia, who make these books—and everything else—possible.

—*David Pogue*

The Missing Manual Series

Missing Manuals are witty, superbly written guides to computer products that don't come with printed manuals (which is just about all of them). Each book features a handcrafted index; cross-references to specific page numbers (not just "see Chapter 14"); and RepKover, a detached-spine binding that lets the book lie perfectly flat without the assistance of weights or cinder blocks.

Recent and upcoming titles include:

- *Google: The Missing Manual by Sarah Milstein and Rael Dornfest*
- *iLife '04: The Missing Manual* by David Pogue et al.
- *iPhoto 4: The Missing Manual* by David Pogue and Derrick Story
- *iMovie 4 and iDVD: The Missing Manual* by David Pogue
- *Mac OS X: The Missing Manual* (Panther Edition) by David Pogue
- *FileMaker Pro 7: The Missing Manual* by Geoff Coffey
- *iPod & iTunes: The Missing Manual, 2nd Edition* by J.D. Biersdorfer
- *Switching to the Mac: The Missing Manual* by David Pogue
- *Mac OS X Hints: Panther Edition* by Rob Griffiths
- *Dreamweaver MX 2004: The Missing Manual* by David Sawyer McFarland
- *Mac OS 9: The Missing Manual* by David Pogue
- *Office X for Macintosh: The Missing Manual* by Nan Barber, Tonya Engst, and David Reynolds
- *AppleWorks 6: The Missing Manual* by Jim Elferdink and David Reynolds
- *Windows XP Home Edition: The Missing Manual* by David Pogue
- *Windows XP Pro: The Missing Manual* by David Pogue, Craig Zacker, and Linda Zacker

Introduction

GarageBand is an extremely powerful, easy-to-use program that lets anyone create professional sounding musical recordings. But as you can imagine, not everybody was thrilled when Apple released it.

"They're putting too much power in the hands of amateurs," complained certain professional musicians. "This is like when Apple came out with desktop publishing. Everybody used all 22 fonts in every document, and every flyer and newsletter looked like a ransom note for the next two years."

And sure enough, on the Web sites where people post their GarageBand compositions, you can find a lot of polished, professional sounding, handsomely processed...dreck.

But Apple has a long history of taking elite creative tools, simplifying them, and making them available to the masses. Yes, iMovie lets amateurs make absolutely terrible films—but it has also open the gates to talented filmmakers who otherwise would have lived in obscurity. One iMovie movie actually won a prize at Sundance last year!

In this regard, GarageBand's cultural effects maybe even more profound. Until recently, the record companies were the gatekeepers to America's pop-music marketplace, and therefore the dictators of musical taste to the masses. After all, the record companies had sole possession of the two things talented musicians needed to build an audience:

- **The production facilities,** like recording studios, equipment, and engineers, and

- **The distribution channels**—namely, record stores.

As you're already aware, the Internet turned out to be a killer replacement, or at least companion, to the traditional distribution systems. A song, photo, or movie can become popular on the Internet without any help from a record company, publisher, or Hollywood studio—in fact, it can be all over the world in a matter of days. So much for the iron grip the record companies once had on the distribution channels.

With GarageBand, the other shoe has now dropped. Suddenly, no-name singers and undiscovered players can produce recordings that sound like they were made at a $1,000-an-hour recording studio. No longer must great talent remain untapped, or recorded on a tape recorder with an accompaniment by the local church organist. In the "American Idol" era, new artists can grow from the grass roots—and inevitably will.

The Two GarageBand Challenges

Before you fill out your Grammy award application, however, two cautions are in order.

First, GarageBand is much more demanding of your Mac than its little i-cousins (iPhoto, iTunes, and so on). Its underlying technology was spun out from a $1,000 professional recording program called Logic, which Apple acquired in 2002 when it bought a company called Emagic.

As one result, GarageBand contains some of the world's most sophisticated musical-instrument and studio-effect simulators. As another result, however, GarageBand craves memory and processor power few other programs you'll ever use. Your first challenge in using GarageBand, therefore, will be making it comfortable on your Mac.

At first, you may find that job about as exciting as feeding a team of sumo wrestlers who've taken up residence in your guest room. But this book, especially Chapter 10, will ease the way.

The second challenge you'll face is understanding the two different kinds of musical information that GarageBand can record, edit, and play back (which, not too long ago, required two different pieces of music software). For more detail, see Figure I-1.

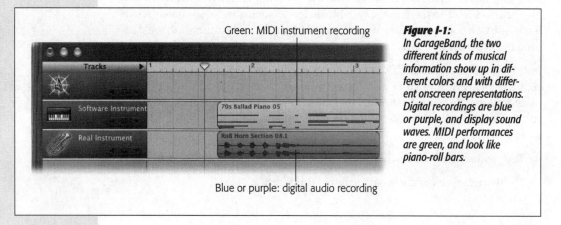

Green: MIDI instrument recording

Blue or purple: digital audio recording

Figure I-1:
In GarageBand, the two different kinds of musical information show up in different colors and with different onscreen representations. Digital recordings are blue or purple, and display sound waves. MIDI performances are green, and look like piano-roll bars.

First, there's digital audio. That's the kind of sound you record with a microphone, like singing or acoustic guitar playing. You may have some experience with recording sounds on the Mac, especially considering most models have a built-in microphone. Digital audio plays back exactly as you recorded it, but doesn't give you much editing flexibility. You can't fix a wrong note, for example, or transpose the whole thing (shift it higher or lower in pitch to a different key).

Second, there's MIDI data, which may be less familiar to you. To record this kind of information, most people hook the Mac up to an electric piano, a synthesizer, or even a MIDI controller (a keyboard that makes no sounds itself). When you play the keys, GarageBand records the notes you play ("OK, you played F-sharp for one second, then G, then A"), but not the sounds themselves. Later, you can edit these recorded notes, erase the bad ones, draw in new ones, transpose them, shorten them, and so on—like word processing for music. And you can change the instrument sound that plays them back at any time.

You'll find much more detail on these two different kinds of musical recordings beginning on page 16.

The point is that if you can overcome these two challenges—the one in your Mac, the other in your brain—GarageBand offers an incredible musical experience. It will let you into a world of music production that was once restricted to people with several thousand, or hundreds of thousands, of dollars to invest.

About This Book

Don't let the rumors fool you. GarageBand may be simple, but it isn't simplistic. It offers a wide range of tools, shortcuts, and professional features. Unfortunately, many of the best techniques aren't covered in the only "manual" you get with GarageBand—its electronic help screens.

This book is designed to serve as the GarageBand manual—the book that should have been in the box. It explores each feature in depth, offers shortcuts and workarounds, and unearths features that the online help doesn't even mention.

Note: This book assumes that you have GarageBand 1.1. If you began with an earlier version, which your Software Update program should have offered to the free update to version 1.1 one day when you were online. If not, you can download this important upgrade from *www.apple.com/garageband*. (Many of the features described here won't make sense if you have an older version.)

About the Outline

This book is divided into three parts, each containing several chapters:

- Part 1, **Building a Hit,** covers the three primary song-construction tools of GarageBand: loops, recordings from a MIDI instrument, and recordings from a microphone or line input. These seven chapters also cover editing these elements, rerecording over parts you messed up, adding effects, using guitar-amp simulators, and so on.

- Part 2, **Beyond the Garage,** takes you from the point of finishing your song into the big, wide world: exporting it to iTunes; burning it to CD; posting it online; using it as background music in iMovie, iPhoto, or iDVD; and so on.

These are also the administrative chapters. They describe how to overcome GarageBand's "I'm gasping for memory and power" messages, how to troubleshoot the program and your gear, how to install new sounds and plug-ins, which free and shareware add-ons are worth trying, and which Web sites to visit for help, in formation, and song swapping.

- Part 4, **Appendixes,** offers three useful references. One describes every menu in GarageBand, to make sure everything's covered in this book. Another shows off all of the program's keyboard shortcuts. Finally, the Music Class Crash Course offers a highly condensed explanation of the sorts of musical concepts you'll encounter in GarageBand: tempo, key, time signature, eighth notes, swing, and so on.

Along the way, you'll get a lot more out of these pages if you have the free GarageBand Examples CD, whose music and narration illustrates some of the most hard-to-explain Garageband concepts. You can download it as described on page 13.

About→These→Arrows

Throughout this book, and throughout the Missing Manual series, you'll find sentences like this one: "Open the System folder→Libraries→Fonts folder." That's shorthand for a much longer instruction that directs you to open three nested folders in sequence. That instruction might read: "On your hard drive, you'll find a folder called System. Open it. Inside the System folder window is a folder called Libraries. Open that. Inside *that* folder is yet another one called Fonts. Double-click to open it, too."

You'll encounter this notation in this book several times. GarageBand's components are scattered in various folder locations, which are useful to visit when you want to add new sounds, effects, or loops to GarageBand's arsenal.

About MissingManuals.com

At *www.missingmanuals.com,* you'll find news, articles, and updates to the books in this series.

But if you click the name of this book and then the Errata link, you'll find a unique resource: a list of corrections and updates that have been made in successive printings of this book. You can mark important corrections right into your own copy of the book, if you like.

In fact, the same page offers an invitation for you to submit such corrections and updates yourself. In an effort to keep the book as up-to-date and accurate as possible, each time we print more copies of this book, we'll make any confirmed corrections you've suggested. Thanks in advance for reporting any glitches you find!

In the meantime, we'd love to hear your suggestions for new books in the Missing Manual line. There's a place for that on the Web site, too, as well as a place to sign up for free email notification of new titles in the series.

The Very Basics

You'll find very little jargon or nerd terminology in this book. You will, however, encounter a few terms and concepts that you'll see frequently in your Macintosh life. They include:

- **Clicking.** This book offers three kinds of instructions that require you to use the mouse or trackpad attached to your Mac. To *click* means to point the arrow cursor at something onscreen and then—without moving the cursor at all—press and release the clicker button on the mouse (or laptop trackpad). To *double-click*, of course, means to click twice in rapid succession, again without moving the cursor at all. And to *drag* means to move the cursor while keeping the button continuously pressed.

  When you're told to ⌘-*click* something, you click while pressing the ⌘ key (next to the Space bar). Such related procedures as *Shift-clicking, Option-clicking,* and *Control-clicking* work the same way—just click while pressing the corresponding key on the bottom row of your keyboard.

- **Menus.** The *menus* are the words in the lightly striped bar at the top of your screen. You can either click one of these words to open a pull-down menu of commands

---

FREQUENTLY ASKED QUESTION

10 Ways to Make GarageBand More Like a Garage Band

In a raging debate on Apple's discussion forum online, GarageBand fans were wondering just how appropriate the name GarageBand was for such a sophisticated piece of software.

Which is when author and programmer Richard MacLemale offered his own top ten suggestions to Apple for making GarageBand more like a real garage band:

10. When you launched GarageBand, the room would fill with nasty cigarette smoke.

9. When you were trying to choose a keyboard sound, the drum loops would get bored and leave for a cig break.

8. When you launched the program, the guitar loops wouldn't be there yet—they'd be late.

7. Using guitar loops too much would result in breaking a string.

6. After a while, the drum loops would go out of tune.

5. Bringing up the Rhodes instrument would require first lifting 100 pounds.

4. While playing a song, each instrument would gradually turn *itself* up.

3. The drum loops would complain when you play too many slow songs in a row.

2. The bass loops would eventually leave the program entirely, because they want to spend more time with their girlfriend.

1. The entire program would be nonfunctional within a year, as the remaining instruments will leave to go to college.

Hmm…maybe GarageBand is good just the way it is.

(and then click again on a command), or click and *hold* the button as you drag down the menu to the desired command (and release the button to activate the command). Either method works fine.

Note: Apple has officially changed it calls the little menu that pops up when you Control-click something on the screen. It's still a contextual menu, in that the menu choices depend on the context of what you click—but it's now called a shortcut menu. That term not only matches what it's called in Windows, but it's slightly more descriptive about its function. Shortcut menu is the term you'll find in this book.

• **Keyboard shortcuts.** Every time you take your hand off the keyboard to move the mouse, you lose time and potentially disrupt your creative flow. That's why many experienced Mac fans use keystroke combinations instead of menu commands wherever possible. ⌘-P opens the Print dialog box, for example, and ⌘-M minimizes the current window to the Dock.

When you see a shortcut like ⌘-Q (which closes the current program), it's telling you to hold down the ⌘ key, and, while it's down, type the letter Q, and then release both keys.

If you've mastered this much information, you have all the technical background you need to enjoy *GarageBand: The Missing Manual.*

Part One:
Building a Hit

1

Setting Up the Garage

GarageBand is a great name. It calls to mind all the great bands that began as amateur acts that rehearsed in some kid's garage. The name suggests the homemade, independent nature of the music you'll be making. It even carries overtones of the us-versus-them, little-guy-against-The-Man, counterculture spirit that Apple has always embraced.

The truth is, though, GarageBand is practically incapable of producing anything but professional, polished music—a far cry, that is, from the slightly out-of-tune, drum-heavy work of true first-time garage bands. That's where the name isn't such a slam dunk.

On the other hand, it's catchier than "GarageDigitalRecordingStudio."

This chapter introduces you to GarageBand. It teaches you how to *play back* music with GarageBand, and goes on to explain the difference between the two kinds of music the program works with (MIDI data and audio recordings). You'll learn how to create *new* music in the following chapters.

Equipment Requirements

Here are the official Apple minimum requirements for GarageBand:

- **A Mac whose processor is a 600MHz G3 or faster.** True, but you can't use the *Software Instruments* (see page 18) unless you have a G4 or later chip.
- **Mac OS X 10.2.6 or later.** Panther (Mac OS X 10.3) is ideal.

- **256 megabytes of memory.** Well, you might be able to record "Chopsticks" with two fingers with this much memory. But if you expect to create compositions much more elaborate than that, 512 MB is the bare minimum. A gigabyte or even more is better.

- **QuickTime 6.5.1 or later.** If GarageBand complains that you don't have this software, download it from *www.apple.com/quicktime.*

- **A screen with at least 1024-by-768-pixel resolution.** That would rule out, for example, blueberry and tangerine iBooks. Then again, they can't run GarageBand anyway.

- **2 gigabytes of hard drive space.** That's what you need to install GarageBand, although there are some sneaky tricks for moving GarageBand onto a different hard drive if necessary (see page 168).

- **Musical equipment (optional).** You can use GarageBand happily for years using nothing but your Mac and its mouse. But if you have even a little musical talent—even the ability to sing in tune—you can get even more out of the program by adding musical gear like a microphone, synthesizer (electronic MIDI keyboard), or guitar (see Chapters 4 and 6).

The point is that GarageBand is a *very* hungry program. It craves memory and horsepower like Donald Trump craves publicity.

If you're getting error messages like "Part of the song was not played," "The hard disk is not fast enough," and "Disk is too slow," flip immediately to Chapter 10 for some explanations and solutions.

Either that, or buy a new Mac.

Installing GarageBand

If GarageBand didn't come preinstalled on your Mac, you can buy it as part of Apple's iLife '04 software suite. You can buy iLife at computer stores or online stores like *www.apple.com.*

iLife is a $50 DVD that includes GarageBand, iTunes, iMovie, iPhoto, and iDVD. (You can't buy GarageBand separately, and you can't download it. Two gigabytes would be a *long* download.)

When you run the iLife installer, you'll be offered a choice of programs to install. Install all five programs, if you like (and if you have the required 4.3 GB of hard drive space), or just GarageBand by itself.

When the installation process is over, you'll find the GarageBand icon in your Applications folder. (In the Finder, choose Go→Applications, or press Shift-⌘-A, to open this folder.) If the GarageBand icon—the little electric guitar—isn't already in the Dock, take a moment to drag it there, so you'll be able to open it more conveniently from now on.

Note: For the moment, don't open GarageBand by double-clicking its icon. (If you do so, the program assumes that you want to create a new piece of music, and asks you to specify a title, time signature, and key signature. If that happens, click Cancel, and then Cancel again, at least for the purposes of this chapter.)

Opening GarageBand

For this guided tour, you need a GarageBand file that's already been completed. You can get yourself one by downloading the GarageBand Examples CD, a "virtual disc" available for free at *www.missingmanuals.com*. (In fact, the rest of this book assumes that you've already done so. For details, see the box on page 13.)

Once you've downloaded the GarageBand Examples disk, open the Chapter 1 folder and double-click the icon called "01—Garage Door." After a moment, GarageBand opens and presents you with the simulated studio shown in Figure 1-1.

Figure 1-1:
GarageBand isn't just the only iLife program that doesn't start with i; it's also the only program made of "wood." (You can move the window around by dragging any of the wood or "brushed aluminum" surfaces.) At first, the program tends to cower in a smallish window. Click the Zoom button to make it fill your screen— much better!

Zoom button   Playhead   Beat ruler   Timeline (track display)

Track headers   New Track   Play   Tempo   Master volume

Playback

You'll probably spend most of your time in GarageBand *playing back* music. That, after all, is the only way to fine-tune and perfect your work.

There's a Play button at your disposal—the big triangle indicated in Figure 1-1—but that's for suckers. Instead, press the Space bar. That's a much bigger target, and a very convenient start/stop control. (You may recognize it as the start/stop control for iTunes and iMovie, too.)

Once you've got the 01—Garage Door file open, press the Space bar to listen to this fonky, fonky piece. It's about a minute long.

Tip: If you hear nothing, it's probably because your Mac's speakers are turned down. You can adjust your Mac's overall volume by pressing the volume keys on the top row of your keyboard.

If you have a very old keyboard (or a very non-Apple one), and you therefore lack these keys, you can also adjust the volume by clicking the speaker *menulet* (the black, right-facing speaker icon in your menu bar).

(If the speaker control doesn't appear on your menu bar, open System Preferences, click the Sound icon, and then turn on "Show volume in menu bar.")

Whenever music is playing back, you can have all kinds of fun with it. For example:

• **Stop the music.** Press the Space bar again.

• **Slow it down (or speed it up).** Use the Tempo control, as shown in Figure 1-2.

• **Adjust the volume.** You can drag the master volume slider shown in Figure 1-1, or you can press ⌘-up arrow (louder) or ⌘-down arrow (softer). (Hey! Those are the same keystrokes as in iMovie and iTunes!)

• **Jump around in the song.** See the next section for navigation techniques. They work equally well whether the music is playing or not.

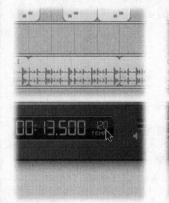

Figure 1-2:
Left: To adjust the tempo (speed) of your piece, position the arrow cursor on the number shown here (which shows how many beats per minute you're getting).

Right: Hold down the mouse button to produce a slider. You're setting the tempo for the entire piece; at least in GarageBand 1.1, you can't program in a change in tempo.

Cycling (Looping)

Looping means playing a certain section of the music over and over again continuously. (That's what musicians call it. Apple calls it *cycling*, because in GarageBand, the word *loop* has a very different meaning. You can read about loops in the next chapter.)

Cycling can be very handy in a number of different situations:

- **Recording.** When you're laying down new music from a MIDI keyboard, Garage-Band merges *everything* you play during all repetitions of the loop. So if your keyboard skills aren't especially dazzling, you can play one hand's part, or even one finger's part, on each "pass" through the loop. GarageBand adds all your passes together.

- **Editing.** In Chapter 5, you'll see that you can edit the notes in Software Instruments sections—adding or deleting notes, rewriting musical lines, and so on. By cycling the section you're editing, you can hear the effects of your edits even while you're making them, in the context of all the other playing instruments.

- **Playing.** Sometimes, it's useful to loop a section just for the sake of listening and analyzing—when a clashing note, for example, is driving you, well, loopy.

To loop a certain section of your piece, start by clicking the Cycle button (identified in Figure 1-3). Or just press the letter C key on your Mac's keyboard.

Either way, the Cycle button lights up, and a yellow stripe appears on the beat ruler (the numbered "ruler" strip at the top of the screen). That stripe—the *cycle region*—tells you which part of the song GarageBand intends to repeat.

UP TO SPEED

GarageBand Examples CD

A few examples make any learning process easier and more fun—and this book is no exception. Throughout this book, you'll find references to GarageBand project files, some finished and some intended for you to complete, on something called the GarageBand Examples CD.

You can download these files right now. First, visit *www.missingmanuals.com*. At the top of the page, click the "Missing CD" button.

You arrive at a page listing the downloadable files for the entire Missing Manual series. Under the GarageBand heading, click to download the "GarageBand Examples CD" disk image. It contains all of the sample music you'll work with in this book.

When the download is complete, you'll find on your desktop a file called GarageBand Examples.dmg. That's a disk image file, shown here at lower left.

When you double-click it, you'll find a second icon on your desktop, resembling a hard drive icon, shown here at lower right. (If Safari is your Web browser, just relax and wait as the icon opens automatically.) This is the actual "CD" icon. If you open it up, you'll find all the files for this book. Copy them to a folder on your hard drive, if you like.

If you're in a hurry or using a slow connection, you can also download the various tutorial pieces one at a time. You'll find them listed under the appropriate chapter numbers.

In a new song, the yellow stripe appears across measures 1 through 4. You can adjust its length and position, though, as shown in Figure 1-3.

If you tap the Space bar now, GarageBand plays *only* the music enclosed by that yellow stripe.

To end the cycling, click the Cycle button again to turn it off, or tap the letter C key again. (You can do that even while the music is playing.)

Yellow stripe: looped region

Figure 1-3:
Drag the yellow stripe to move it elsewhere in the song. It maintains its existing length. Or drag the ends of the yellow stripe to adjust its length. Either way, you're identifying which part of the song you want repeated endlessly.

Cycle button

letter C

Preroll Before the Loop

It's all well and good that GarageBand can endlessly repeat a certain section of music. In many circumstances, though, it would be even nicer if you could hear the looped section in context—that is, if you could hear the music leading up to it. In the music biz, you could say that you'd like to hear some preroll.

Trouble is, once you click the Cycle button, playback always begins right at the beginning of the looped region, even if you position the Playhead somewhere else first. You're deprived of the chance to hear the music leading up to the cycled chunk.

The solution: Turn cycling off (press the C key again). Position the Playhead where you want it—two measures before the loop, for example. Then begin playback, and turn cycling on (by tapping the letter C key) while the playback is under way.

GarageBand now does what you hoped: It waits to begin the loop until the Playhead reaches the yellow stripe.

Navigating the Music

Your current position in the song—that is, the spot from which you'll start recording or playing—is always indicated by the *Playhead* (Figure 1-1) and the moving vertical line beneath it.

You can drag the Playhead around manually, of course; you can also click anywhere in the beat ruler to make the Playhead snap to that spot. You can even jump to a spot in your piece by typing in its time or measures-and-beats position into the digital time display (page 59).

But you'll feel much more efficient if you take the time to learn GarageBand's navigational keyboard shortcuts:

- **Jump back to the beginning.** Pressing either the letter Z key or the Home key rewinds the piece to the beginning without missing a beat.

letter Z

Tip: On Mac laptops, the Z key is easier to press than the Home key, because triggering the Home function requires first pressing the Fn key in the lower-left corner. Too much trouble.

- **Jump to the end.** Press Option-Z or the End key. That's a great technique for people who like to build up their songs section by section. After you've finished the first part, you can jump to the end of it, ready to begin recording the second.

Note: As far as GarageBand's playback is concerned, the *end* of your piece isn't necessarily where the music stops. It's the point indicated by the small left-pointing triangle on the ruler.

Sometimes you'll trim a piece to make it shorter—and wind up stranding the End marker way off to the right, so that GarageBand "plays" a minute of silence after the actual music ends. In that case, you can fix the problem by dragging the End marker inward until it lines up with the end of the colored musical regions. (You can never drag it inward past the end of the music, though.)

- **Jump back, or ahead, a measure at a time.** As you may recall from your childhood music lessons, a *measure* is the natural building block of musical time. It's usually two, three, or four beats long. (You can think of a *beat* as one foot-tap, if you were tapping along with the music.)

  In GarageBand, the measures are indicated on a numbered *beat ruler* (identified in Figure 1-1) that helps you figure out where you are in the music. You can jump forward or back a measure at a time by pressing the left and right arrow keys. (Clicking the Rewind and Fast-forward buttons serves the same purpose.)

Tip: You can also *hold down* the arrow keys, or the onscreen Rewind and Fast-forward buttons, to zoom faster through the piece. Both of these techniques work even when the music is playing.

- **Jump right or left one screenful at a time.** Press the Page Up or Page Down key. (It may feel a little odd to press *up/down* keys to scroll *right/left*, but you'll get used to it.)

- **Zoom in or out.** Once you begin editing your own music, you'll occasionally want a God's-eye view of your whole piece for a visual overview of its structure. Or you'll want to zoom in to see the individual soundwaves or notes of a certain musical passage.

That's what the Control-right arrow and Control-left arrow keystrokes are for. They stretch and collapse the ruler, respectively, making the onscreen representation of your music take up more or less space. (You can also drag the Zoom slider beneath the instrument names, but that's more effort.)

Two Kinds of Music

If you've been reading along with half your brain on the book and half on the TV, turn off the TV for a minute. The following discussion may be one of the most important you'll encounter in your entire GarageBand experience.

Understanding how GarageBand produces music—or, rather, the *two* ways it can create music—is critically important. It will save you hours of frustration and confusion, and make you sound *really* smart at user-group meetings.

GarageBand is a sort of hybrid piece of music software. It can record and play back music in two different ways, which, once upon a time, required two different music-recording programs. They are:

Digital Recordings

GarageBand can record, edit, and play back digital audio—sound from a microphone, for example, or sound files you've dragged in from your hard drive (AIFF files, MP3 files, unprotected AAC files, or WAV files, for example).

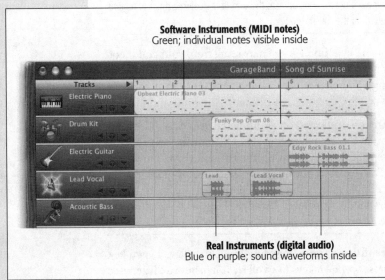

Software Instruments (MIDI notes)
Green; individual notes visible inside

Real Instruments (digital audio)
Blue or purple; sound waveforms inside

Figure 1-4:
GarageBand can process two very different kinds of musical material, which Apple calls Real Instruments and Software Instruments. Each offers advantages and drawbacks—but learning the difference is a key part of learning to love GarageBand.

If you've spent much time on computers before, you've already worked with digital recordings. They're the error beeps on every Mac, the soundtrack in iMovie, and whatever sounds you record using programs like SimpleSound, Amadeus, and ProTools. The files on a standard music CD are also digital audio files, and so are the ones you can buy at iTunes.com.

Digital recordings take up a lot of room on your hard drive: 10 MB per minute, to be exact (stereo, CD quality).

Digital recordings are also more or less permanent. GarageBand offers a few rudimentary editing features: you can copy and paste digital audio, chop pieces out, or slide a recording around in time. But in general, you can't *transpose* these recordings (make them play back at a different pitch), and you can't change their tempo (make them play back faster or slower).

Now then: To avoid terrifying novices with terminology like "digital recordings," Apple calls this kind of musical material *Real Instruments*.

On the GarageBand screen, Real Instrument recordings show up in blue or purple blocks, filled with what look like soundwaves (Figure 1-4).

MIDI Recordings

You know what a text file is, right? It's a universal exchange format for typed text.

In the early '80s, musicians could only look on longingly as their lyricists happily shot text files back and forth, word processor to word processor, operating system to operating system. Why, they wondered, couldn't there be a universal exchange format for *music*, so that Robin in Roanoke, with a Roland digital piano, could play back a song recorded by Susan on her DX-7 synthesizer in Salt Lake City?

Soon enough, there was a way: the *MIDI file*. MIDI stands for "musical instrument digital interface," otherwise known as "the musical version of the text file." To turn your Mac into a little recording studio, a musician had to rack up three charges on the Visa bill:

- **A MIDI keyboard,** such as a synthesizer.

- **A MIDI interface,** a little $40 box that connects the keyboard to the computer.

- **A MIDI sequencer,** which is software capable of recording, editing, and playing back what you play on the MIDI keyboard.

Although Apple would go bald in horror at using such intimidating language, Garage-Band is, in fact, a *MIDI sequencer*. It can record your keyboard performances; display your performance as bars on a grid, piano-roll style; allow you to edit those notes and correct your mistakes; and then play the whole thing back.

Behind the scenes, GarageBand memorizes each note you play as little more than a bunch of computer data. When it's playing back MIDI music, *you* might hear "Three Blind Mice," but your *Mac* is thinking like this:

```
01|01|000 E3 00|01|000    60
01|02|000 D3 00|01|000    72
01|03|002 C3 00|02|240    102
```

From left to right, these four columns tell the software when the note is played, which note is played, how long it's held down, and how hard the key was struck. That's everything a computer needs to perfectly recreate your original performance.

Musical information that's stored this way has some pretty huge advantages over digital recordings like AIFF files. For example, you can *change the notes*—drag certain notes higher or lower, make them last longer or shorter, or delete the bad ones entirely—whenever you like. You can also *transpose* a MIDI performance (change its key, so it plays higher or lower) with the click of a button. You can even speed up or slow down the playback as freely as you like. When you make such an adjustment, the Mac just thinks to itself, "Add 3 to each pitch," or "Play this list of notes slower."

The downside of MIDI recordings is, of course, that you can't *capture sound* with them. You can't represent singing, or rapping, or sound effects this way. A MIDI file is just a list of notes. It needs a *synthesizer* to give it a voice—like the synthesizer built into GarageBand.

Apple refers to the sounds of GarageBand's built-in synthesizer as *Software Instruments*. They show up in GarageBand as green blocks, filled with little horizontal bars representing the MIDI notes that will be triggered. Figure 1-4 makes this distinction clear.

Why It Matters

Why is it important to learn the difference between Real Instruments (sound recordings) and Software Instruments (MIDI data)? Because if you confuse the two, you can paint yourself into some very ugly corners.

For example, suppose you "lay down" (record) the background music for a new song you've written. But when you try to sing the vocals, you discover that the key is way too high for you.

If most of your accompaniment is constructed of MIDI (green) musical material, no big deal. You can transpose the entire band down into a more comfortable range.

But if you'd recorded, say, a string quartet as part of the backup group, you're out of luck. Those are Real Instruments (digital recordings), and you can't change their pitch.

The bottom line: If you began your work by constructing a backup band out of green Software Instruments, you should always finalize your song's key and tempo *before* you record live audio.

Another common example: GarageBand lets you perform a neat trick with Software Instruments. After recording a part using, for example, a MIDI keyboard, you can reassign the whole thing to a different instrument whenever you like, freely fiddling with the orchestration. You can drag a blob of notes from, say, the Electric Piano track into the Country Guitar track. The Mac doesn't care which sound you use; its job is simply to trigger the notes for "Three Blind Mice" (or whatever).

But although you can drag a blue or purple Real Instrument region into a different Real Instrument track, its instrument sound won't change (see Figure 1-5). In fact, you can *never* change the instrument sound of a Real Instrument.

Figure 1-5:
You can drag a Software Instrument recording into a different Software Instrument track, thereby changing which sound plays those notes. But GarageBand won't let you drag a Real Instrument snippet into a Software Instrument track.

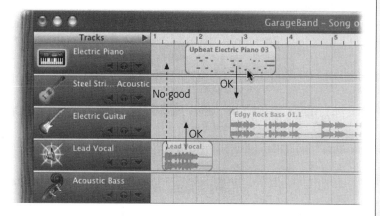

Tracks

When you work in GarageBand, the *timeline* is your primary canvas. It's something like the timeline view in iMovie: a scrolling map of the overall project, marked at the top by a *beat ruler* that helps you figure out where you are in the song.

Tracks are the horizontal, parallel stripes that represent instruments playing simultaneously. Which is lucky, because if this software could play only one instrument at a time, it would have to be renamed GarageSolo.

You'll learn how to *fill* these gray stripes in the following chapters. For the moment, though, it's useful to learn your way around the tracks themselves. After all, like the musicians in a real garage band, they're paid very little, but respond well if you treat them with a little respect.

As you read the following instructions, you might want to follow along by working with the Garage Door song you opened in the previous section (page 11).

Creating a Track

You can add a track in any of three ways.

- **Click the + button below the track names.** You can see this button in Figure 1-1.

- **Choose Track→New Track.** Or press Option-⌘-N.   Alt ⌘ N

  Both of these methods open the New Track dialog box shown in Figure 1-6. Click the appropriate tab—Real Instrument or Software Instrument—and then, on the right side of the dialog box, click the *name* of the kind of instrument you plan to add.

(If you intend to record sound—that is, if what you need is a Real Instrument track—you can bypass the dialog box by simply choosing Track→New Basic Track. Details in Chapter 6.)

You can read much more about this process in the tutorial at the end of the next chapter.

Tip: A track's *header* is the dark area at the left edge of the track, where you see its name and icon. To find out which kind of track you're dealing with—Real Instrument or Software Instrument—click the track header. If it turns greenish, you're dealing with a Software Instrument (MIDI) track. If it's purplish, you've clicked a Real Instrument (live recording) track.

You can select one track after another, "walking" through the list of them, by pressing the up or down arrow keys on your keyboard.

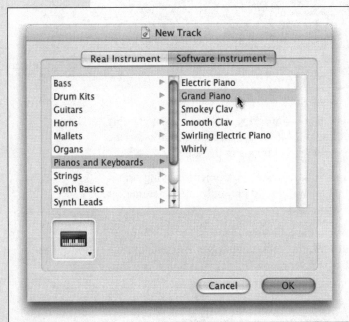

Figure 1-6:
A certain track can handle either a Real Instrument (sound file) or a Software Instrument (MIDI notes), so you have to tell GarageBand which sort of instrument you intend to add. If you're going to record a Real Instrument, also specify which effects you want GarageBand to add to the track, like reverb or EQ (equalization). Details in Chapter 7.

• **Drag a loop into an empty gray spot in the** timeline **(the track display area).** Chapter 2 covers this method in delicious detail.

In any case, a new track appears *below* all the existing tracks.

Tip: If you have a standard, preferred "combo"—drums at the bottom, bass line above that, then piano, then guitar, and so on—you can save a lot of time by building an empty GarageBand template with this track structure. Save this empty file to your desktop. Each time you want to work from this template, open it—and then before filling it with music, choose File→Save As and name the song you're about to create.

The number of simultaneous tracks that GarageBand can play depends on the horse-power of your Mac and which *kind* of tracks they are; Software Instruments make the Mac work a lot harder than Real Instrument recordings. On slower Macs, four or five tracks is about the limit; ten or twelve tracks is typical on a Power Mac G4. If you have a fully tricked-out, top-of-the-line Power Mac G5 loaded with RAM, then you can build tracks into the dozens.

Fortunately, there's a whole chapter's worth of tips and tricks for helping GarageBand overcome the strain of track-intensive compositions waiting in Chapter 10.

Tip: As you add and work with tracks, keep your eye on the Playhead handle. As described in Figure 1-7, it's an early-warning system that lets you know when you're overwhelming your Mac.

Figure 1-7:
As you play and record music, the Playhead triangle darkens—from white, to yellow, to orange, and finally red—to indicate how much trouble your Mac is having. If it spends a lot of time in the red, you're approaching your maximum track limit.

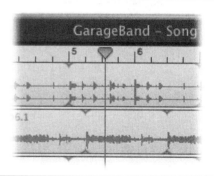

Rearranging Tracks

You can rearrange your tracks' top-to-bottom order just by dragging them vertically. You might, for example, like to keep the track you're working on up at the top where it's easy to find. Or maybe you like to keep your tracks in traditional "score order" (that is, as the instruments would appear in standard full-orchestra sheet music).

Deleting a Track

Before you nuke one of your tracks, scroll through the whole thing to make sure you're not about to vaporize some important musical material. (Consider zooming out—tap Control-left arrow repeatedly—until the entire track fits on your screen.)

Then click the track header to select it. Choose Track→Delete Track, or press ⌘-Delete, to send the track into the great sheet music stack in the sky. (Of course, GarageBand's amazing Undo command can resurrect it if necessary; see the box on page 22.)

Renaming a Track

Click a track's header to select it, and then click carefully, once, on its name. It's now a simple matter to edit the track's name, as shown in Figure 1-8.

Figure 1-8:
If a track header is already selected, click once on the track's name to open its "renaming rectangle." If not, click inside the track header's colored area first, then click the track name. (Just don't double-click the track name; you'll open up a dialog box by accident.) Hold your breath and remain very still. At last, the name-editing box appears.

Edit the name by typing. Then press Return or Enter, or click somewhere else in GarageBand, to make the new name "stick."

Track Characteristics

The importance of the New Track dialog box shown in Figure 1-6 depends on what kind of musical material you intend to record (that is, which of the two tabs you click):

- **Real Instrument.** This tab lists instruments, all right, but they actually refer to *effects presets* that contain canned settings for reverb, echo, and other processing

---

GEM IN THE ROUGH

There's Undo, and Then There's Undo

GarageBand offers a multiple-level Undo command. That is, you can take back more than one editing step, backing up in time. GarageBand, in fact, can take back the last 30 steps. Choose the Edit→Undo command (or press ⌘-Z), you can rewind your file closer and closer to its condition when you last saved it. (Or if you haven't saved the file, Undo takes you closer and closer to the moment when you opened it.)

That fine print may startle people who are used to, say, Microsoft Word, which lets you keep undoing even past the point of saving a document. It's a good argument for saving a GarageBand file less frequently—because once you save the document, you lose the ability to undo changes up to that point.

Of course, if you really do want to rewind your work all the way back to the instant when you last saved the piece, you can bypass all of those Edit→Undos and choose instead, File→Revert to Saved. GarageBand tosses out all the work you've done since the last save.

And one last thing: If you rewind too far, and you Undo your way past a good edit you made, you also have a multiple Edit→Redo command at your disposal. In effect, it undoes the Undos.

---

effects that have been optimized for each instrument type. The actual instrument sound is determined by your microphone or whatever electronic instrument you hook up to your Mac. Chapter 6 has details.

- **Software Instrument.** This tab also lists instruments, but here, you're choosing an instrument *sound* that will play when you press the keys of your MIDI keyboard. Details in Chapter 4.

Tip: Either way you can also choose an icon for the track, using the pop-up menu at the lower-left corner. Apple gives you 68 little graphics to choose from—every instrument in GarageBand, plus silhouettes of singers. (These are purely graphic ornaments; they don't affect the sound in any way.)

To open this palette of icons, by the way, you don't have to click the tiny, down-pointing triangle, as you might expect. Instead, click squarely on the icon itself. The broader target means quicker access.

The appearance of the New Track dialog box is not, fortunately, the only chance you get to adjust these parameters.

You can summon the same box at any time, even after recording into the track, by double-clicking the track header, by double-clicking the track header, or, if a track is already selected, by choosing Track→Track Info (⌘-I). The resulting dialog box is now called Track Info, but it looks overwhelmingly familiar.

Note: In fact, when you open the Track Info dialog box, you get a Details button at the bottom that you *don't* get in its New Track dialog box. Details on effects in Chapter 6.

You also get a Master Track tab at the top of the dialog box; it's described in Chapter 7.

Muting and Soloing Tracks

Most of the time, GarageBand plays all of your tracks simultaneously—and most of the time, that's what you want.

Sometimes, though, it's useful to ask one track to drop out for a minute. You might want to mute a track when:

- You've recorded two different versions of a part, and you want to see which one sounds better.
- You're trying to isolate a wrong note, and you want to use the process of elimination to figure out which track it's in.
- The Playhead is bright red, indicating that the Mac is gasping under its load of tracks. So you'd like to lighten its burden by shutting off a couple of tracks without deleting them forever.

Silencing a track is easy: Just click the little speaker icon below the track's name (see Figure 1-9). Or, if the track header is selected, just tap the letter M key on your keyboard.

The speaker, officially called the Mute button, "lights up" in blue, which means: "I'm shutting up until you change your mind." The regions of notes in that track grow pale to drive home the point. (You can turn the Mute button on or off *while* the music is playing—a great way to compare your mix with and without a certain instrument.)

There's nothing to stop you from muting *more* than one track, either. If you need the entire percussion section to sit out for a minute, so be it.

Of course, if you find yourself muting more than half of your tracks, you should be using the *Solo* button instead. That's the tiny pair of headphones right next to the Mute button.

Here again, the point is to control which tracks play, but the logic is now reversed. When you click the headphones (or, if the track header is selected, press the letter S key on your Mac's keyboard), that's the *only* track you hear. The note regions in all *other* tracks grow pale.

UP TO SPEED

The Weirdness of the Files

Veteran Mac fans know that some programs, like Word and TextEdit, create documents—that is, individual file icons on the hard drive.

Other programs, like iMovie, create project folders filled with supporting elements like sound and movie clips.

GarageBand falls into a third category unto itself.

When you save a new GarageBand song, it appears to be a standard, self-contained document file. You'll soon discover, though, that it doesn't act like a document file. For example, you can't attach it to an outgoing email message in Entourage unless you first compress it as a .zip or .sit file.

Turns out GarageBand creates a sort of hybrid, a cross between a folder and a file, known as a package. A Mac OS X package looks like an icon, but acts like a folder, in that it contains other files and folders.

In times of troubleshooting—for example, when you're trying to figure out why a certain GarageBand "document" is

so big—you can actually open up one of these packages to see what's inside.

To do so, Control-click the GarageBand song icon and, from the shortcut menu, choose Show Package Contents, as shown here. Lo and behold, a new window opens, exactly as though you'd opened a folder.

Inside you'll find two important elements. First, there's the project-Data file, which is the actual "edit list" that tells GarageBand what to play when. (If you're familiar with iMovie, the projectData file is the equivalent of the iMovie project document.)

Second, there's the Media folder (again, exactly as in an iMovie project folder). Here, GarageBand stashes several kinds of song component: any digital audio files you've recorded (singing tracks, for example); copies of sound files you added to a composition by dragging them into the program from the Finder; and in some cases (page 171), copies of any loops you've used in your masterpiece.

Oxymoronic though it may sound, you can actually Solo as many tracks as you like. All *other* tracks are silent.

To turn a track's Mute or Solo button off again, click it again (or press the M or S key a second time).

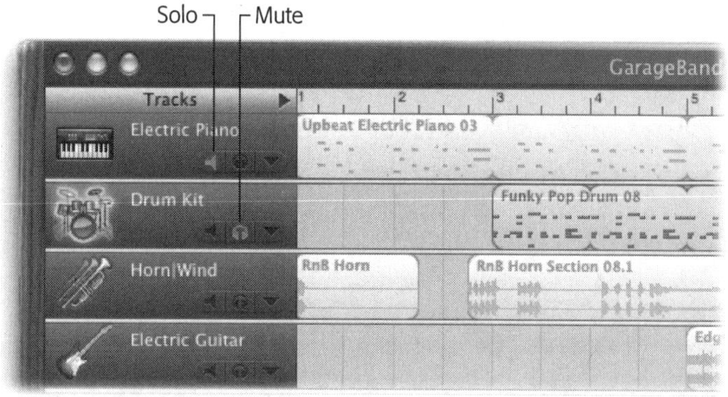

Figure 1-9:
You can tackle the on/off status of your tracks in two ways: either by specifying which ones don't play (by turning on their Mute buttons), or by specifying which tracks are the only ones that play (by turning on their Solo buttons).

Loops

Apple claims that GarageBand can be a blast even if your mastery of music never even progressed to the "Chopsticks" stage. And it's true: GarageBand lets you create authentic-sounding, studio-quality music even if you can't carry a tune, let alone a tuba. This chapter, dear nonmusicians, is sure to be one of your favorites.

That's because GarageBand comes with over 1,100 *loops*—short, prerecorded snippets performed in recording studios by professionals who most certainly do know their instruments. According to Apple, some of GarageBand's Motown drum loops, in fact, were played by the original studio musicians who recorded classic Motown hits like "My Girl" and "I Heard it Through the Grapevine."

Loops are only a few seconds long, but they're designed to repeat seamlessly for as long as you specify. That's a serious help when you want to create a drum part, for example.

Using some extremely advanced technological mojo, GarageBand manages to make every loop sound good with almost any other. So all you have to do is choose the drum beat, bass line, and guitar noodling you like (for example), and trust GarageBand to make them all sound like they were recorded in perfect sync. As you'll see, it's all about dragging and dropping.

Starting a New GarageBand Project

The first time you open GarageBand—or whenever you choose File→New—you get the dialog box shown in Figure 2-1.

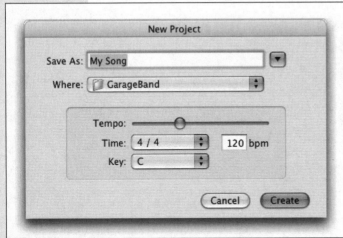

Figure 2-1:
The overwhelming majority of Garage-Band masterpieces that people have posted online are built with these settings: 120 beats per minute, 4/4, key of C. Clearly, most people do not, in fact, ever get around to changing these parameters.

Incidentally, if you're interested in learning about time signatures, keys, tempo, and so on, see Appendix A for a crash course.

If you *do* know a little bit about music or the Mac, you can use this dialog box to specify details like this:

- **What to call your new piece.** You'll almost certainly want to type a new title into the Save As box—"My Song" gets old fast.

- **Where to file it.** The program always hopes that you'll keep all your compositions in your Home→Music→GarageBand folder, which the iLife installer created. You can, of course, choose to file it anywhere else (press ⌘-D, for example, to save it onto your desktop). But you'll have to redirect GarageBand in this way each time you create a new piece.

- **The song's tempo.** That is, how fast or slow it is, expressed in beats per minute. You can either drag the Tempo slider or type a new number into the "bpm" box just below it.

  You don't really have to know what you're doing at this stage. You can adjust a song's tempo at any time, even after you've recorded it.

- **The song's time signature (meter).** Now you're getting into musician territory; this setting specifies how many *beats* (foot-taps, you might say) there are in a measure. Put another way, the first number in a time signature—like the upper digit in the time signature 4/4—is what you'd count off to your garage band to get it off to a synchronized start. ("And-a one! Two! Three! Four!")

  This is a rather important decision. You *can* change your mind later (page 147), but not introducing a good bit of chaos into whatever music you've already recorded. (You can't change the time signature midway through a piece, either.)

Note: GarageBand offers a choice of some less common time signatures like 9/8 (think "Jesu, Joy of Man's Desiring"), 2/4 (every march you've ever heard), and 12/8 ("Everybody Wants to Rule the World"). GarageBand's *loops,* however, are designed to work only in 4/4. For most of the other time signatures, no loops at all are available. A couple show up for 2/4 and 6/8, but they're actually mislabeled and don't fit into the beats. The GarageBand Jam Pack (page 40) expands the selection slightly.

In short, GarageBand is prepared to handle time signatures other than 4/4—but only if you intend to record your *own* music performances, as described in the following chapters. So, if you want to work with loops, you're stuck with 4/4.

- **What key your piece is in.** The *key* of a piece specifies where it falls on the piano keyboard (for example)—how high or low it is, in other words. (See Appendix A for details.)

  If you have enough musical knowledge to understand keys, now is the time to choose the one you want. You can *transpose* GarageBand's loops and your MIDI-instrument performances at any time (page 92)—that is, move them into a different key. But some of GarageBand's loops start to distort if you shift them too far from their starting points. Furthermore, anything you record into a Real Instrument track, using a microphone or electronic instrument, remains locked in pitch forever.

Note: The key you choose also affects which loops are available to you, because GarageBand ordinarily hides the loops that are far from the key you choose. More on this topic on page 40.

Once you've made your choices, click OK. After a moment, you see a screen that looks something like Figure 1-1 on page 11. GarageBand is now a blank canvas—ready to receive input, captain! It starts you off with a $50,000 Yamaha C7 grand piano sound and (if no external keyboard is attached) a 29¢ onscreen keyboard to "play" it.

For the moment, close the little keyboard by clicking the tiny, round Close button at its top left corner. When you get time, you can read all about it on page 68.

The Loop Browser

If you're following along with this chapter, leave the one empty Grand Piano track on the screen. Close the onscreen keyboard for the moment. (If you've been fooling around on your own, start a fresh project by choosing File→New.)

Now, if the plan is to build a piece of music out of 1,100 musical spare parts, you'd better have a *very* organized toolbox. Sure enough, GarageBand offers an extremely clever loop-finding system called the Loop browser. To open it, use one of these three methods:

- Click the eyeball icon below the list of tracks, as shown in Figure 2-3.
- Choose Control→Show Loop Browser.
- Press ⌘-L.

Later, you can hide the Loop browser by repeating the same step (except that the menu command will say Hide Loop Browser).

Tip: When you first open the Loop browser, you're seeing only a sampling of the musical smorgasbord Apple has prepared for you. Only about *half* of the Loop browser buttons—35 of them—are visible.

To view the rest of the buttons, drag the dark gray brushed metal divider bar upward into the Track area, as shown in Figure 2-2.

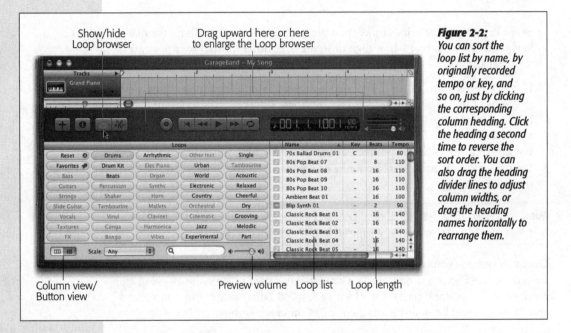

Figure 2-2:
You can sort the loop list by name, by originally recorded tempo or key, and so on, just by clicking the corresponding column heading. Click the heading a second time to reverse the sort order. You can also drag the heading divider lines to adjust column widths, or drag the heading names horizontally to rearrange them.

At this point, GarageBand offers three different ways to search its massive database of juicy sonic tidbits to locate the one you're seeking: Button View, Column View, and the Search box.

Loop Quest 1: Button View

Here's how to use the grid of oval Loop browser buttons:

1. **Click the oval button named for the instrument you want.**

   Eventually, you'll cultivate your own work routine. But in the recording biz, it's common to lay down the *rhythm tracks* first—the bass, guitar, and drums, for example—and then, later, record the melodic lines, like the vocals or instrumental solos, on top of that background.

   Suppose, then, that you're hunting for just the right drum pattern for a new song you're writing. Click Drums.

At this point, the Drums button remains lit in blue, and the other instrument buttons fade out. The right side of the Loop browser displays a long, scrolling list of drum riffs. These are your loops.

The light gray readout next to the volume slider at the bottom of the window displays how many of GarageBand's 1,100 loops are in the category you're now browsing ("282 items," for example).

2. **To listen to a loop, click its name.**

Immediately, GarageBand begins playing that prerecorded snippet—cleverly adjusting the loop's speed to match the current tempo of your piece—and then repeating it endlessly. (Now you know why it's called a loop.) A little speaker icon, as well as some colored highlighting, lets you see at a glance which loop is playing.

Drag the slider at the bottom edge of the window to adjust the loop volume.

To stop the playback, either click the name again, or click a different loop name to hear *it*.

GEM IN THE ROUGH

Redesigning the Button Browser

The buttons of the Loop browser are a nifty way to hunt through hundreds of loops. Only trouble is, you now have to hunt through dozens of buttons.

Fortunately, you can rearrange the buttons in the browser in either of two ways.

The point, of course, is to arrange the buttons so they're easy to find. For example, you might want to install the most useful buttons into the cluster of the top 35, making them visible when you initially open the Loop browser. That way, you needn't expand the Loop browser manually every time you open GarageBand.

Method 1: If you grab a button with the mouse and drag it on top of another button, the two buttons swap places when you let go.

Method 2: Control-click any button that you'd like to replace with another. From the shortcut menu that appears, choose the new button name, as shown here. You've just changed the name and function of the button you clicked.

The advantage of this approach is that those shortcut menus offer the complete list of GarageBand buttons, including many that don't generally appear. (The drag-to-swap method, by contrast, only lets you shuffle buttons that are already on the screen.)

Oh, and if you ever want to put all the buttons back where Apple had them, choose GarageBand→Preferences, click General, and click the Reset button.

Tip: Whenever you find a loop that you especially like, or think you'll use again, turn on its Fav checkbox, usually located in the rightmost column. (Make your GarageBand window wider if you don't see this column of checkboxes.) You've just added it to your list of Favorite loops.

At any time, you can recall these favorite loops by clicking the Favorites button at the left edge of the Loop browser. You've just saved yourself the effort of crawling through the 1,100 choices to find that awesome Nordic Fiddle again.

Now, you can have hours of fun just scrolling through this vast list of drum loops, muttering, "Hey! That's the one from 'Brick House'!" But over 275 drum loops come with GarageBand. By the time you find just the right hip-hop beat, hip-hop wouldn't be hip anymore.

That's why GarageBand comes equipped with features that help narrow the loops to just the one that suits the piece you're building:

3. **Click a category or adjective button: Country, Jazz, Relaxed, Acoustic, and so on. In fact, click as many as you like.**

MUSIC CLASS

Scale: Any

The pop-up menu on the bottom edge of the Loop browser, called Scale, offers another way to filter GarageBand's list of loops. It lets you view only the loops that, musically speaking, "go" with certain kinds of scales.

A scale is the series of notes—you know, "Do, re, mi," and so on—that fits a particular key. Most simple melodies are constructed of only the seven notes in a particular scale.

Most GarageBand loops sound good when played simultaneously with other loops—but not all of them. For instance, a guitar loop playing in a major key and a piano loop in a minor key will clash horribly. That's why the Scale pop-up menu exists—so that you can match your loops, major with major or minor with minor.

Your options are:

Any: You're seeing all loops. None are hidden.

Minor: A minor key, and its associated scale, is one that sounds sad or angry. (To hear a melody played using a minor scale, set the Scale pop-up menu to Minor. Then, in the Loop browser, click Reset and then Guitars. Click the

loop called Acoustic Noodling 03.)

Minor keys are fairly rare in pop music, but when you're feeling a little depressed, GarageBand can accommodate you. Choose this option to display only loops played on minor scales.

Major: A major key, and its associated scale, sounds happy. Most pop music uses this kind of scale. To hear the idea, set the Scale pop-up menu to Major. Then click Reset, Guitars, and Acoustic Picking 02.

Neither, Good For Both: Many loops don't have any particular key, pitch, or scale. Drums, for example, have no pitch, so they "go" with music in any key without clashing. Certain bass, guitar, and string loops are more or less scaleless, too—meaning they could go with either major or minor music. (Musicians' Note: Octaves, unisons, and open-fifth "power chords" are some examples. The common thread: you don't hear the third of the chord.)

In any case, after fiddling with this pop-up menu, be sure to set it back to Any, so you won't later wonder what happened to your huge master list of loops.

Each time you click one of these buttons, GarageBand filters its list of loops to show you only the ones that match your description—and dims another set of oval buttons. For example, if you click Drums, and then Electronic, and then Distorted, you wind up with a list of only five loops.

This method isn't utterly foolproof; you might disagree with the categorization of some of the loops. It's not crystal clear how GarageBand is doing its filtering, either. For example, once you've clicked Drums and then Jazz, turning on the Part and Clean buttons doesn't produce any changes in the list.

Still, most of the time, you can find your way to your desired loop in just a few clicks.

Tip: Most people start drilling down by clicking the instrument button (like Piano) first, followed by the category buttons (Clean, Cheerful, and so on). But in fact, you can start with *any* button and work backward: Click Cheerful first, then Piano, and so on.

4. **Once you've added a loop to your piece (see page 35), or if you give up on your hunt and want to start over, click the Reset button to turn off all buttons and start anew.**

On the other hand, you don't have to return quite that far. It's often less time-consuming just to *back up* in your button-clicking.

To do that, just turn *off* the most recent blue buttons that you've turned *on*. For example, suppose you click Drums, then Electronic, then Cheerful, only to find that there's just one loop in this category. If you decide you've barked up the wrong tree, just click Electronic (for example) to backtrack to the intersection of the Drums/Electronic categories. This way, you can begin drilling down again.

Loop Quest 2: Column View

This business of narrowing your loop quest by clicking successive descriptive buttons is a pleasure, but it isn't right for everyone. Because all 63 of the loop buttons are

Figure 2-3:
Start by clicking the Column View button. Click a "folder" in the first pane (like By Instruments) to see its contents (like Banjo or Bongo). Click an instrument to see, in the third column, the loop categories within that instrument (Clean, Dark, and so on). Finally, choose from the far-right list.

Column view

displayed in one big nonhierarchical pile, it's not always clear which are instrument categories, which are mood categories, and so on.

Column view solves that problem rather quickly. It turns the Loop browser into a close cousin of the Finder column view, so that you can drill down in successive panes and never lose track of the path you took (Figure 2-3).

Because the third column shows, in parentheses, how many loops fall in each category, Column View provides a good deal of insight into how GarageBand's loops come categorized. There are 11 categories in the Flute group, for example (Cheerful, Orchestral, Acoustic, and so on), but that doesn't mean that you've got dozens and dozens of flute samples. In fact, GarageBand comes with only four flute licks, and the same set of four appears in each of the 11 Flute categories.

Loop Quest 3: The Search Box

Once you've worked with GarageBand awhile, you may not feel quite so browsy as you did when you first began fooling around with it. Eventually, you come to know which loops you have, and then wish for a more direct way to pluck them out of the haystack of music.

That's what the Search box is for (on the bottom edge of the Loop browser). You may not remember, for example, that a certain hyper-funky keyboard loop was played on something called a clavinet; you remember only that its name was something like "Cop Show."

POWER USERS' CLINIC

Auditioning: The Loop's Big Break

Once your GarageBand skills grow beyond staying up into the wee hours just clicking loop names and giggling with power-mad glee, you may begin to hunt down the little efficiencies that mark the skilled software master. And when it comes to choosing just the right loop for the piece you're building, that means learning to use loops with cycling.

As described on page 12, cycling is when GarageBand repeats a certain section of the music endlessly. Cycling is a great feature when you're experimenting to find just the right loop to add, or as you practice what you're going to record on top of it.

To loop a certain section of your piece, click the Cycle button (identified on page 14), or press the letter C key. The Cycle button lights up, and a yellow stripe appears on the beat ruler to identify which part of the song GarageBand will repeat. Adjust its length and position, as shown back in Figure 1-3.

If you tap the Space bar now, GarageBand plays only the music indicated by that yellow stripe.

Now here's the cool part: If you click a loop's name in the Loop browser, you'll hear the loop begin playing in perfect sync with the music you've already installed in the piece. It may even wait a moment to start playing the loop, to ensure that the loop will play together with the rest of the "band."

Now, previewing loops by selecting them as the music plays works whether cycling is on or off. But with cycling on, it's easier to audition (listen to) one loop after another, just by clicking each one's name, without having to keep rewinding and starting the playback over. Better yet, just press the up- or down-arrow key to walk through the list of loops, listening to each in turn.

To stop playback, press the Space bar; to turn off cycling, click the Cycle button again to turn it off, or tap the letter C key again.

So you type *cop* into the Search box and press Return or Enter. Instantly, GarageBand reveals all eight of its Cop Show loops, without requiring that you drill down through the categories (see Figure 2-4).

Figure 2-4:
In light gray lettering, the text just to the right of the Search box lets you know how many loop names match your search. (It's sometimes a wake-up call to let you know that you need to scroll the list in the far-right column.)

And now, three notes about the Search box:

- It searches only within the *currently selected* Loop browser category (Bass→Acoustic, for example). It you intend to search the entire GarageBand loop collection, therefore, click the Reset or All button first.

- You can use it to search either for a loop's name or for its category. That is, you can search for terms like *intense* or *strings,* even if those words don't actually appear in any loop names.

- To empty the Search box (and return to seeing all loops), click the circled X at its right end.

Placing a Loop

Suppose that you've used one of the three loop-finding techniques, and you've homed in on just the right loop. Now it's time to install it into your song.

To do that, drag the loop's name upward and into position, as shown in Figure 2-5. The leftmost edge of the loop will align with the spot where you release the mouse.

What happens when you release the mouse depends on *where* you release the mouse.

Drag into a Blank Gray Area

If you drag into an empty track area, you create a brand new track, already set to play the instrument whose name you dragged (Figure 2-5). At the beginning of your song-building session, this is the technique you'll probably use the most. (It makes no difference whether you release the mouse in the light gray area beneath the existing music or the darker gray area beneath the existing track headers.)

Tip: If you *Option*-drag a green Software Instrument loop into an empty track area, GarageBand *converts* that green Software Instrument into a blue Real Instrument loop—and creates a Real Instrument track to hold it.

This is an important trick when your Mac is wheezing under the weight of too many tracks. See the box on the facing page for the explanation.

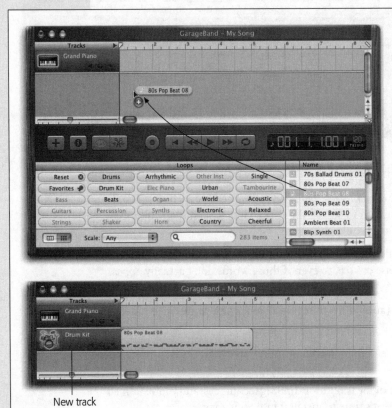

Figure 2-5:
If you drag a loop into an empty track area (top), you create a new track and fill it with one repetition of the loop (bottom). You can save time by dragging it carefully into the horizontal position you want, using the beat ruler at the top of the window as your guide. Of course, you can always adjust the loop's position after placing it, just by dragging it from side to side.

New track

On the other hand, once you've added a track for Cool Upright Bass, for example, there's little point in creating a second or third Cool Upright Bass track for bass licks that occur later in the song. Simply keep all of your Cool Upright Bass in a single track. That's why you can also drag into an existing track (read on).

Drag into an Existing Track

If you drag a loop into a track that's assigned to the *same* instrument sound, you get just what you'd expect. For example, if you drag the Acoustic Noodling 04 loop into an Acoustic Guitar track that you created earlier (by dragging Acoustic Noodling 01 into place, for example), you get more Acoustic Noodling, just as you'd expect.

But suppose you drag a loop into a track whose instrument *doesn't* match the loop you're dragging. For example, suppose you drag Dreamy Guitar Pattern 01 into a Grand Piano track. What now?

GEM IN THE ROUGH

The Secret Lives of Green Loops

If you've managed to grasp the difference between Garage-Band's two kinds of musical building blocks, congratulations. If you've never worked with music on the Mac before, getting over this conceptual hurdle is a huge accomplishment. (To review: Software Instruments = green = MIDI data = editable notes. But Real Instruments = blue or purple = digital audio = frozen as is.)

But wait—there's more.

It turns out that GarageBand's green loops have a little secret. Yes, each contains MIDI note-trigger information, represented by those horizontal bars. But behind the scenes, each one also contains a digital-audio representation of itself—a true-blue AIFF recording. (For proof, switch to the Finder, press ⌘-F, and search for the name of a green GarageBand loop, like Deep Electric Piano. You'll find out that each Software Instrument loop shows up as an .aif file—an AIFF sound file—as it sits in a folder on your hard drive. Each is also far larger than a pure MIDI file would be.)

Go ahead, ask it: What's the point?

Turns out it's actually easier for the Mac to play back digital recordings (blue or purple) than MIDI material (green), because it doesn't have to synthesize the sound itself, in real time. Therefore, if your Mac is having trouble playing back the number of tracks you need, converting green loops into blue ones makes them easier for the Mac to play back. Blue loops require less processing power to play back, so you can use more tracks and effects in a piece.

The downside is that you lose all the great features of MIDI loops, like the freedom to change its notes, transpose it into any key you like, make different notes play louder or softer, adjust its post-processing effects (like reverb), and so on. You're freezing it as it is, complete with whatever effects it came with.

Now, if your Mac isn't having trouble managing all your tracks, you can ignore this entire discussion. But if this MIDI-to-AIFF conversion interests you, here's a summary of the three ways to pull it off.

First, you can drag a green loop into a blue (Real Instrument) track.

Second, you can Option-drag a green loop out of the Loop browser into an empty spot in the gray timeline area. GarageBand converts the loop into digital audio and creates a new Real Instrument track to hold it.

Finally, you can request that GarageBand always convert green loops into noneditable blue ones, every time you drag one into your piece. Just choose GarageBand→Preferences, click the Advanced tab, turn on "Convert to Real Instrument" (shown here), and close the dialog box.

At that point, the effect of the Option key changes. Now, Option-dragging a green loop does not make it change into a blue one; GarageBand leaves the green loop green.

To sum up, the Option key always reverses the status of the "Convert to Real Instrument" checkbox in GarageBand's preferences.

Here's where things can get wacky—and confusing. To understand what's going on, you must understand the distinction between Real Instruments (digital recordings—blue or purple in GarageBand) and Software Instruments (MIDI note data—green); see page 16 for a refresher.

In any case, here's what happens when you drag:

- **Green loop→Green track with different sound.** Suppose you drag a Software Instrument loop into a Software Instrument track—but the instrument doesn't match. To use the example above, let's assume you drag Dreamy Guitar Pattern 01 into a Grand Piano track.

  In that case, something rather cool happens: GarageBand plays the *notes* of the loop using the *instrument sound* of the track. Suddenly you're hearing that dreamy guitar pattern played on a piano. See Figure 2-6.

  This simple twist vastly multiplies your options as you build a song. When you think about it, you can reassign any green loop to any of dozens of instrument sounds. Apple's categorization is only a starting point for your creativity.

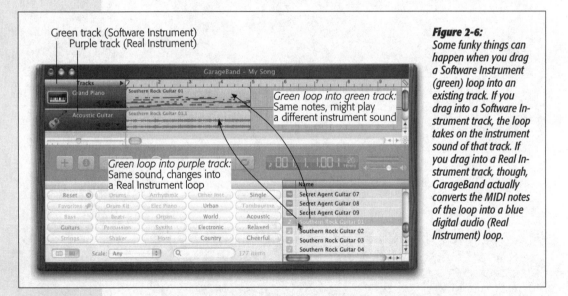

Green track (Software Instrument)
Purple track (Real Instrument)

Green loop into green track:
Same notes, might play
a different instrument sound

Green loop into purple track:
Same sound, changes into
a Real Instrument loop

Figure 2-6:
Some funky things can happen when you drag a Software Instrument (green) loop into an existing track. If you drag into a Software Instrument track, the loop takes on the instrument sound of that track. If you drag into a Real Instrument track, though, GarageBand actually converts the MIDI notes of the loop into a blue digital audio (Real Instrument) loop.

- **Green loop→Blue track.** If you drag a Software Instrument loop into a Real Instrument track, something weird and wonderful happens: GarageBand turns the MIDI loop into a digital recording! Right before your eyes, the green loop turns blue, and its horizontal bars turn into soundwaves, indicating that its transformation is complete. Once again, see Figure 2-6.

  This behavior isn't exactly consistent with the blue-loop-to-green-track "no go" behavior described above, but it's rather cool nevertheless. It may just give you the speed relief you need when your Mac is straining under the load of your composition; see the box on page 37 for complete details.

- **Blue loop→Blue track with different sound.** This combo produces yet another surprising effect. Dragging a digital-audio (blue) loop into an existing digital-audio track has no effect at all on its instrument sound. Figure 2-7 illustrates this phenomenon.

Note: Although blue loops always play back with their original instrument sounds when added to an existing blue track, they are still affected by the effects and settings of that track—echo, reverb, stereo, and so on. See Chapter 7 for more on track effects.

Figure 2-7:
You can drag any number of different digital-audio loops back-to-back into the same Real Instrument track, as shown here (see the second track): Effected Drum Kit, Alternative Rock Bass, and Shaker 4, for example. They'll all play back with the proper instrument sounds, even if the track is called, for example, Acoustic Guitar.

- **Blue loop→Green track.** If you drag a blue loop (Real Instrument) into a green track (Software Instrument), nothing happens at all. GarageBand shakes its little software head "no" and throws the loop back where it came from. You can't park digital audio in a track that expects the horizontal bars of MIDI notes.

All Together Now

In any case, the magic of loops is that most of them sound amazing together, as you'll discover when you try the tutorial on page 56.

Now, if your GarageBand window is wide enough, you'll see columns of information for your loops: Key, Tempo, and so on. And you might wonder how a bass loop that's listed as 80 beats per minute, key of D, would sound good with a piano loop that says it's 110 beats per minute, key of C.

Ah, welcome to the magic of software. The listings of tempo and key in the Loop browser indicate the originally recorded tempos and keys. When you actually install a loop into your piece, though, GarageBand automatically tweaks it, nudging into the key and tempo of *your* piece, no matter how it was originally recorded.

Tip: See Chapter 3 for details on working with loops you've placed into your tracks: making them actually loop (repeat), moving them around, shortening them, and so on.

GEM IN THE ROUGH

More Loops Than You Bargained For

When you first peruse the loops that come with GarageBand, you may be pleasantly surprised by how many you have. You may be vaguely aware that you can buy an add-on pack of loops in the form of the Apple GarageBand Jam Pack, but you may not realize that you've got a bunch more loops already on your hard drive. They're just hidden at the moment.

The problem is that GarageBand's different loops were recorded in different keys. (Inspect the Key column in the Loop browser for proof.) If you've ever heard a tone-deaf, slightly drunk karaoke singer at a party, you know how painful it is to listen to clashing keys (two different ones at once). And Apple firmly believes in the old Chinese proverb, "May all your loops sound good together."

Now, one of GarageBand's most amazing features is its ability to transpose its loops (shift them up or down in pitch). If you find a bass loop recorded in the key of D, and drag it into a piece that's in C, it will still sound great, because GarageBand will automatically process it to fit the neighboring key—yes, even if it's a blue (digital-audio) Apple Loop.

So why does GarageBand start out hiding loops that don't match your key?

Apple worries that you might get greedy with that auto-transposing feature. If you choose a blue key-of-F guitar loop, well, that key is rather distant from the key of C. GarageBand's magic software-processing elves will dutifully transpose it into C for you, but the result occasionally sounds

funny—slightly distorted, or, more often, inappropriate for the instrument. (This caveat applies only to blue Real Instrument loops. Green Software Instrument loops sound great in any key.)

Therefore, GarageBand comes set to hide all Real (blue) loops that don't match the key of your piece, to protect you against madcap transpositions.

You can request that it not be such a diva, and show you all of the loops in its bag of tricks. To do that, choose GarageBand→Preferences, click the General icon, and turn off "Filter for more relevant results." Close the dialog box, return to the Loops browser, and click Reset.

Now examine the loops again. As you can see, many more loops appear in the list. For example, if your piece is in C, you now see seven loops in the Bass→Jazz→Cheerful category instead of four.

You may notice that even when "Filter for more relevant results" is turned on, by the way, the listed loops aren't all in your piece's key. For example, scrolling through the list of Bass loops reveals that many of the bass licks were indeed recorded in the key of C. Yet the list also offers you blue loops in keys like C# and D.

The "Filter" option leaves you with blue loops in your song's key and in keys within two half-steps (piano keys) of it. (It also shows you *green* loops in all different keys, because GarageBand can transpose these into any key with no loss of fidelity.)

More Loops

GarageBand comes with 1,100 loops. That should be plenty—for the first half-hour or so!

As your lust for greater musical expression grows, though, you might find yourself wishing you had a more comprehensive sonic palette. You might have noticed, for example, that GarageBand comes with a healthy selection of rhythm parts (bass, drums, guitars, keyboards, mallet instruments), plus some strings and brass—but no solo instruments, like trumpet, clarinet, harp, or solo violin. As noted earlier, GarageBand is also heavily slanted toward music in 4/4 time.

Fortunately, expanding the possibilities is easy enough, since you can add more loops in any of these forms.

Note: As noted at the end of this chapter, you can add almost any sound file to a GarageBand composition just by dragging it into the timeline area. That doesn't make it a loop, however.

A true GarageBand loop comes in *Apple Loop* format. That's basically a dressed-up AIFF file with built-in tags that specify its original length, key, category, and so on. See page 165 for instructions on converting any plain-vanilla loop into a true-blue, smart Apple Loop.

The GarageBand Jam Pack

This $100 expansion pack from Apple offers 2,000 more loops, 15 more guitar-amp simulations, 100 more audio effects, and 100 additional instrument sounds.

That's a lot of add-on fun. It's worth noting, though, that most of the new instruments are in the same categories as the original GarageBand set: guitars, vibraphones, drums, basses, and keyboard instruments. Many of the "100 new instrument sounds" are actually processed or combined versions of the sounds you already have; only a few wholly new instrument sounds join your squad. Fortunately, they're well worth having: a couple of new solo saxophones, a solo flute, plus new guitars and bass samples. There's also a few sound effects, like a car starting, vinyl record scratching, and phone sounds.

Soundtrack

Think of Apple's $300 soundtrack-creation program, Soundtrack, as GarageBand's grandpappy, as it comes with 4,000 Apple Loops of its own. If you've bought Soundtrack—or any of the commercial add-on loop packs for Soundtrack—then you can share its musical riches with GarageBand. Just drag the Soundtrack loops from the desktop into GarageBand's Loop browser, as described below.

Apple Loops from Other Companies

Apple isn't the only company getting into the loop-selling act. There are a few other sources of loops in the Apple Loop format. Some, mercifully, are free. (You'll even find a few free samples on the "Missing CD" page for this book at *www.missingmanuals.com*.)

Tip: The beauty of visiting the Web sites listed below is, of course, that you can actually listen to the loops before you buy them. Most of them offer free samples, too, so you can tweak your orchestra without spending a nickel.

- **BandMateLoops.com.** If you're into drums, there's a good chance you'll find what you're looking for among these loop packs: Rock Drums, Electro Beats, Funk Drums, Scratches, and House Beats. Each set costs $18.

- **TuneupLoops.com.** Tune-Up for GarageBand includes 500 loops for about $35.

GEM IN THE ROUGH

Insta-Samples: Canned Sound Without Loops

Now you know where to find additional loops to buy, download, and install into GarageBand.

In many cases, though, going to all that trouble and expense isn't worth it when all you need is a quick sound effect, or even a sample of a pop song already in your iTunes library. What many Garage-Band aficionados don't realize is that you can use any MP3 file, AIFF sound, AAC file (except copy-protected ones), or even Windows-format WAV file right in a GarageBand composition just by dragging it there, as illustrated here.

Need a breaking-window sound to open your new love ballad, "When You Left Me, There Was Only One Way Out"? Zoom over to Google.com, conduct a search for free AIFF sound effects, download a choice candidate, and simply drag its icon off your desktop into the GarageBand Timeline window. That sound effect now plays right along with your music.

Want to sample a killer drum hit from a pop song in your

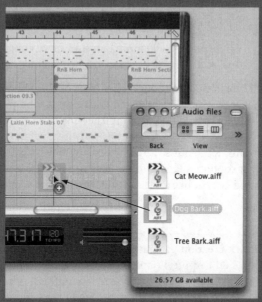

iTunes music library? No problem. Position your iTunes and GarageBand windows so you can see them both at the same time. Drag the MP3 file's name right out of iTunes and into the GarageBand Timeline window. After the importing dialog box disappears, edit the imported file just as you would any region (see Chapter 3), chopping it up until only the choice moment remains.

Or, similarly, want to create your own version of a pop song? Your first step might be to drag the song into GarageBand from the iTunes window to use as a reference. Adjust the GarageBand tempo control, for example, until the metronome more or less clicks right along with the imported song. Try playing the bass line along with the imported song, or lay down your own singing track on top of it, even if you ultimately intend to delete the imported reference track.

(About that business of copy-protected AAC files, like the ones you buy from the Apple Music Store: If you're desperate to include one, burn a CD of the song, leaving a non-copy-protected copy on the disc. Once when you insert the CD into your Mac, just drag the appropriate song file right out of its desktop window and into GarageBand.)

- **Samples4.com.** This British Web site offers a complete line of GarageBand expansion packs at various prices, starting at about $50.

- **BitShiftAudio.com.** 40 free GarageBand loops, all up-to-the-minute in terms of pop-music style.

- **Access-music.de.** This German company offers a 46 MB set of "punchy arpeggiator patterns, fat filter flows, and amazing pad sounds exclusively generated with a Virus C synthesizer"—for free.

And that's just the beginning. Fire up your Web browser, visit Google.com, and search for *free Apple loops.* You'll find plenty of downloads to keep you busy.

How to Install New Loops

Once you've got your hands on a new set of loops, install them into GarageBand just by dragging them there, as shown in Figure 2-8.

What happens now depends on *where* the loops are coming from. In each case, Garage-Band tries to do the smartest thing:

- **From a hard drive.** Some Mac fans have enormous loop collections that they've amassed using other software (like Apple's Soundtrack). These power users are understandably reluctant to let GarageBand *copy* their hundreds of megabytes of loops into its own private loop folder, thus duplicating the loops on the hard drive.

  That's why, when you drag a folder of loops from a hard drive (whether your own built-in one, an external one, or even a networked one), you get the dialog box shown in Figure 2-8. It's asking how you want to handle this new set of loops. You can opt to have them copied into GarageBand's own Loops folder, or you can have GarageBand *index* them (add them to its list of available loops) but leave the actual files where they are, for the sake of conserving hard drive space.

FREQUENTLY ASKED QUESTION

The Case of the Lost Loops

Hey! I installed some new Apple Loops that I downloaded from the Web, and now they're lost somewhere among the 1,100 original GarageBand loops, filed away into the proper instrument or mood categories. How am I supposed to identify which ones are the new ones?

Most loop companies are smart enough to name their supplementary loops with an identifying prefix ("XYZ-Piano Riff 03," for example).

If they don't, then sure enough, you may have a hard time finding your newly installed loops.

One investigative tip is to study the GarageBand folder on your hard drive, where Mac OS X automatically stashes newly installed loops (and instruments and effects).

Open the Library→Application Support→GarageBand→Apple Loops folder on your hard drive. Inside, you should find your newly installed loops in a separate folder of their own. Take note of the loops' names, so that you'll remember them when you return to GarageBand.

And if all else fails, you can always use Mac OS X's Find command to search for the loops by Date, assuming you remember when you installed them.

• **From a CD or DVD.** GarageBand copies the loops into your existing loops folder. It's assuming that this particular disc may not always be in your Mac when you use GarageBand, and that therefore the loops may not always be available—so it copies them to your hard drive for safekeeping.

Once you've installed a loop by dragging into the Loop browser, it becomes available to every GarageBand project you ever work on, a permanent addition to your collection (until you choose to delete it, of course).

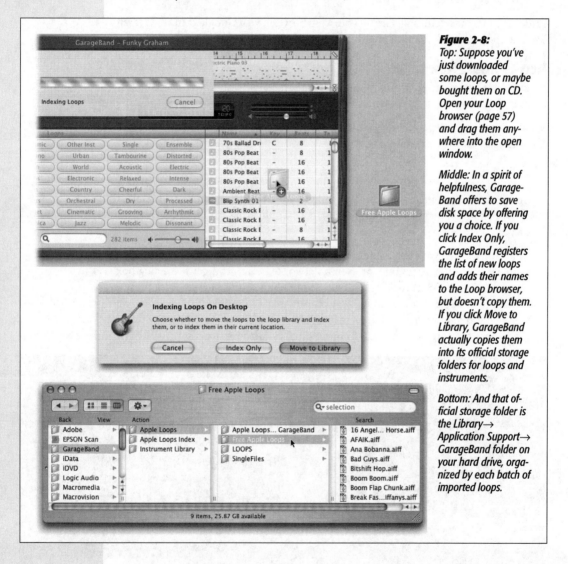

Figure 2-8:
Top: Suppose you've just downloaded some loops, or maybe bought them on CD. Open your Loop browser (page 57) and drag them anywhere into the open window.

Middle: In a spirit of helpfulness, Garage-Band offers to save disk space by offering you a choice. If you click Index Only, GarageBand registers the list of new loops and adds their names to the Loop browser, but doesn't copy them. If you click Move to Library, GarageBand actually copies them into its official storage folders for loops and instruments.

Bottom: And that official storage folder is the Library→ Application Support→ GarageBand folder on your hard drive, organized by each batch of imported loops.

Removing Loops and Rebuilding the Index

Not everybody feels straitjacketed by the meager 1,100 loops that come with Garage-Band. Some people actually feel overwhelmed. For them, the trick is not finding new loops to add to their collections—it's deleting the loops they know they'll never need. After all, if your specialty is composing lush, romantic waltzes, it's not immediately apparent how Vinyl Scratch 09 will be useful to you.

Removing loops is a matter of finding them on your hard drive. Open your hard drive→Library→Application Support→GarageBand→Apple Loops folder to find them.

Ordinarily, fooling around with these behind-the-scenes GarageBand folders isn't such a hot idea. Moving, deleting, or renaming the wrong file could profoundly confuse GarageBand.

But if you make your way directly to the Apple Loops folder and don't do anything but remove the loops you really don't want to see, you'll be all right. For sanity's sake, don't simply delete them. Instead, drag them into some other folder on your hard drive, so you can put them back in the unlikely event that you're commissioned to write "The Record Scratching Waltz."

Now, just moving loops out of the Apple Loops folder doesn't actually delete their names from GarageBand's Loop browser. Their names will still appear the next time you fire up GarageBand, because they're still in GarageBand's master *index file* of loops.

But the moment you click the loop's name, you see the dialog box shown in Figure 2-9. Click OK, wait a moment, and then relish your newly pruned collection of loops.

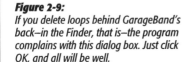

Figure 2-9:
If you delete loops behind GarageBand's back—in the Finder, that is—the program complains with this dialog box. Just click OK, and all will be well.

Apple Loop not found!

This Apple Loop was not found. Your Apple Loops will be reindexed to make sure that you only see existing Apple Loops. This may take a while.

OK

Regions

A *region,* in GarageBand lingo, is one of the round-ended green, blue, or purple music blocks in the timeline. These are your GarageBand building blocks. A region may contain musical material or silence. Each may last only a fraction of a second, or the entire length of a song. Just by chopping, copying, pasting, and dragging regions around, you can build an infinite number of compositions that have never been heard before.

Loops, described in Chapter 2, are one kind of region (green or blue), but they're not the only kind. In subsequent chapters, you can read about how to record material of your own. Regions containing MIDI note information are always green, Apple Loops containing digital audio recordings are blue, and audio recordings you make yourself (or audio files you drag in from the Finder) are always purple.

The following discussions tell you how to manipulate regions in general—but these techniques are especially useful for manipulating loops.

Selecting Regions

Before you cut, copy, delete, split, join, or move regions around, you must first select them. This isn't rocket science, of course—you perform the same "Select, then apply" ritual in just about every Macintosh program.

Here's the complete GarageBand region-selecting handbook:

- **Select one region** by clicking it.

- **Select an additional region** by Shift-clicking it. If you Shift-click one by accident, Shift-click it again to deselect it.

- **Select all the regions in one section of the piece** by drag-selecting (Figure 3-1).

- **Select all the regions in one track** by clicking the track header (on the left side, where the track's name and icon appear).

- **Select the entire song** by choosing Edit→Select All (or pressing ⌘-A).

You can tell when a region is selected because its color deepens and its text darkens.

To deselect everything and start over, simply click in any empty gray spot in the timeline.

Figure 3-1:
By dragging enormous chunks of your song, you can rearrange sections and experiment with musical arrangements. The trick is selecting so many regions all at once. To do so, start by zooming out. Then, drag a box around the entire area you want to select. Now you can drag any of the selected regions to move them all at once, exactly as with icons in the Finder.

Zoom slider (drag left to zoom out)

Renaming Regions

Regions usually begin life named after their tracks or instruments. But giving them more descriptive names—like "Vocal Intro," "Bridge," or "Zither Solo"—goes a long way in helping you recognize where you are in your song at any given moment.

To change a region's name, double-click it. As shown in Figure 3-2, an editing window appears. You'll read more about this Track Editor in subsequent chapters, but for now, what you care about is the Track Name box (Figure 3-2).

Dragging Regions

You can change when a region plays by shifting its horizontal position. Just drag it by its center.

Dragging is a very handy tactic. When you drag a region *horizontally,* you make it play earlier or later in time. When you drag it *vertically,* you move it to a different track, according to the rules described on page 38.

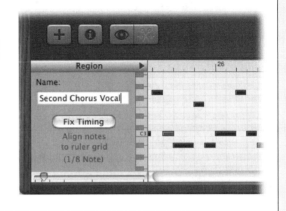

Figure 3-2:
When you double-click any region, the Track Editor appears at the bottom of the window. One key feature is the Track Name box, where you can type a new name for the region. Press Return or Enter to make the name stick.

(Try not to worry about the inconsistency of having to edit the region's name so far away, and not right on the region itself.)

Figure 3-3:
This pop-up menu determines how fine or how coarse the underlying drag-and-drop grid is. It lists basic musical rhythmic units, from largest to smallest (that is, slowest to quickest). In 4/4 time, a region will snap only to the beginnings of measures if you choose "1/1 Note" (that is, a whole note); it will move much more freely if you choose "1/16 Note" (a sixteenth note).

And when you select a huge chunk of your song (Figure 3-1), you can rearrange huge chunks of your piece at once.

The Grid

You may notice that a dragged region tends to snap to positions on an underlying grid, whose vertical lines correspond to the markings on the beat ruler across the top of the window. Here are the keys to understanding this snapping motion:

- In general, the snapping is a good thing. It keeps your loops aligned with one another, so that your GarageBand players have a virtual conductor keeping them together.

- A region you're dragging snaps to the nearest measure, quarter note, and so on. One way to control the fineness of this invisible grid is to use the Grid pop-up menu at the upper-right corner of the GarageBand window, as shown in Figure 3-3 on the previous page.

- If you choose Automatic from the Timeline Grid pop-up menu, the grid expands or contracts according to how much you've zoomed in. As you magnify your music, you get more gridlines per measure, which offers you finer positioning options. (The onscreen gray gridlines show you where GarageBand intends to snap.)

- If you want complete dragging freedom—no snapping grid at all—choose Control→Snap to Grid, or just press ⌘-G. Now you can drag a region wherever you like. (Repeat the command to turn the grid on again.)

Looping Regions

If you install a loop, hit the Home or Z key to rewind, and then press the Space bar to play, you may wonder why you went to all the trouble. The newly installed loop plays once—and then stops.

Fortunately, they're not called loops for nothing. The first and second illustrations in Figure 3-4 show how you can make a loop repeat (or any region, for that matter).

You can make a region repeat as many times as you like. In many songs, for example, you might want the drums to play continuously for the entire song. You can even stop dragging halfway through a repetition, giving you, for example, one-and-a-half repetitions. That might be useful if, say, you want those drums to stop short halfway through a measure to create a dramatic break.

Tip: When you make a loop repeat by dragging its upper-right edge, you're *cloning* the original loop, and the copies remain genetically linked to their progenitor. If you edit the first occurrence, all attached repetitions also change.

If you'd prefer the ability to edit each repetition separately, duplicate the loop region by copying and pasting (or Option-dragging) instead. That way, you create fully independent regions that you can edit independently.

Shortening Regions I

You don't have to use Apple's canned loops in their entirety. By shortening a region from its right end, you can isolate only a favorite first portion of it.

Shortening a region is simple enough: Drag the end inward, as detailed at bottom in Figure 3-4. You'll know you've grabbed the right spot when the cursor changes to a vertical bar with a rightward arrow. (Contrast with the curly cursor that appears when you make a loop repeat.) If you've used iMovie 4, this movement should feel distinctly familiar. It's exactly the same cropping motion you can use on clips in the Movie Track.

Tip: If the region is blue or purple—a Real Instrument region—you can drag *either* end inward. That is, you can shorten it either from the beginning or end. (You can't shorten a green Software Instrument loop except from its *right* end.)

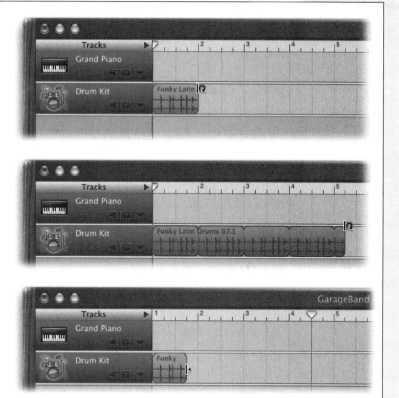

Figure 3-4:
If you drag a region by its upper-right corner (top), you make it repeat seamlessly (bottom); the curly cursor tells you that you've grabbed the correct corner. The farther to the right you drag, the more repetitions you get.

Middle: The little notches—four of them shown here—illustrate where the region will repeat.

Bottom: If you grab the middle or bottom of a region's right side, you can shorten it by dragging it to the left. (See the difference in the cursor shape?) You can also grab the left side of a blue or purple region and drag inward, cropping out the beginning of the region.

And now some cool mix-and-match editing pointers:

- Once you've shortened a region, you can then drag its upper-right corner to make *just that shortened version* repeat over and over. This trick does amazing things for drum and bass loops, for example, creating fresh, shorter, more repetitive loops that never existed in Apple's imagination.

- The advantage of shortening a region by dragging its end—as opposed to splitting the region and deleting the unwanted portion, as described below—is that you can always restore the region to full length by dragging its end outward again.

- If the *middle* of a blue or purple region is your favorite part, use this technique to crop out both the beginning and ending of it.

Shortening Regions II

If your goal is to shorten a certain drum loop and then place a different region right next to it, try this shorthand: Drag the second region *right on top* of the one you want to shorten, so that they overlap. When you release the mouse, you'll see that you've vaporized the overlapped portion of the stationary region.

In some cases, you'll just leave the dragged region where it is now, so that it plays side-by-side with the shortened one. But once the chopping is done, you don't *have* to leave it where you dropped it. You can drag it right back where it started from, having used it as only a temporary chopper-offer.

Lengthening Regions

You can also make a region longer by dragging its right end to the right. That's not the same thing as dragging the top *right* corner, which makes the loop *loop*. Instead, dragging the loop's right edge extends the loop's width without making it repeat.

You might wonder what the point is, since the extended area of the region is filled with silence. But this trick can be handy when, for example, you recorded only seven measures, but want to loop the region so that it repeats every *eight* measures. By making the region an even eight measures long, you can now drag its upper-*right* corner to make it loop evenly.

Splitting Regions

You don't have to use a region in its entirety. Drum loops, in particular, are fun to split down the middle; the resulting half-loops or quarter-loops often serve as useful *fills* (drum riffs right before a musical moment).

All you have to do is position the Playhead precisely where you want the split to occur; click the region to select it; and then choose Edit→Split (or press ⌘-T). You'll see that the region is now in two separate pieces. You can manipulate, cut, copy, drag, shorten, repeat, or otherwise process each of these two pieces independently.

As noted earlier, what's especially intriguing is that you can split off a snippet of a region, and then make *that* repeat over and over, creating a whole new effect.

And now, some important region-splitting tips:

- It helps to zoom in on your loop before splitting it, so you can see exactly where your knife is about to fall. Drag the zoom slider beneath the track list, or just press Control-right arrow or Control-left arrow key to zoom in or out.

- You can simultaneously split *stacked* regions—that is, parallel regions in several tracks at once. Just make sure that you've first selected the ones you want to split by Shift-clicking each one (Figure 3-5).

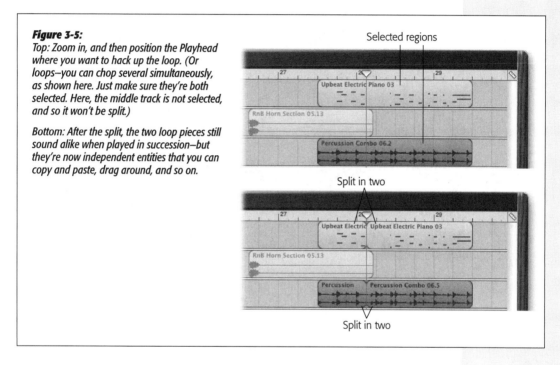

Figure 3-5:
Top: Zoom in, and then position the Playhead where you want to hack up the loop. (Or loops—you can chop several simultaneously, as shown here. Just make sure they're both selected. Here, the middle track is not selected, and so it won't be split.)

Bottom: After the split, the two loop pieces still sound alike when played in succession—but they're now independent entities that you can copy and paste, drag around, and so on.

- After you split a region, both pieces of it remain highlighted. That's great if you now want to copy, delete, or move both pieces as a unit—but if *that* were your aim, why would you have just split them?

  No, most of the time, you want to handle them individually. And that's why it's important, just after a split, to click an *empty* track area to deselect them. Only then can you drag or click one of the split pieces all by itself.

You'll use this technique in the tutorial that concludes this chapter.

Joining Regions

What the Split command hath rendered asunder, the Join Selected command shall restore.

Combining two or more regions on a track into a single, unified one has a number of benefits. For example, musical riffs that you've painstakingly assembled and positioned turn into a single, easy-to-manipulate block. Copying, pasting, and dragging regions around is much simpler, too, if you can select the music in question with one quick click, without having to select a bunch of itty-bitty individual regions one at a time. And, of course, you can *loop* a region that you've created by joining them.

There is, however, one condition: The Join Selected command is dimmed if you've selected *blue* regions—that is, Real Instrument Apple loops. It works only on two green regions (MIDI, aka Software Instruments) or two purple ones (those you've recorded yourself, or sound files you've dragged in from the Finder).

Tip: According to GarageBand's online help, there are other conditions, too—but don't believe it. For example, the regions you're about to join do *not* have to be adjacent. In fact, you can even Shift-click two regions that are separated by *other* regions! They'll still merge into one long region that appears to float behind the intervening ones—the only time you'll ever see superimposed regions in GarageBand. Weird!

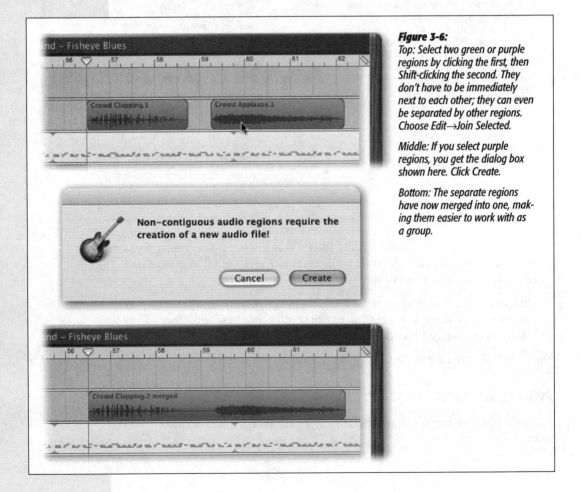

Figure 3-6:
Top: Select two green or purple regions by clicking the first, then Shift-clicking the second. They don't have to be immediately next to each other; they can even be separated by other regions. Choose Edit→Join Selected.

Middle: If you select purple regions, you get the dialog box shown here. Click Create.

Bottom: The separate regions have now merged into one, making them easier to work with as a group.

Figure 3-6 shows the routine.

Copy and Paste

Let's face it: copy and paste form the cornerstone of the personal-computer religion. If you couldn't copy and paste, where would word processing be? Where would Photoshop be? Where would college students be?

It works with regions just as it does with fields in FileMaker, objects in a drawing program, or icons in the Finder:

1. **Select the region or regions you want to copy.**

   Click to select the first one, Shift-click to select additional regions, either in the same track or in other tracks. Or just "drag out" a huge selection rectangle, as shown in Figure 3-1.

2. **Press ⌘-C (or choose Edit→Copy).**

   You've just placed a copy of the selected music on your invisible Macintosh Clipboard; the original regions remain where they are. If you press ⌘-X (or choose Edit→Cut) instead you place a copy on the Clipboard and *remove* the selected regions from the piece.

3. **Click in the beat ruler to indicate where you want the Clipboard regions to reappear.**

   Or move the Playhead to the proper spot using the arrow keys, the time display, or any other navigation technique.

Note: If your aim is to paste the music at the very end of the piece, you may find that you're not allowed to move the Playhead beyond the end of the existing music. The trick is to first drag the end-of-song marker farther to the right. (It's the tiny, dark purple, left-pointing triangle in the beat ruler.)

---

4. **Press ⌘-V (or choose Edit→Paste).**

   The cut or copied music appears at the position of the Playhead.

The regions always reappear in the tracks from which you cut or copied them; you can't paste into a different track.

Option-Drag

Copy and paste is all very well, but it's a four-step procedure. When you want to copy a region into a nearby spot, there's a much more efficient technique—Option-dragging.

Press the Option key (called Alt on non-U.S. keyboards). While it's down, drag a region to a new position. You peel off a perfect copy of the original. (You may recognize this technique from working with icons in the Finder.)

As with copy-and-paste, this feature is very useful when you drag *horizontally,* because:

- Unlike looping (page 50), Option-dragging offers a quick and easy way to make a region repeat *periodically,* as opposed to immediately.

- As noted earlier, Option-dragging creates a separate, fully independent region. That's a handy tactic when you want to *edit* the copy or copies, creating slight variations from the original.

But Option-dragging (or copy-and-paste, for that matter) is also useful when you drag a region vertically into a different track. For example, you can:

- **Set up part doubling.** *Doubling,* in orchestration parlance, means "two instruments playing the exact same notes." Setting up two of the same instrument gives the melody a more intense, louder sound.

But dragging a green Software Instrument region into a different Software Instrument track gives you the sound of two different *instruments* playing the same line, which creates a new, hybrid sound. Try, for example, dragging the loop called 80s Dance Bass Synth 08 into a track of its own, and then Option-dragging it straight up or down into a green piano or bass track. Because it's now played simultaneously by two different instruments, suddenly the lick has more kick.

- **Chorus yourself.** It's an age-old studio trick made famous by the Beatles: Option-drag a region vertically into a second track; then offset the copy by a fraction of a beat by dragging it a hair to the right. (You'd want to turn off the grid as described on page 50 before you drag.)

The result is a cool, reverby, sound-bouncing effect that you can heighten by slightly reducing the volume of the duplicate.

Delete

To delete a selected region or regions, press the Delete key (or, if you're in no particular hurry, choose Edit→Delete).

Tutorial: Funk for Nonmusicians

GarageBand can be extremely addictive, as you're about to find out. Even if you don't know a quarter note from a Quarter Pounder, you'll be able to create amazing, professional-sounding compositions just by dragging loops around.

The piece you're going to create sounds awfully cool, considering it doesn't involve a single bit of actual playing on your part. But constructing it will nonetheless be an educational process, because you'll learn something about *arranging:* the art of making music build, relax, and surge forward again, and knowing when to add instruments and when to take them away.

Tip: If you're using a laptop, choose ⊞→System Preferences, click Energy Saver, click Options, and make sure that the Processor Performance pop-up menu says "Highest." If it says Reduced, GarageBand may not have the horsepower to process the sonic wall you're about to build.

That's a good piece of advice any time you work in GarageBand.

If you'd like to compare your work with the finished file, download the "GarageBand Examples CD" as described on page 13. The file you want is called "02 Loop Tutorial."

Phase 1: Clean Up the Garage

The following steps assume that (a) you know how to find a certain loop, as described starting on page 29, and (b) you know your way around the beat ruler (page 15).

1. **In GarageBand, choose File→New. In the New Project dialog box, type** *Funky Graham,* **press ⌘-D to choose the desktop as the file's home, and click Create.**

   You've just accepted a tempo of 120 beats per minute, a meter of 4/4, and the key of C. That's all fine, even if you don't know what it means (page 220).

Tip: You could have pressed the Return or Enter key instead of clicking Create. In fact, you can press Return or Enter to "click" the blue pulsing button in just about any dialog box.

   You arrive at an almost empty GarageBand screen. There's a Grand Piano track waiting for you, probably accompanied by the GarageBand onscreen keyboard. You won't need either one.

2. **Close the onscreen keyboard by clicking the tiny Close button (the tiny droplet button at top left of the keyboard window). Get rid of the Grand Piano track by pressing ⌘-Delete.**

   Or choose Track→Delete Track, if you like doing things the long way.

Tip: At this point, you may want to make the GarageBand window fill your window for more elbow room by clicking the green Zoom button at its top left corner.

3. **Open the Loop browser.**

   Do so by clicking the eyeball button at lower-left, by choosing Control→Show Loop Browser, or by pressing ⌘-L. In any case, the Loop browser should now appear at the bottom of your window.

Phase 2: Install Some Loops

At last you're ready to start filling that great gray expanse with some actual music.

1. Find the loop called Upbeat Electric Piano 03.

   One quick way would be to type *upbeat* into the Search box at the very bottom of the window. Another would be to click the Elec Piano and Clean buttons, and then scroll down a tad. See Chapter 2 for the full scoop on finding loops.

2. Drag the words Upbeat Electric Piano 03 into the upper-left corner of the empty gray timeline area.

   You've just installed it at the beginning of measure 1. GarageBand creates a new track, called Electric Piano, to hold it.

   Your piece is so far only two measures long. Alas, nobody ever won a Grammy for a two-measure piece.

3. Grab the upper-right corner of your new green region, so that the cursor turns curly. Drag to the right; release when you reach measure 9 (see Figure 3-7).

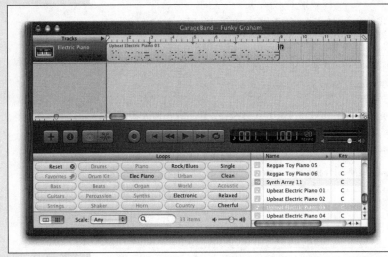

Figure 3-7:
You've just told your keyboard player to play the same thing four times in a row. So far, the music is funky, all right, but a bit monotonous. Time to start laying down some more tracks.

To hear your creation so far, press the letter Z key and then the Space bar. (Both the Home key and the Z key mean "rewind to the start." But learn the Z key. First of all, it's right there near the Space bar, so you can easily go *Z-space!* whenever you want a playback. Second, if you're a roving musician, there's no dedicated Home key on a laptop.)

Press Space again to stop the playback.

4. In the Loop browser, click Reset. Find the loop called Funky Pop Drum 08. Drag it up below the first track; release your mouse at measure 3.

   As you drag, a vertical positioning line appears so you'll know where the loop will sit when you let go.

5. Drag the upper-right corner of this drum loop so that it ends at measure 7.

Do a quick Z–Space bar. Feel how the music takes a giant leap forward in interest, propulsion, and funkiness when the drums enter? This business of *layering* your compositions, bringing in new elements gradually, is a cornerstone of music making. If you'd just begun the song with *both* the piano and the drums, it wouldn't have been nearly as interesting.

Tip: The piano turns out to be a tease or a preview. You've just figured out why the audio of some movie scenes sometimes begins *before* the picture changes, and why some novels begin with teaser sentences like, "Casey put down the tweezers and walked out the door, never to be seen again."

Only trouble is, the piece so far begins a bit *too* timidly. It's just noodling on an electric piano. That's hardly going to get the attention of the murmuring jazz-club audience as they finish dessert. You need something right up front, something commanding that says, "I'm about to play some funk, and *you will listen.*"

6. **Find RnB Horn Section 05. Drag to the beginning of the piece beneath the first two tracks, so that GarageBand creates a third track.**

When you play this back, you'll discover that RnB (that is, "rhythm and blues") Horn Section 05 begins with a single note—a brass *sting* or *stab*. It's just the attention-grabber you need.

Trouble is, this loop *also* contains a bit of melody a few beats later—and you want to delay that particular gratification. It would be better if you could split this loop in half, and save the second part for later.

But how is a poor author to show you exactly where to wield the scalpel without actually coming over to your house?

Easy: By teaching you about the Time display.

Phase 3: Meet the Time Display

The Time Display is the blue "LED" number counter just below the timeline.

As shown in Figure 3-8 at top, this display can express the position of the Playhead in either of two ways:

- **As measure and beats.** If you're musically inclined, you'll probably prefer the standard musical notation that appears here. It's this format: 025.15.3.100, which refers to measures, beats, *sub-beats* (that is, quarters of a beat), and *ticks* (of which there are 240 per sub-beat).

  That's probably *way* more precision than you'll ever need, but hey—overkill is in these days. (Just ask anyone who's bought a Hummer.)

- **As hours, minutes, and seconds.** The Time display can also show you your position in pure time code—that is, how many hours, minutes, seconds, and thousandths of a second you are into the song.

This mode is especially handy when you're preparing music to accompany, say, an iMovie movie, because you can use it to make sure that the music fits the important moments in the movie exactly.

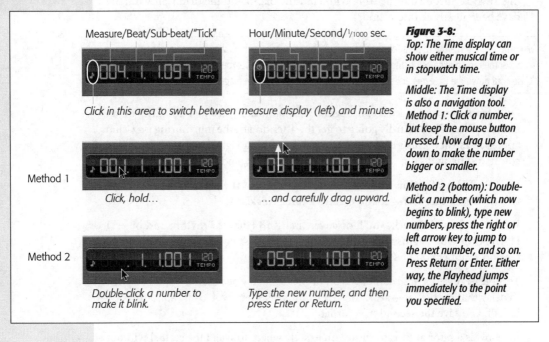

Measure/Beat/Sub-beat/"Tick"   Hour/Minute/Second/¹/₁₀₀₀ sec.

Click in this area to switch between measure display (left) and minutes

Method 1

Click, hold...   *...and carefully drag upward.*

Method 2

Double-click a number to make it blink.   *Type the new number, and then press Enter or Return.*

Figure 3-8:
Top: The Time display can show either musical time or in stopwatch time.

Middle: The Time display is also a navigation tool. Method 1: Click a number, but keep the mouse button pressed. Now drag up or down to make the number bigger or smaller.

Method 2 (bottom): Double-click a number (which now begins to blink), type new numbers, press the right or left arrow key to jump to the next number, and so on. Press Return or Enter. Either way, the Playhead jumps immediately to the point you specified.

To switch between these two displays, click to the left of these digits, where you see the tiny clock (absolute time) or musical note (measures:beats).

So how will you split the new horn lick at just the right spot? Like this:

1. **Using the Time display, position the Playhead at 002.2.1.001 (that is, measure 2, beat 2).**

   If it's easier, you can just drag the Playhead handle and keep an eye on the Time display as you drag.

2. **Click the RnB Horn Section 05 loop to select it (if it isn't already selected). Then choose Edit→Split (⌘-T).**

   You've just cut the loop in two. You've separated the melody from the initial sting.

3. **Shift-click the first piece to deselect it, then choose Edit→Cut (⌘-X).**

   You've just socked away the melodic second part of this loop on your invisible Clipboard. You'll return it to the piece it in just a minute.

4. **Find the loop called RnB Horn Section 08. Drag it into the existing Horn/Wind track, measure 3.**

That's not actually where this loop is going to wind up, but that's as close as you can get with your initial drag. GarageBand doesn't let you drag a loop anywhere except at the beginning of a measure (the numbered "inches" tick marks on the beat ruler).

If you want one to begin *partway* through a measure, you have to adjust it afterward, like this:

5. **Put the Playhead at 002.4.1.001 (measure 2, beat 4). Drag your newly installed Horn Section 8 loop slightly to the left, until its left edge aligns with the Playhead.**

This horn lick now begins on the *fourth beat* of measure 2. A quick Z-Space will prove how great it sounds. And while your brass players are on a roll, you can finally permit them to finish the loop you split a moment ago.

6. **Position the Playhead at 006.2.1.001 (measure 6, beat 2). Choose Edit→Paste (⌘-V).**

The melodic portion of RnB Horn Section 05 reappears, neatly trimming off an empty piece of the preceding horn region. When you play all this back, it sounds like one smooth brass part. Nobody would ever guess that you built it out of chopped-up canned music product.

If you now try to listen to the piece with fresh ears, you can sort of tell that the piece is building up to something musically important at measure 9. (Most mainstream music is built out of four-, eight-, or sixteen-measure sections.)

At the moment, though, your drum part peters out at measure 7. To complete the drumming for the first section, you'll add a slightly different drum loop, one whose sound suggests the major new musical section that's about to begin.

7. **Find Funky Pop Drum 07. Drag it into the second track at measure 7, right next to the original Funky Pop Drum loop.**

Now then: Where has the bass player been all this time? Time to add another layer of interest.

8. **Find the loop called Edgy Rock Bass 01. Drag it beneath the other tracks so that it lines up with measure 5.**

Doing so creates a new Electric Bass track.

You've just completed the first eight bars (measures) of what may be the funkiest music your Mac has ever played. Do a Z-Space bar to play it back.

Note: Take a moment, if you haven't already done so, to save your work (choose File→Save, or press ⌘-S). The dark dot inside the window's red Close button (upper-left) lets you know that your project has unsaved changes; make a habit of saving your work every few minutes.

Phase 4: The Big Finish

You *could* stop now, of course. You can press ⌘-S (or choose File→Save) to preserve your work, which you should do every ten minutes or so, and move on to other work.

You *could* also eat just one potato chip, read just one email message, or open just one birthday present.

In any case, if you decide to finish the piece, you'll be building the next section of the piece—the *bridge*. The bridge, as the name suggests, is the piece of contrasting music that connects two major sections. Ordinarily, the bridge (or the "B" section, as it's sometimes called) connects to another important section, often a repetition of the first ("A") part. In the case of this short tutorial, though, the bridge just builds into the climactic end of the piece.

1. **Find Groovy Electric Bass 04. Drag it up to measure 9 in the Electric Bass track.**

   Now there's a twist! You're probably accustomed to creating a *new* track with every loop you install. But blue Real Instrument recordings can go end-to-end in the same track, even if they're recordings of totally different instruments. They maintain their original sound, but share the same effect settings (like reverb or echo).

2. **Drag the upper-right corner of the new loop to the right. Stop at measure 21.**

   If measure 21 isn't currently on the screen, no problem; the window scrolls automatically as your cursor reaches the right edge of the window. (Otherwise, you can always zoom out, using the slider below the track names.) The point is that you want this bass player to keep going and going to the end of the song.

3. **Find Shaker 04. Drag it below the other tracks, measure 9.**

   Your fifth track is born.

4. **Drag the Shaker loop's upper-right corner all the way to the beginning of measure 15.**

   Your percussion player is going to start gently, using only the shaker. But then, as the frenzy builds, he'll start getting funky and Latin:

5. **Find Funky Latin Drums 08. Drag it up to measure 15, in the same track as the Shaker. Extend its upper-right corner to the beginning of measure 19.**

   Between the bass and the percussion, you've got yourself a smoking rhythm section. But after a couple of measures of this, your ears will crave the entrance of some new musical interest:

6. **Press the Z key (to scroll back to the beginning). Click the blue RnB Horn Section region in measure 1, and choose Edit→Copy.**

   You'll be recycling this brass sting several times.

7. Move the Playhead to measure 11. Choose Edit→Paste (⌘-V). Paste another copy at measure 13, measure 17, and measure 21.

   These horn stabs are your musical punctuation marks.

   This is all sounding plenty funky, but it's time to reintroduce our friend the electric piano player. Remember, the magic of good arranging is knowing when to add, and when to take away. In this case, *building* the instrumentation builds excitement.

8. Hit the Z key and copy the Upbeat Electric Piano loop at the top. Click in the beat ruler at measure 13, and paste.

   Oops—it's a tad too long. You'd set it up for four complete repetitions, and you need only three here.

9. Grab the right end of the newly pasted Electric Piano loop. Drag inward to measure 19.

   That's right—you can drag not only outward to create more repetitions, but also inward to decrease the number.

10. In the Loop browser, find RnB Horn Section 08. Drag it into the Horn/Wind track, measure 23.

    Now, measure 23 is actually a moment after the song is over. But you need to perform some surgery on this four-measure-long horn lick, and there's nowhere else to put it. (If you were to drag it between two other horn licks, it would erase them anywhere it overlaps.) So you're going to use measure 23 as an operating table. After the trim, you'll move it into its final position.

11. Carefully grab the left end of the newly placed horn loop. Drag to the right as shown in Figure 3-9.

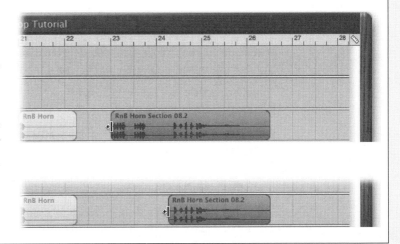

Figure 3-9:
Top: You've parked this horn loop here as a temporary staging area while you make it shorter. Position your cursor at the left edge of the region, so that the special trimming cursor appears.

Bottom: Trim away everything up to the final batch of soundwaves, like this.

You've just cut away the two bursts of repeated horn notes that begin this lick, leaving behind only the melody part.

12. **Double-click the first blue numbers in the time display, so that they start blinking (see Figure 3-8 on page 60). Type 14, and press the right arrow key. Type 3, and press the right arrow again. Type 1; right arrow again. Type 1, and press Return.**

    You've just placed the Playhead at a very precise spot: Measure 14, beat 3. By placing this horn fragment at a position that's *not* the beginning (downbeat) of a measure, you'll be putting the accent on a different "syllable," giving it a different sound from its earlier incarnation when you used it in measure 3.

13. **Drag the shortened horn loop to the left, so that its left end aligns with the Playhead.**

    Now scroll back to measure 9 and give your second half a listen. Pretty cool— especially the way the bass player gets her own little solo at the end, right?

Phase 5: The Big Finish

At the moment, the only payoff you get for all of this musical genius is a single brass stab at the beginning of measure 21. It does seem to say, "That's all, folks," but could use a little beefing up. You want your ending to *land,* not to just fizzle out.

The way to give the final note more oomph is to back it up with bass and drums. It so happens that a loop called Distorted Finger Bass 01 begins with a perfect two-note lick that would sound great when played together with your brass "exclamation point." (Listen to it now to see.)

1. **Find Distorted Finger Bass 01. Drag it into a gray area beneath your other tracks, measure 21.**

   You've just created a new track that contains nothing but this loop.

   Unfortunately, the *instrument* used by that loop is some weird, synthesized bass sound that doesn't really match the rest of your instrumentation.

   Fortunately, it's a Software Instrument (green), so you can change the instrument that plays its notes. That's what you're about to do:

2. **Double-click the track header (where it says "Electric Bass" and bears the picture of a bass).**

   The Track Info dialog box opens (Figure 3-10, bottom). This is where you can change a Software Instrument's sound.

3. **In the left-side list, click Bass. In the right-side list, click Slapped Electric Bass. Close the dialog box.**

   When you play back this loop, you'll discover that it's now played on an electric bass like the one you've been hearing all along.

4. **Drag the right side of the Distorted Finger Bass inward until only the first two notes remain.**

Finally, a little help from the drummer would help to nail this last chord.

5. **Find Single Open High Hat 01. Drag it into your Shaker track at measure 21.**

Now you've got yourself an ending! Hit Z, then Space, to play back your masterpiece.

In later chapters, you'll find out how to fiddle with the relative volumes of these tracks. But as a quick Z-Space bar will tell you, using GarageBand can produce some pretty slick results even if you don't do anything more than choose the right loops and slice up a few regions.

Figure 3-10:
Top: When you try to change instruments, this dialog box may appear. In it, "the file" refers to the instrument-and-effects preset listed in the right-side list. GarageBand is just checking to make sure that, if you've fiddled with any of the effects, as described in Chapter 7, you have the opportunity to save those settings, so they'll still be there the next time you choose this instrument sound.

Bottom: Choose a new sound for this Software Instrument track.

Do you want to save the file before switching to a new one?

If you don't save, the current setting will be lost.

☐ Never ask again

Save   Cancel   Don't Save

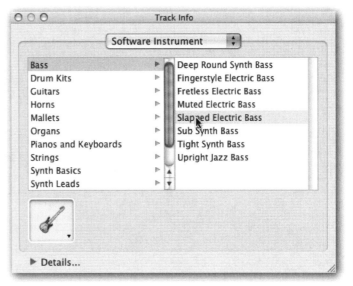

Track Info

Software Instrument

Bass	▶	Deep Round Synth Bass
Drum Kits	▶	Fingerstyle Electric Bass
Guitars	▶	Fretless Electric Bass
Horns	▶	Muted Electric Bass
Mallets	▶	Slapped Electric Bass
Organs	▶	Sub Synth Bass
Pianos and Keyboards	▶	Tight Synth Bass
Strings	▶	Upright Jazz Bass
Synth Basics	▶	
Synth Leads	▶	

▶ Details...

Software Instruments (MIDI)

As you know from the previous chapters, GarageBand's loops can provide hours of fun and profit even if you don't have a lick of musical training. If you have some semblance of musical chops, though, GarageBand can quickly take you to the next level of creativity. It can record your live keyboard performances, whether you're a painstaking, one-note-at-a-time plunker or a veteran of Carnegie Hall.

To generate the notes that GarageBand records, you can play either an external musical keyboard or an onscreen one. Either way, the cool part is that you can combine your own performances with GarageBand's other tools. For example, some people use GarageBand's loops to create a rhythm section—a backup band—and then they record a new solo on top. Other people ignore the loops altogether and play all of the parts themselves, one instrument at a time, using GarageBand as a multitrack "tape recorder."

Anything you record like this shows up in *green* GarageBand regions. If you made it through Chapter 1, you now know that these regions contain MIDI information (that is, note data that you can edit). If you played a wrong note, no biggie—just drag it onto a different pitch, or delete it altogether. If your rhythm wasn't perfect, so what? No human being's rhythm is perfect (at least compared to a computer's), not even that of rock star millionaires. GarageBand can fix it for you.

How to Feed a Hungry GarageBand

To record a musical performance in this way, you need some way to feed GarageBand a stream of live musical data. You can do so in any of several ways:

• **Use the onscreen keyboard.** That is, click the mouse on the keys of GarageBand's own, built-in, onscreen piano keyboard. Until Apple invents a ten-button mouse, however, this onscreen keyboard limits you to playing only one note at a time. Unfortunately, it's very clunky; it's like playing a piano with a bar of soap.

But it's free, it's built-in, and it's handy for inputting the occasional slow solo line or very brief musical part.

• **Use your Mac's alphabet keyboard.** A free program called MidiKeys turns your regular typing keyboard into a *musical* keyboard. The downside is that you don't get much expressive capability, since pressing the letter keys harder or softer doesn't produce any difference in sound. Still, at least you can play chords this way, and you can use your fingers instead of the mouse.

• **Connect a MIDI controller.** MIDI (pronounced "middy"), you may recall from Chapter 1, stands for *musical instrument digital interface*. It's an electronic language that lets musical equipment and computers communicate over a cable.

Because your Mac is perfectly capable of playing any of hundreds of musical-instrument sounds (like the ones built into GarageBand), you don't really need an electronic keyboard that can *produce* sounds; all you really need is one that can *trigger* them.

That's the point of a MIDI *controller;* it looks and feels like a synthesizer keyboard, but produces no sounds of its own. It makes music only when it's plugged into, for example, a Mac running GarageBand.

Apple sells (or, rather, resells) a MIDI controller for $100 called the M-Audio Keystation 49e. If you can live with 49 keys, it's a very nice keyboard. It draws its power directly from your USB jack, so you don't need a power adapter, and it's *velocity-sensitive,* which means that its keys are touch-sensitive. The harder you play, the louder the piano sound, for example.

• **Connect a MIDI synthesizer.** If you already own a MIDI synth—an electronic keyboard that provides an assortment of sounds and has MIDI connectors on the back—there's no point in buying a MIDI controller. You can connect the keyboard directly to your Mac and use it the same way, and simply ignore the keyboard's own sound banks.

Some synthesizers can connect straight to your Mac with a USB cable. Most, however, require a *MIDI interface,* a box with nickel-sized MIDI In and Out connectors on one side, and a USB cable for your Mac on the other.

The following pages explain these musical input methods one by one.

Your FREE! Onscreen Digital Piano

When you fire up a new GarageBand document (on a Mac with no physical MIDI keyboard is connected), the GarageBand keyboard appears automatically in a floating window. This onscreen piano is a gift from Apple to people who would like to record notes of their own (instead of just using loops), but don't own a physical MIDI keyboard (Figure 4-1).

Your FREE! Onscreen Digital Piano

Clicking the keys of this little keyboard with your mouse plays the instrument sound of whatever Software Instrument (green) track is currently selected. (The corresponding instrument name appears at the top of the keyboard.)

The onscreen keyboard is a pretty bare-bones beast. For example, it lets you play only one note at a time.

But the onscreen keyboard also harbors two secrets that you might not discover on your own. First, it actually has more keys than the 88 of a real piano—well over 10 octaves' worth of keys! To reveal the keyboard's full width, drag its lower-right ribbed resize handle. Or just scroll the keyboard by clicking the tiny gray triangles on either end.

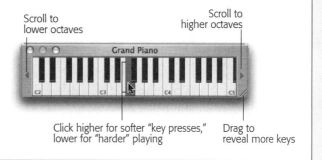

Figure 4-1:
You can make this keyboard appear at any time by pressing ⌘-K (or, if you're charging by the hour, choosing Window→Keyboard). Hide it by clicking its tiny upper-left Close button.

Scroll to lower octaves

Scroll to higher octaves

Grand Piano

Click higher for softer "key presses," lower for "harder" playing

Drag to reveal more keys

MUSIC CLASS

A Different Kind of Velocity

As you get to know GarageBand, and as you get to know the language of electronic music, you'll encounter one term with increasing frequency: velocity or key velocity.

That's a measurement of how hard you struck the keys of your MIDI controller or synthesizer. After all, GarageBand is required to notice and record that information; if it didn't, how could it play back what you recorded with perfect accuracy?

Now, if you're like most people, your first question is: "Um, why don't they just say volume? I mean, the harder you hit the key, the louder it plays, right?"

And that's where things get tricky. It's true that on a piano, hitting the keys harder makes the music louder. In fact, most

of the instrument sounds in GarageBand work like that.

But in the wacky world of computerized music, your key velocity might not affect the loudness of the note. It might change the quality of the sound instead, or even what notes are played.

For example, in most of GarageBand's acoustic-guitar sounds (Auditorium Acoustic, for one), pressing a key harder adds a little slide into the note—a grace note, a glissando up the fretboard from the next lower note. In the Fuzz Clav sound, banging harder gives the notes more of an Austin Powers-era "wah wah" sound.

In short, "velocity" means the velocity of your finger coming down on the key. It says nothing about the resulting sound, which is just the way MIDI linguists like it.

CHAPTER 4: SOFTWARE INSTRUMENTS (MIDI)

69

Second, you can actually control how hard you're "playing" the keys. No, not by mashing down harder on the mouse button. Instead, you control the pressure on the keys by controlling the position of your mouse when it clicks. Click higher up on the key to play softer; click lower down to play harder.

Playing harder usually means playing louder, but not always. Depending on the Software Instrument you've picked, hitting a key harder may change the *nature* of the sound, not the volume. More on this topic in the box on page 69.

For instructions on using the onscreen keyboard to record, skip ahead to page 75.

The Mac Keyboard as Piano

It's nice that Apple provided a little onscreen keyboard so that even the equipment-deprived can listen to GarageBand's amazing sound collection. But you'll never make it to the Grammy Awards using nothing but that single-note, mouse-driven display.

Fortunately, a program called MidiKeys costs the same as the GarageBand keyboard ($0), but lets you trigger notes by playing, rather than clicking. You can download MidiKeys from the "Missing CD" page at *www.missingmanuals.com*.

MidiKeys turns your *Mac* keyboard into a *piano* keyboard:

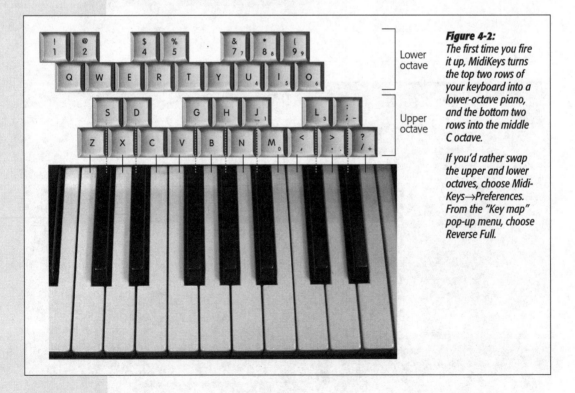

Figure 4-2:
The first time you fire it up, MidiKeys turns the top two rows of your keyboard into a lower-octave piano, and the bottom two rows into the middle C octave.

If you'd rather swap the upper and lower octaves, choose Midi-Keys→Preferences. From the "Key map" pop-up menu, choose Reverse Full.

- The top two rows of keys are the "left hand" piano area—that is, a lower octave. The row beginning with the letter Q represents the "white keys," and the number keys are the "black keys."

- The bottom two rows make up the "right hand"—an upper octave. The Z row is the white keys, starting with middle C; the A row just above it represents the "black keys."

Tip: You can reassign these octave positions by choosing MidiKeys→Preferences.

As shown in Figure 4-2, having every other row serve as "black keys" means that some computer keys produce no sound at all. That's because a real piano doesn't have a black key next to *every* white key. It's no wonder using MidiKeys takes some getting used to.

Nonetheless, it's a powerful tool for scratching out GarageBand pieces when you're on a plane, on a bus, in bed, and anywhere else where lugging along an external keyboard would get you arrested, expelled, or divorced.

Trying Out MidiKeys

To use MidiKeys, create a Software Instrument (green) track in GarageBand. (One way is to choose Track→New; in the New Track dialog box, click Software Instrument. Choose an instrument from the right-side column, and then click OK.)

Now open MidiKeys. Once its keyboard appears (Figure 4-2), try playing a few "keys" on the bottom row of your Mac's keyboard. You'll see the MidiKeys piano keys change color, you'll hear the corresponding notes play in GarageBand, and you'll see a flickering "light" in the time display. It tells you that GarageBand is receiving MIDI musical data.

At this point, you can use MidiKeys like it's a MIDI controller keyboard, including making GarageBand recordings (page 75).

Sending MidiKeys to the Background

There are only two problems with using MidiKeys as you've read about it so far. First, it doesn't communicate with GarageBand unless its window is in *front* of GarageBand's, which means that you can't get at GarageBand's controls. Second, you can't control the key velocity (page 69) unless you drag the MidiKeys Velocity slider as you play, which is not exactly a simple task when you're using both hands in the middle of a Rachmaninoff concerto.

By putting MidiKeys into background mode, you eliminate both problems—sort of. You can play your Mac's keyboard even when GarageBand is in front, and you can use the up and down arrow keys to adjust the key velocity while you play.

Note: Having to press arrow keys isn't exactly the expressive ideal either, but let's face it: Your Mac's keys just aren't touch-sensitive. If you record one hand at a time, riding the arrow keys with the other hand, it's a manageable arrangement.

Of course, you may also want to record your track with *no* velocity adjustments, and then adjust the key velocities later by editing the track (page 97).

The downside of background mode is that it only works if you keep a modifier key of your choice—Control or Shift, for example—pressed while you play. That's how MidiKeys knows when you want it to play, as opposed to when you're just tapping GarageBand keystrokes.

If you're willing to make that tradeoff, see Figure 4-3 for instructions in setting up background mode.

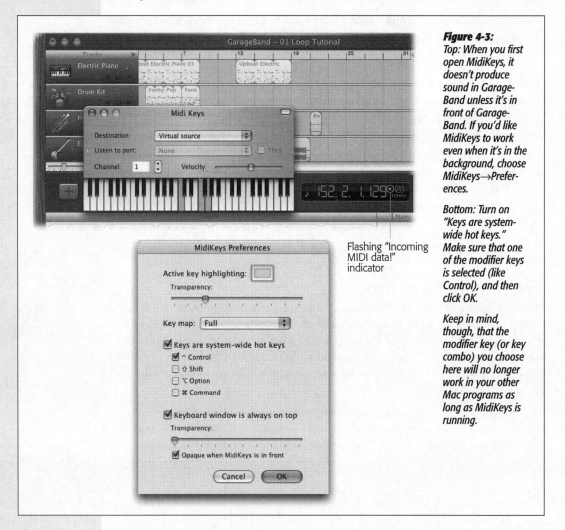

Flashing "Incoming MIDI data!" indicator

Figure 4-3:
Top: When you first open MidiKeys, it doesn't produce sound in Garage-Band unless it's in front of Garage-Band. If you'd like MidiKeys to work even when it's in the background, choose MidiKeys→Preferences.

Bottom: Turn on "Keys are system-wide hot keys." Make sure that one of the modifier keys is selected (like Control), and then click OK.

Keep in mind, though, that the modifier key (or key combo) you choose here will no longer work in your other Mac programs as long as MidiKeys is running.

Thereafter, MidiKeys does the best conceivable job of turning your Mac into a bona fide musical instrument. Here are some of its finer points:

- MidiKeys lets you play *polyphonically*. In plain English, that means you can play more than one note at a time. Most Macs can handle six-note chords with ease; on faster Macs, eight-note chords seem to be the maximum.

  The Mac's keyboard was never intended to be chorded, however. Indeed, it's been carefully engineered to process only one keypress at a time, for word processing purposes. Therefore, playing chords using MidiKeys results in a subtle, mandatory rolling effect, as each note sounds a few milliseconds after the preceding one.

  If the effect becomes noticeable, you can always clean up the chords after recording, using GarageBand's *quantizing* feature (page 94).

- While MidiKeys is quite useful for recording new tracks, it's also extremely handy when choosing an instrument sound for a track.

  Think about it: Ordinarily, when the New Track dialog box appears (Figure 4-4), GarageBand offers no way for you to *hear* what each listed sound sounds like (unless you have an external MIDI keyboard). Most people wind up laboriously clicking a sound's name, closing the dialog box, clicking the keys on the Garage-Band onscreen keyboard, double-clicking the track name to reopen the Track Info dialog box, and then repeating the whole ritual over and over.

Figure 4-4:
This dialog box appears when you choose Track→New Track. These instrument sounds all look delicious, but how are you supposed to know which one sounds exactly right for your piece? Simple: Press a few keys on your MIDI controller (or, if you're using MidiKeys, the bottom row of your keyboard). Use your arrow keys to "walk" through the instrument list, and "play" a few more keys to hear the next sound.

But with MidiKeys in background mode, you can click an instrument's name and then "play" a few notes on your Mac's keyboard to hear what it sounds like (while pressing the designated MidiKeys modifier key, of course)—all without leaving the Track Info dialog box.

If you fool around here long enough, you'll find some surprising selections, including sound effects, exotic percussion instruments, and traditional instruments that have been processed in wild, sometimes musically inspiring ways.

Tip: A very similar program called LoudK is also available on the Missing CD page at *www.missingmanuals. com.* It offers even more flexibility, like the ability to draw up your own map of keys-to-notes, but is also much more expensive ($70).

MIDI Synths and Controllers

The best way to record keyboard performances, though, is to bite the bullet, break the bank, and buy an actual, external MIDI musical instrument. As noted earlier in this chapter, it might take any of these forms:

• **A MIDI controller.** Apple, for instance, sells an M-Audio keyboard for $100. The only cable required is its USB cable, which connects directly to your Mac's USB port.

That's not the only controller worth considering, of course. If the idea of 49 keys strikes you as a bit confining, the same company also makes a 61-key model that Apple sells for $200. Online music stores like *www.samash.com* sell both of these models and many others, including a full 88-key model (the same number of keys as a real piano) for $300. These more expensive keyboards have semi-weighted keys that feel more like a piano than the spring-loaded plastic keys of the 49-key model.

• **A MIDI keyboard.** This category includes synthesizers, electric pianos, Clavinovas, and so on. Some connect directly to your Mac's USB port, but most require an adapter known as a *MIDI interface,* which costs about $40 at music stores.

• **Another MIDI instrument.** Keyboards aren't the only MIDI instruments. There are also such things as MIDI guitars, MIDI drum sets, and even MIDI gloves. They, too, generate streams of note information that GarageBand can record and play back.

Once you've hooked up a MIDI instrument, create a Software Instrument track and try playing a few notes. You'll hear whatever sound you established for that track, and you'll see the little MIDI activity "light" blinking in GarageBand's time display (Figure 4-2). Now you're ready to record.

Tip: An external instrument is also great when it's time to *choose* a sound for a new track, because you can walk through the various instrument names without ever having to close the Track Info dialog box. See Figure 4-4 for more information.

Recording a MIDI Track

Whether your keyboard is on the screen or on your desk, virtual or physical, you use it to record in GarageBand the same way. Here's the routine:

1. **Click the track you want to fill with music.**

   Remember, it must be a Software Instrument (green) track.

   If you don't already have a green track ready to record, choose Track→New Track to create one. In the New Track (Track Info) dialog box, click the Software Instrument tab, and then choose the instrument sound you want (Figure 4-4). Click OK.

2. **Turn on the metronome, if you like.**

   A *metronome* is a steady beat clicker that's familiar to generations of musicians. By clicking away "1, 2, 3, 4! 1, 2, 3, 4!" it helps to keep you and GarageBand in sync.

   Use the Control→Metronome command, or the ⌘-U keystroke, to turn the metronome clicker on or off. (See the box below.)

UP TO SPEED

When Not to Use the Metronome

GarageBand is perfectly capable of recording a keyboard performance without clicking away at you with its metronome. In fact, there's a very good reason you may not want the metronome turned on: If the piece you intend to play speeds up and slows down with the mood and the spirit. In those musical situations, a rigid, inflexible tempo would rob your music of all its spontaneity and feeling.

Of course, playing without the metronome means that your sense of where the beats and measures fall won't correspond with GarageBand's. Your measure 1, 2, and 3 won't line up with the beat ruler at the top of the GarageBand window.

That's not necessarily a bad thing. Listen to "03-Expressive Tempo," for example. (It's one of the songs on the Garage-Band Examples CD—see page 13.) It's a perfectly lovely piece. True, its beats and measures are all out of whack with GarageBand's sense of beats and measures. But when people listen to the music, they'll never know or care.

Playing without the metronome does mean, however, sacrificing some very useful GarageBand features. For one thing, you may find it difficult to add another track to the same piece. It's hard to play together with a free-form, flexible-tempo track that you've already recorded.

You lose much of the drag-and-drop region-editing flexibility described in Chapter 3, too. Remember how GarageBand regions' ends snap neatly against the underlying grid of beats and measures? If your more expressive grid doesn't align with GarageBand's, you're out of luck.

Finally, you won't be able to adjust the rhythm of your performance using GarageBand's Fix Timing button (13).

In more expensive recording programs (like Digital Performer, for example), you can actually teach the program to follow your own expressive tempo curve as you speed up and slow down; that is, you can make its conception of beats match what you play.

GarageBand, however, is a much more basic program that offers no way to automate a tempo change in the course of a piece. If you're trying to record anything that's more expressive than, say, a typical pop or rap song, you may be forced to go off the grid.

Tip: On the General pane of GarageBand→Preferences, you can indicate whether or not you want the metronome to play during *playback,* or only when you're recording.

3. **Choose a tempo for recording.**

   This is a very important step. Because you're using a *sequencer* (recording software) instead of a tape recorder, it makes no difference how slowly you record the part. You can *record* at 60 beats per minute, for example, which is basically one note per second—and then *play back* the recording at a virtuosic "Flight of the Bumblebee" tempo (229 beats per minute, say). Your listeners will never be the wiser.

   This isn't cheating; it's exploiting the features of your music software. It's a good bet, for example, that quite a few of the pop songs you hear on the radio were recorded using precisely this trick.

   So how do you find a good tempo for recording? First, just noodle around on your keyboard. Find a speed that feels comfortable enough that the music maintains *some* momentum, but is still slow enough that you can make it through the part without a lot of mistakes.

   Then adjust the GarageBand tempo slider to match. Hit the Space bar to play the music you've already got in place, if any, and adjust the Tempo control (page 76) during the playback until it matches the foot-tapping in your head.

Tip: If you haven't recorded *any* music, one way to hear the tempo as you fiddle with the Tempo control is to turn the metronome on during playback, as described in the preceding tip. Then play back your empty song, using the clicks as your guide while you adjust the Tempo slider.

   Once you've found a good recording speed, stop playback.

4. **Position the Playhead to the spot where you want to begin recording.**

   If that's the beginning, great; just press the letter Z key or the Home key. If it's in the middle of the piece, click in the beat ruler or use the keyboard shortcuts (page 15) to position the Playhead there. (Most often, though, you'll want to put the Playhead a couple of measures before the recording is supposed to begin, as described in the next step.)

5. **Set up your countoff.**

   It's very difficult to begin playing with the right feeling, volume, and tempo from a dead stop. That's why you always hear rock groups (and garage bands) start each other off with, "And a-one! And a-two!" That's also why most orchestras have a conductor, who gives one silent, preparatory beat of his baton before the players begin.

   GarageBand can "count you in" using either of two methods. First, it can play one measure full of beats, clicking "one, two, three, go!" at the proper tempo so you'll know when to come in. That's the purpose of the Control→Count In command.

When this command has a checkmark, GarageBand will count you in with those clicks.

If you intend to begin playing in the middle of existing music, though, you may prefer to have the music itself guide you to your entrance. This is the second method. For example, you might decide to plant the Playhead a couple of measures *before* the spot where you want to record. As long as doing so won't record over something that's already in your track, this is a convenient way to briefly experience the "feel" or "groove" of the music before you begin playing.

6. **Get ready to play—hands on the keyboard—and then click the red, round Record button.**

   Or just press the letter R key on your Mac keyboard.

   Either way, you hear the countoff measure, if you've requested one, and then the "tape" begins to roll. Give it your best, and try to stay in sync with the metronome, if you've turned it on.

7. **When you come to the end of the section you hoped to record—it might be the entire piece, or maybe just a part of it—tap the Space bar (or click the Play button) to stop recording.**

   On the screen, you'll see the new green region you recorded.

FREQUENTLY ASKED QUESTION

The Pickup Artist

Hey, how do I make the countoff work if my piece begins with a pickup?

Ah, there's an experienced musician in the audience. Welcome.

A pickup, in musical terms, is a note that begins a melody but doesn't fall on the downbeat (first beat) of the tune; it actually sounds right before the downbeat. In the Broadway song "Tomorrow" (from Annie), the lyrics go, "The sun'll come out, tomorrow." In this case, the word "The" is a pickup (and the downbeat is on the word "sun").

"Tomorrow" a little obscure for you? All right then, what about the national anthem? In "Oh-oh say can you see," that "oh-oh" is a pair of pickup notes. The *"say"* is the landing note, the beginning of the first full measure.

The reason GarageBand's countoff feature confuses the recording of pickups is that the program always counts off

one full measure of beats before it starts to listen to, and record, your playing. But if you're playing the melody for "Tomorrow," you'd actually count silently "one, two, three," and begin singing on "four." In that situation, GarageBand wouldn't record the first note of the song, because its countoff clicker insists that all four beats be silent.

Even if this discussion leaves you, a musical novice, out in the cold, the bottom line should be clear: If you find that GarageBand keeps not recording the first note or two that you play when the countoff feature is turned on, let a second nearly full measure of clicks go by before you play. That is, let the countoff go "1, 2, 3, 4, 1, 2, 3"–and then play your pickup.

In that case, GarageBand will "record" empty beats at the beginning of measure 1, so that your pickup will be heard at the end of it.

---

8. **Play back your recording to see how you did.**

Rewind to the spot where you started recording. If you recorded *under tempo* (that is, slower than you intend the playback to be), boost the tempo slider to a better setting. (Because you recorded a stream of MIDI note information and did not record actual digital audio, you can adjust the playback tempo at any time without changing the pitch of the notes. You couldn't get an "Alvin and the Chipmunks" effect if you tried.)

Tap the Space bar to hear your performance played back just as you recorded it.

Tip: Do what the pros do: Record a section at a time. The odds of a good take are much greater when the segment is short. Remember, too, that if your song contains repeating sections, you can reuse one perfect take by copying and pasting it to a different spot in the song.

Retakes

Even before you play back a new recording, you may know if it was a great performance, a good candidate but not necessarily your best effort, or a real stinker that must be deleted immediately. Maybe you messed up a portion of the playing. Maybe you had trouble keeping up with the metronome, or you felt as though it was holding you back.

The beauty of a MIDI sequencer like GarageBand, though, is that you can keep your take, redo it, or trash it, instantly and guilt-free, having used up no tape or studio time.

Here's how to proceed after recording a MIDI performance:

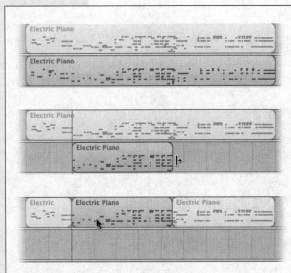

Figure 4-5:
Top: You've recorded this take twice, with mixed results each time.

Middle: Suppose the middle section of the second take was the best performance. Chop off both ends.

Bottom: Drag the remaining middle section upward onto the first take; this obliterates the corresponding moments of the first take. The result: A hybrid final track containing the best portions of each recording.

- **Trash the whole thing.** If the whole thing stank, press ⌘-Z to trigger the Edit→ Undo command. The new green region disappears. Adjust the tempo, if necessary, and try recording again.

Note: Before you go nuts deleting "bad" performances, though, remember that it's sometimes more time-efficient just to manually fix what was wrong with it, using the GarageBand track editor. See the next chapter.

- **Trash part of it.** Use the Edit→Split command (page 52) to cut the region into pieces, so that you can preserve the good parts but rerecord the bad ones.

- **Keep it.** If the whole thing was great, or mostly great, save your file (⌘-S) and move on to the next track.

- **Mark it "best so far."** Press the letter M key to mute the track you just recorded. Then create a new track and repeat the entire process, hoping to do better this time. After this second attempt—or your third, fourth, or fifth—you can compare your various takes by muting and un-muting them as they play back. You can also chop up these various regions and use only the best parts of each attempt, yet another extremely common practice in professional recording studios (Figure 4-5).

Tip: One great way to create a new track for the next attempt is to duplicate the first one (choose Track Duplicate→Track). GarageBand creates a new, empty track just below the first one—with the same instrument sound and effects (reverb and so on) already selected.

Spot Recording (Punch In/Punch Out)

If you're able to record an entire song perfectly the first time, with no mistakes—well, congratulations. Sony Records is standing by.

Most people, though, wind up wishing they could redo at least part of the recording. Usually, you played most of it fine, but botched a few parts here and there.

In the professional recording business, patching over the muffed parts is so commonplace, it's a standard part of the studio ritual. Clever studio software tools can play back the track right up until the problem section, seamlessly slip into Record mode while the player replays it, and then turn off Record mode when it reaches the end of the problem part, all without missing a beat. Recording engineers call this *punching in and out.*

Believe it or not, even humble GarageBand lets you punch in and punch out. Once you master this technique, you'll be very grateful.

Here's how it goes:

1. **Turn on cycling.**

    Page 12 describes *cycling* in the context of playing a section of music over and over again. For recording, the steps are much the same (see Figure 4-6). In this case, though, the beginning and end of the yellow Cycle bar designate your punch-in and punch-out points—the part you're going to rerecord.

2. **Set up your metronome and tempo. Turn on the Count In command (in the Control menu).**

See page 75 for details on setting up a recording. In this case, Count In is very important; it makes GarageBand play the one measure of music that precedes your punch-in point. (You don't have to position the Playhead for this exercise. Whenever Cycling is turned on, the Playhead always snaps to the beginning of the yellow stripe when playing or recording begins.)

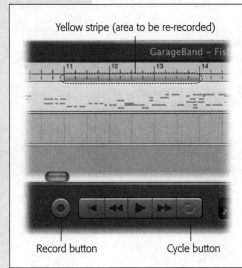

Yellow stripe (area to be re-recorded)

Record button   Cycle button

Figure 4-6:
Click the Cycle button—or press the letter C key—to make the yellow "repeat this much" bar appear at the top of the screen. Drag the ends of the yellow bar to identify the musical section you'll be loop-recording. (If you don't see the yellow bar, or if you want it to appear in a totally different section of the piece, drag through the lower section of the beat ruler.)

3. **Begin recording (by pressing the letter R key, for example).**

During the countoff measure, you don't just hear metronome clicks—you also hear the *existing* music in that preceding measure. GarageBand begins recording after the countoff, as the Playhead reaches the yellow cycle area.

As you record, you'll also hear the *old* material—the part you're trying to rerecord. Don't worry, though; it will disappear after you replace it. (If it bothers you, delete it manually before punching in.)

GarageBand doesn't play past the end of the yellow bar. Instead, it loops back to the beginning of the yellow bar and keeps right on recording. (This loop-record feature is the key to *cumulative recording,* described next.) If you nailed it on the first take, just stop playing.

4. **Press the Space bar (or click the Play button) to stop recording.**

When you play back the piece, GarageBand flows seamlessly from your original take to the newly recorded "patch" section.

Tip: This punch-in/punch-out routine is the only way to go if your goal is to rerecord precisely measured sections.

When the parts you want to rerecord have nicely sized "bookends" of silence before and after, though, there's a more casual method available. Just play the piece from the beginning—and "ride" the letter R key on your keyboard. With each tap, you jump into and out of Record mode as the piece plays. This *manual* punch-in/punch-out method offers another way to record over the bad sections and preserve the good ones.

Cumulative Recording

GarageBand's tricks for people with less-than-stellar musical ability don't stop with the slow-tempo-recording trick and the ability to rerecord certain sections. The Cycle button described earlier is also the key to cumulative recording, in which you record *one note* at a time, or just a few, building up more complexity to the passage as GarageBand loop-records the same section over and over (Figure 4-7).

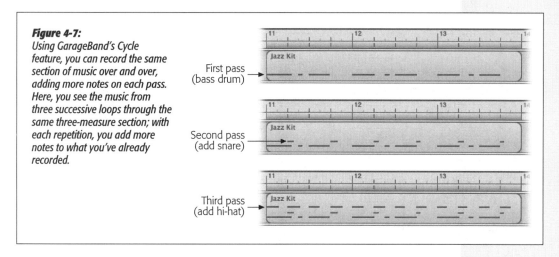

Figure 4-7:
Using GarageBand's Cycle feature, you can record the same section of music over and over, adding more notes on each pass. Here, you see the music from three successive loops through the same three-measure section; with each repetition, you add more notes to what you've already recorded.

First pass (bass drum)

Second pass (add snare)

Third pass (add hi-hat)

This trick is especially useful for laying down drum parts. In real life, drummers are surrounded by different kinds of drums; they're constantly reaching out and twisting to hit the different instruments at different times.

When you want to perform your *own* drum parts, you'll probably be using a MIDI keyboard. It turns out that GarageBand's various drum sounds—bass drum, snare drum, tom-toms, and so on—are "mapped" to the various keys of the keyboard (see Figure 4-8). Unless you have an extraordinarily unusual limb structure, you'll probably find it very difficult to play all the drums you want in a single pass, since they're scattered all over the keyboard.

It's much easier to record drum parts in successive passes, as GarageBand continues to record: the bass drum the first time, the snare on the next pass, and so on.

Here's how to set up loop recording:

1. Turn on cycling.

See step 1 of the preceding instructions. Figure 4-6 explains how to adjust the yellow Cycle bar. The point here is to "highlight" the portion of music you want to record.

2. Set up the recording.

Adjust the metronome, the Count In option, and the tempo, just as described in the previous pages. If you plan to record in the middle of a piece, place the Playhead to the left of the cycled region to give yourself a running start. (GarageBand will be in playback-only mode until it reaches the yellow Cycle bar.)

Click a track header to indicate which track you want to record. If you intend to lay down a drum track, fool around with your keyboard to identify which key plays which drum sounds. (The basic setup for GarageBand's drum kit is shown in Figure 4-8.)

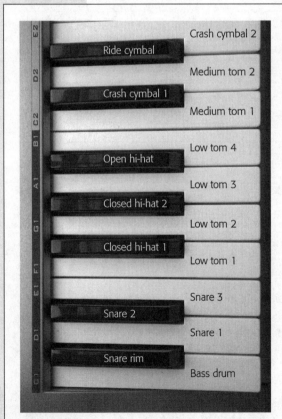

Figure 4-8:
Cumulative recording is especially useful for drum parts, because it lets you focus on only one drum sound at a time. This diagram illustrates how GarageBand's drums are mapped to the keys of your keyboard. (The different drum kits are all mapped identically, although what constitutes a snare or a low tom in the Jazz kit may not sound anything like the one in the Techno kit.)

The bass drum (kick drum), snare, and ride cymbals are the foundation of most drum parts, so these may be the keys you want to "ride" with three fingers as you record.

3. **Click the Record button (or press the letter R).**

   Each time GarageBand plays through the yellow-striped section, it will record any notes you play. Remember, GarageBand accumulates *all* the notes you play, adding them to the piece even if you play them on different repetitions of the looped passage.

Tip: It's OK to let a pass or two go by without playing anything. You just haven't added anything to the recording in progress, so no harm done. In fact, you might want to consider routinely sitting out a couple of repetitions between recording bursts.

Each time GarageBand loops back to the beginning of the section, you'll notice that it's already playing back what you laid down on previous passes. And when you finally stop (tap the Space bar) and play back the new passage, you'll discover that every note you played during the various repetitions plays back together.

Tip: Believe it or not, you can stop the playback, listen, do other work on your piece, and return much later to add yet another layer of cumulative-recording notes—as long as you haven't disturbed the yellow cycling bar in the beat ruler. Once you move that yellow stripe or turn off cycling, GarageBand ends your chance to record additional material in that region. The next recording you make there will wipe out whatever's there.

Mod Wheels and Other MIDI Fun

Many of GarageBand's built-in sounds are *samples*—brief recordings of actual instruments. That's why the grand piano sounds so realistic: because it *is* a grand piano (a $50,000 Yamaha, to be exact).

But behind the scenes, GarageBand's sounds have been programmed to respond to various impulses beyond just pressing the keys. They can change their sounds depending on what other MIDI information GarageBand receives from your keyboard.

For example:

- **Sustain pedal.** If you have a sustain or damper pedal, you can ride it with your foot just as you would on a piano. (It's designed to hold a note or a chord even after your hands have released the keys.) Almost any MIDI keyboard—including the $100 M-Audio Keystation—has a jack on the back for a sustain pedal, which costs about $15 from online music stores like *www.samash.com*.

- **Key velocity.** As noted earlier in this chapter, a number of GarageBand sounds respond to key velocity (that is, how hard you strike the keys). Most of the instrument sounds just play louder as you hit the keys harder, but some actually change in character. Acoustic guitars feature a little fingerboard slide; clavichords get more of a "wah" sound; Wah Horns also "wah" more; and many of the synthesizer keyboard sounds sound "rounder" as you hit the keys harder.

  Using the correct technical language, you would say that these instruments are velocity-sensitive.

- **Pitch and mod wheels.** Some keyboards, including that $100 M-Audio controller that Apple sells, have one or two *control wheels* that also affect GarageBand's sounds (Figure 4-9).

Figure 4-9:
On the M-Audio MIDI controller keyboards that Apple sells, two control wheels liven up the MIDI proceedings. The pitch-bend wheel actually bends the note's pitch. Just turn the wheel either before or after striking the note, depending on the effect you want. The modulation wheel, meanwhile, produces sound-changing effects, or does nothing, depending on the GarageBand sound you've selected.

For example, a *pitch bend* wheel makes a note's pitch slide up or down while you're still pressing the key. It's an essential tool for anyone who wants to make brass or wind instruments sound more realistic, since those instruments are capable of sliding seamlessly from pitch to pitch—something a keyboard, with its series of fixed-pitch keys, can't ordinarily do.

You can use the pitch wheel in either of two ways. First, turn the wheel downward, for example, and hold it (it's spring-loaded). Then, play the key you want—and simultaneously release the key. What you hear is a slide *up* to the desired note.

Second, you can strike the key first and *then* turn the wheel, or even wiggle the wheel up and down. The sound winds up wiggling or bending away from the original note, which is a common technique when you're trying to simulate, for example, the bending notes of a blues harmonica.

Tip: You can hear these effects in the sample file called 04-Control Wheels. It's on the GarageBand Examples CD described on page 13.

The pitch wheel affects *all* GarageBand sounds.

- Your keyboard may also have a *mod wheel,* short for modulation wheel. It's an all-purpose control wheel that produces different effects in different sounds. For example:

Instrument Name	Mod-Wheel Effect
Bass instruments	Brightens the sound
Choir sounds	Vibrato
Drum kits	No effect
Guitars	Vibrato
Most horns	Vibrato
Funk horns	"Fall-off" (slide down) at end of note
Mallets	Vibrato
Most organs	No effect
Vocoder Synth Organ	Searing distortion
Most pianos	No effect
Strings	Vibrato
Most Synth Basics	Vibrato
Star Sweeper	"Sweeps" the sound's phase
Synth Leads	Vibrato
Most Synth Pads	No effect or vibrato
Angelic Organ	"Clicks" through the sound
Aquatic Sunbeam	"Sweeps" the sound's phase
Electric Slumber	"Sweeps" the sound's phase
Liquid Oxygen	"Clicks" through the sound
Tranquil Horizon	"Sweeps" the sound's phase
Woodwinds	Vibrato

Note: *Vibrato* is the gentle wavering of pitch that's characteristic of most professional instrumental soloists and singers. (Real-world pianos and drum sets can't produce vibrato, which is why GarageBand's corresponding sounds don't react to the mod wheel.)

Learning to use your mod wheel can add a great deal of beauty, realism, and grace to your GarageBand recordings. Note, in particular, that you don't have to turn it all the way up; you can turn the wheel only part way for a more subtle effect. Remember, too, that the mod wheel is usually most effective when you turn it *after* the note has begun sounding. It's the contrast of the mod wheel (versus the unaffected note) that produces the best effect.

Editing Software Instrument Parts

Recording MIDI data, as described in the previous chapter, has a huge advantage over recording with a microphone: The results are almost infinitely *editable*. For example, you can delete wrong notes or drag them onto the right ones. If you played a section too loud, you can lighten it up after the fact. You can change the tempo or key of the music, making it faster, slower, higher, or lower, without distortion. If you discover a more appropriate instrument sound for a certain part, you can reassign the whole part.

In fact, GarageBand even lets you edit the invisible data generated by the foot pedal and control wheels.

The key to all of this freedom is the nature of the recordings you make with a MIDI keyboard: GarageBand stores your performance as a series of scheduled note triggers. When you play back your piece, GarageBand plays its own built-in synthesizer in real time. It's not playing back a sound recording.

The Track Editor

The doorway to all of this editing magic is the Track Editor, shown in Figure 5-1.

You can open this window in any of several ways:

- **Double-click a green region in the timeline.** This is the best way to open the Track Editor, because it appears prescrolled to the notes in the region you clicked.

- **Click the scissors icon ( ) beneath the track headers.** The Track Editor opens to the beginning of the first region on the track.

• Choose Control→Show Editor, or press ⌘-E. Once again, the Track Editor opens to the beginning of the track.

Tip: When the Editor window first appears, it shows only about an octave's worth of vertical space. Fortunately, you can drag upward on GarageBand's dark gray "brushed metal" divider strip—see Figure 5-1—to double the Editor's height. (You might remember having to do this when using the Loop browser, too. Unfortunately, you'll have to do it again each time you open GarageBand.)

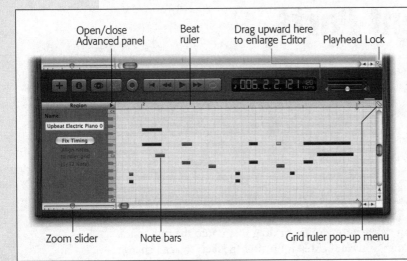

Open/close Advanced panel   Beat ruler   Drag upward here to enlarge Editor   Playhead Lock

Zoom slider   Note bars   Grid ruler pop-up menu

Figure 5-1:
The Track Editor reveals a close-up of your MIDI performance. Like an old-time piano roll, it resembles a grid. Time goes by horizontally, while the bars indicate the recorded notes on a vertical grid representing pitch. (The little piano-keys "ruler" at left should help you gain your bearings.)

Once you know your way around the Editor window, the editing itself is very easy. You can tug on the little note bars with your mouse to move, stretch, or shrink them. More about this in a moment.

For now, gain your bearings by noticing these controls:

• **Note bars.** These are the notes in the green MIDI region. (MIDI regions can be either GarageBand loops or music you've recorded yourself, as described in this chapter.) Longer bars represent longer notes.

Darker bars represent notes with greater *key velocity*—that is, keys that were hit harder (see the box on page 83). The lighter the shade of gray, the lighter that note was played.

• **Beat ruler.** These are the same measures of your piece that are represented by the beat ruler at the top of the GarageBand window.

But in designing the Track Editor, Apple's programmers faced a quandary. Should this Track Editor window be matched to the timeline area above it, so that when you scroll the top window, the Track Editor scrolls too? Or should you be able to scroll the top and bottom parts of the GarageBand window independently?

As it turns out, Apple gives you a choice (read on).

- **Playhead Lock button.** When this little icon looks like this 🔒, you can scroll the Track Editor independently of the main GarageBand window. In fact, during playback, the Playhead in the Track Editor screen may chug merrily right off the screen. In this situation, GarageBand scrolls automatically only when the *upper* Playhead hits the edge of your window.

  But when you click the icon so that it looks like this 🔒, both parts of the window scroll together. The Playhead line moves across (and autoscrolls) both parts of the window.

- **Zoom slider.** You can see more of the song at once in the Time Editor by dragging this slider to the left, which causes the beat ruler (and all the notes) to get smaller. To zoom in for finer editing, drag the slider handle to the right, which makes the ruler and the note bars grow.

Tip: You don't have to drag the little slider's handle. It's often faster simply to click *in* the slider. The handle jumps to the spot of your click. (In fact, this tip applies to *all* GarageBand sliders.)

- **Scroll bars.** These scroll bars work like any Macintosh scroll bars, but they're especially important in the Track Editor. If you open the Editor using either the scissors icon or the Show Editor command, the Track Editor window often appears to be completely *blank*. It opens to some portion of the track that has no notes in it. You're left to wonder whether the notes are higher or lower than what's currently on display, or sooner or later. In both of those situations, you'll wind up doing a lot of scrolling.

  This sense of Editor disorientation is a good argument for opening it using the first method described above: by double-clicking a region in the timeline.

Tip: You can also scroll the Track Editor by dragging your cursor through it in the direction you want to go. (Avoid beginning your drag directly on a note bar, though.)

- **Advanced panel.** You can read about the editing controls of this panel in the following pages. For now, just note the tiny triangle that opens and—when you need more space—closes it, as identified in Figure 5-1.

- **Grid ruler pop-up menu.** This little+ menu works just as it does in the Timeline window. It's a list of basic rhythmic values (1/4 Note, 1/2 Note, and so on) that adjusts the fine vertical grid lines in the Track Editor.

  This rhythmic grid comes into play in several situations. First, the beginnings and endings of your note bars automatically snap against these gridlines when you drag, as described below. Second, GarageBand makes *all* selected notes snap to the nearest gridline when you use the Fix Timing command (page 94). Third, this setting determines the value of any new notes you create by ⌘-clicking, as described in the next section.

The Encyclopedia of MIDI Editing

Now that you know how to navigate the Track Editor, you can get down to the business of using it to rewrite history: changing the recorded music.

Note: Any edits you make to a MIDI region that you've *looped* (by dragging its upper-right corner) appear in *all repetitions* of that loop, which may take you by surprise.

If you'd like to edit only *one* repetition, create it by copying and pasting the original region, so that it's no longer related to the original.

- **Hear a note** by clicking it. (Clicking a note bar also turns it bright green to show that it's selected.)

- **Delete a selected note** by pressing the Delete key.

- **Change a note's pitch** by dragging its note bar up or down, using the center of the note bar as a handle. (If the note won't seem to budge, try zooming in. GarageBand probably considered the note bar too small to make a decent handle.)

- **Shorten or lengthen a note** by dragging the right end of its bar. You'll discover that GarageBand forces the note's end to align with the current note grid, described above. (Once again, try zooming in if you're having trouble.)

Note: You can't shorten a note from its left side. If your intention is to lop off the "front" of a note, drag the entire note, as described next, and then shorten the *right* side.

- **Make a note play sooner or later** by dragging its center horizontally.

  You'll notice that as you drag a note, it snaps to the next rhythmic grid line (quarter note, eighth note, or whatever value you've selected from the Grid Ruler pop-up menu shown in Figure 5-1). That's GarageBand's attempt to help keep your music in sync.

  If you'd like to be able to drag freely, choose Control→Snap to Grid (⌘-G), so that the checkmark no longer appears.

- **Duplicate a note** by Option-dragging its bar. This trick works whether you drag vertically or horizontally.

- **Insert a new note** by ⌘-clicking at the appropriate spot. (As soon as you press the ⌘ key, the cursor turns into a little pencil to let you know what's about to happen.)

  Use the vertical, left-side piano keyboard ruler as a guide to pitch, and the beat ruler to help you figure out where you are in the song.

  You'll soon discover, by the way, that you can't ⌘-*drag* to determine the length of the note you insert. Every new note you create has the same duration. That value (eighth note, for example) is determined by the setting in the Grid Ruler pop-up menu shown in Figure 5-1.

You can always adjust a note's length once it appears in the Track Editor, of course, by dragging its right end. But when you intend to insert a bunch of notes of similar value, it's worth taking the time to select that duration from the Grid Ruler pop-up menu first.

Tip: Very often, the fastest way to create a new note is not to use the ⌘-click trick at all. Instead, Option-drag an existing note bar to duplicate it; then, before you release the mouse, move it to the proper pitch and time. The first advantage here is that you can duplicate a note that already has the duration and velocity you want; the second is that you can duplicate a *batch* of selected notes at once.

- **Select a few notes** by clicking one, then Shift-clicking each additional note. (Shift-click a second time to remove a note bar from the selected group.)

- **Select a lot of notes** by dragging a selection box around them (Figure 5-2).

Either way, once you've selected notes, you can perform several editing maneuvers to all of them at once. For example, you can cut or copy them (described next), delete them, Option-drag to duplicate them, stretch or shorten them (drag the right end of any *one* selected note bar), drag them up or down in pitch, drag them left or right in time, and so on. They retain their original timings and relationships.

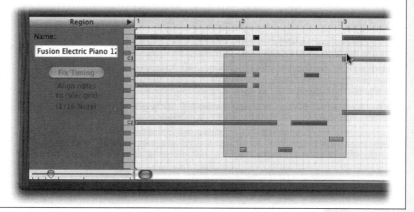

Figure 5-2:
To select a batch of notes, begin dragging diagonally from a blank spot of the Track Editor. Your selection will include any note bar that's even partly enclosed by the resulting box.

When you drag them, they remain in perfect formation.

- **Cut/copy and paste notes to a different spot** by selecting them, choosing Edit→Copy (⌘-C) or Edit→Cut (⌘-X), clicking in the Editor's beat ruler to place the Playhead, and then choosing Edit→Paste (⌘-V). The notes you copied or cut appear at the Playhead position.

GarageBand *adds* pasted notes to whatever already occupies the paste position, rather than wiping out what's there.

Transposing Notes or Regions

To *transpose* music means to shift it up or down into a different key, raising or lowering its pitch. The ability to transpose recordings and loops is a key advantage that Software Instruments (green) have over digital recordings from a microphone. You can also transpose Apple's own digital recordings (blue loops), although they sound funny if you move them too far from their originally recorded pitches.

Transposing is a very useful feature. For example, it lets you:

- Adapt a song that was in the perfect singing key for somebody else into the perfect singing key for *you*, without rerecording it.

- Reuse Apple's canned loops in other keys, greatly expanding your palette of chords and harmonies (see Figure 5-3).

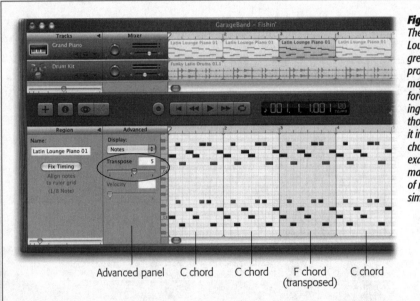

Figure 5-3:
The loop called Latin Lounge Piano 01 is a great little lick. The only problem is that it's a C major chord, now and forever. By transposing copies of this loop, though, you can turn it into any other major chord—F and G, for example—and thereby make it fit the harmonies of many harmonically simple compositions.

Advanced panel   C chord   C chord   F chord   C chord
(transposed)

- Quickly create an "echo" of a certain musical lick that plays back an octave higher or lower than the first occurrence of that melody.

Now, if you want to transpose only *some* of the notes in a green Software Instrument region, open the Track editor and use any of the selection techniques described in the previous section. Then drag them up or down, using any one of them as a handle.

The official GarageBand Transpose slider, though, works only on *entire regions*. It goes like this:

1. **Select the region you want to transpose.**

If you've opened a region for editing in the Track Editor, GarageBand will transpose all of it, regardless of which notes are selected.

You can click a region in the timeline, select a number of regions simultaneously (Shift-click them in the timeline), select all the regions in a track (click the track header), or select the entire piece at once (click in the timeline area and then choose Edit→Select All, or press ⌘-A).

2. **Open the Advanced panel, if necessary.**

You open it by clicking the little triangle identified back in Figure 5-1.

3. **Specify how far you want to transpose the region(s).**

Use the Transpose slider—drag right to transpose the notes higher, left to make them play lower—or type a number into the box just above the slider.

Both of these controls display the number of *half steps* by which you're about to transpose the selected notes. (A half-step is one piano key to the right or left.)

For example, typing *1* here would transpose a middle C up to C sharp, which is the black key just to its right. If you type *2* here, you'd transpose a middle C up to D, the *white* key just to its right.

If you know a little bit about music, you may find the following equivalents handy: To transpose up a major third, enter *4*. Up a fourth, enter *5*. Up a perfect fifth, type *7*. Up an octave, enter *12*.

And to transpose the selection *down,* either drag the slider handle to the left, or type a *negative* number into the box (*-12* for an octave down, for example).

You can transpose green Software Instrument regions up to 36 half-steps in either direction (that is, three octaves up or down). You can transpose blue Real Instrument loops 12 half-steps up or down (one octave).

Tip: If you transpose a Real Instrument loop upward and it sounds a little funny—because you've shifted it out of its natural range—try transposing it down a whole octave, so that it lands on the same pitch but in a lower register.

For example, suppose you transpose a bass lick down 4 half-steps, from C to A flat, and it winds up sounding muddy. Think to yourself: *I transposed it by -4; what would be the equivalent pitch 12 half-steps higher? Well, -5 plus 12 = 8.* Drag the slider to 8, and sure enough, you get the same notes, but in a more natural-sounding range.

---

4. **Remain calm.**

What's slightly alarming about transposing in GarageBand is that there's *no visible change,* which is especially puzzling when it comes to green Software Instruments. You might expect to see the note bars move higher on the Editor grid when you transpose them upward, or lower when you transpose downward. But instead, the note bars remain exactly where they are (Figure 5-3 proves the point). Blue loops don't look any different, either.

Even though they don't *look* different, they do *sound* different. Play back a section that you transposed, and you'll hear the difference immediately.

You'll just have to get used to the audio-visual disconnect.

Tip: If, much later in the editing process, you can't seem to figure out why some notes don't seem to play-ing on the proper pitches, click one of them. The Transpose slider reveals whether or not you've transposed the region.

If you ever want to restore a region to its original recorded pitch, select it and set the Transpose slider to its center position (or type *0* into the box above it).

Quantizing (Fix Timing)

When Apple representatives demonstrate GarageBand in public, the feature that often gets the most oohs and aahs from the audience is the Fix Timing button. With one quick click, it magically cleans up any recording that has less-than-perfect rhythm. What sounds at first a little ragged, a bit stumbling, suddenly plays back with clean, perfect timing.

Among computer-based musicians, the term for this cleanup is called *quantizing* or *quantization.* In GarageBand, you quantize your music using a button in the Track Editor called Fix Timing.

When you click this button, GarageBand automatically moves all of the notes in a region into perfect alignment with the underlying rhythm grid. In effect, it "rounds off" each note's attack to the nearest eighth note, sixteenth note, or whatever rhythmic value you've specified in the Grid Ruler pop-up menu.

When Not to Quantize

This all sounds wonderful, of course—who wouldn't want a magic button that makes you sound like a better player?—but quantizing is a delicate art. It *can* make your music sound better and cleaner. But it can also create a cacophonous mess.

Many musicians regard quantizing with a certain degree of skepticism. Here's what can go wrong:

- If Fix Timing nudges some notes into alignment with the *wrong* gridlines, your recording may turn into a horrible sounding, clashing crash (Figure 5-4).

- Quantizing drains a lot of the humanity out of a performance. After all, the tiny quirks and inconsistencies are what give a performance its personality; they make a performance *yours.* When you make every note snap against a fixed-rhythm grid, the music can wind up sounding machine-generated and robotic.

The invention of quantizing software in the '80s helped usher in musical styles that are *supposed* to sound rigidly rhythmic, like disco and rap. But after a while, many musicians grew disenchanted with the way quantizing reduces everything to a machine-gun stutter. Today, professional sequencing programs offer features like *partial* quantization, which lets you specify what *degree* of quantizing you want, and *reverse* quantization (or "humanizing"), which deliberately introduces minor rhythmic inaccuracies into an overly quantized recording to make it sound more human.

GarageBand lacks these less severe quantizing options. It's an all-or-nothing take on quantizing.

Figure 5-4:
Top: These notes were supposed to be running sixteenth notes (four fast notes per beat), but they're not quite precise.

Bottom: One click on "Fix Timing" later, they're precise, all right, but they don't sound anything like the original music. They've turned into ugly, clomping chords.

(Part of the problem was the quarter-note grid—selected for comic purposes to make this point.)

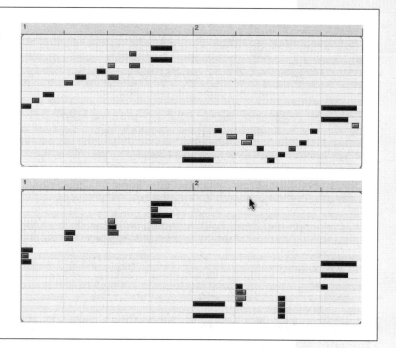

- Quantizing flattens out musical effects like grace notes (a lightly played, very quick note right before the main note), glissandos (sliding down the keyboard with a finger), and rolled chords (rolling the hand through a chord rather than striking all notes of it at once). All of the notes in these musical figures get pushed to the nearest eighth-note or sixteenth-note gridline, thereby changing them from delicate special effects into clashing, wrong-note chords.

Tip: On the GarageBand Examples CD (page 13), listen to the file called 05-Quantizing. Double-click the piano region, set the Grid Ruler pop-up menu to "1/8 Note," and then click Fix Timing.

Now play the file back again to see what's become of the piano part. Let this sample file be a lesson about when *not* to use quantization.

How to Quantize

These downsides notwithstanding, quantizing can still be a very useful cleanup maneuver, especially in the kinds of rock, rap, and hip-hop music for which GarageBand is so well suited. Subtlety and nuance are not necessarily the most prized qualities in those styles.

Here's how to go about fixing the timing of your performance:

1. **Select the music you want to quantize.**

   To quantize an entire region, click its green, rounded rectangle in the timeline (and don't click inside the Track Editor). You can even select more than one region for quantizing just by Shift-clicking them, or an entire track by clicking its header. (You can't quantize more than one track at a time.)

   To quantize only some of the notes in a region, open the Track Editor and select the bars as described on page 91.

2. **Using the Grid Ruler pop-up menu (the tiny ruler icon just above the Editor window's vertical scroll bar), choose the kind of grid you want.**

   If you choose too large a value, like "1/4 Note," all of the faster notes in the region will wind up clumped around the quarter-note gridlines in big, ugly, clashing chords (see Figure 5-3). But if you choose too fine a value, like "1/32 Note," then GarageBand may nudge some of your notes into alignment with the *wrong* gridline—for example, moving certain notes forward instead of backward where you meant them to go—resulting in a stuttering, halting disaster.

   The "correct" setting depends on the tempo of your piece, what kind of notes are in it, and the effect you're looking for. Experimentation is the only way to find a setting that works.

UP TO SPEED

Beyond Pitch Bend

It's kind of neat that GarageBand records, displays, and edits streams of MIDI information like pitch bend, key velocity, and pedaling. But in the real world of MIDI, those kinds of data are only the beginning. Professional music software can record and play back dozens of other kinds of invisible MIDI data.

Aftertouch, for example, is a measurement of how much pressure you apply to a key after you've pushed it down. Of course, a real piano doesn't respond to aftertouch at all; once you've pressed down a key, pressing harder doesn't give you anything but a thumb-ache. But on some synthesiz-

ers, bearing down harder on a key after it's already down triggers, say, the vibrato sound on a trumpet.

Program Change data lets you switch to a different synthesizer sound in mid-performance. Breath controller data is generated by a special attachment that, yes, you breathe into, giving you yet another way to change the "shape" of the sound.

GarageBand doesn't record or let you edit these MIDI data types (not that most GarageBand musicians would even care).

Fortunately, if the Fix Timing button makes a mess of things, you can always choose Edit→Undo (⌘-Z) and try a different setting—or just drag the offending note bars into grid alignment by hand.

Velocity, Pedaling, and Other MIDI Data

As you've probably started to gather by now, there's more to a musical performance than deciding which notes to play when. A keyboard player, for example, adds nuance and interest to a performance using a number of other tools. The *velocity* of the playing (how hard each key is struck), the pedaling (using a sustain pedal connected to the keyboard), and the control wheels (pitch and modulation) can all affect the way the music sounds.

GarageBand records all of this information as you play and lets you edit it later. The key to viewing and editing these kinds of MIDI information is the Advanced panel of the Track Editor (Figure 5-5).

Editing Key Velocity

As you know from the box on page 69, key velocity is a digital record of how hard you pressed each key when you recorded a MIDI region. On some instruments, greater key velocity just means "louder," as it does on a piano. But in others, greater velocity means "more vibrato," "crunchier sound," and so on.

Key velocity is measured on a scale of 0 to 127, which may not seem like an especially logical scale to *you,* but (because it's a power of 2) it's very convenient for the Mac to understand. In any case, a velocity of 1 indicates a key pressed with all the force of a falling pigeon feather; a velocity of 127 reflects the force of, say, a second piano falling onto the first. (GarageBand doesn't actually let you change a note's velocity to 0, because that would be a nonsensical value for most musical purposes.)

In the Track Editor, a note bar's *color* indicates its key velocity, as you can see here:

Note color	Key velocity
Light gray	0–31
Medium gray	32–63
Dark gray	64–95
Black	96–127

To edit your notes' key velocities, first open the Track Editor's Advanced panel identified in Figure 5-5. Then proceed as shown in the same figure.

Note: Things can get tricky when you've selected multiple notes with different velocities. In that case, the slider and the number box show the *highest* key velocity among the selected notes. But as you make the adjustment, you're adding or subtracting the *same* amount from all other notes.

If you select three notes, therefore, that have velocity settings of 20, 30, and 40, the Velocity box will say 40. If you drag the slider to shave 10 off the heaviest note, the first two notes will also have decreased by 10. The three notes will now have velocity settings of 10, 20, and 30.

By adjusting key velocities in this way, you can perform a number of different musical-surgical procedures:

- Make an entire *lick* (short musical passage) play with more emphasis. Or less.

- Change the "color" of a chord by lightening up on some notes, and bringing out others.

- Add vibrato to the *money note* (the highest, longest, most important note) of a flute solo.

- Edit an acoustic guitar part so that the sliding grace notes play only where you want them to. (When struck with a key velocity of 124 or higher, most GarageBand acoustic-guitar samples add a little sliding grace note upward from the next lower note.)

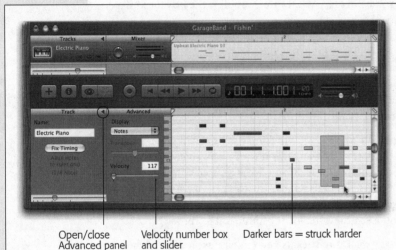

Figure 5-5:
To edit key velocity, first select the note or notes you want to affect, as shown here. Then, change their velocity using either the Velocity number box—type in a new number from 0 to 127—or the slider beneath it.

Open/close Advanced panel

Velocity number box and slider

Darker bars = struck harder

Editing Pedaling

If your MIDI keyboard has a sustain pedal—the electronic equivalent of the rightmost pedal on a regular piano—then GarageBand records your foot-presses right along with the key-presses. In the Track Editor, it draws a map of the ups and downs of the pedal, as shown in Figure 5-6. Each little ball represents one change in the sustain pedal's status.

Note: As with key velocity, sustain-pedal motion is recorded on a scale of 0 to 127. Unlike key velocity, however, there's no such thing as a sustain-pedal setting *between* 0 and 127. After all, in the real world, there's no such thing as *half*-pressing the pedal on a piano. So every value is either 0 or 127—which GarageBand tries to simplify by labeling the lines 0 and 1—and your pencil cursor will snap either to the "up" line or the "down" line.

You can use the Track Editor to edit pedaling you recorded during a performance, of course. But you can also use it to add pedaling to a performance that didn't have any to begin with—a performance you created using MidiKeys (page 70), for example, or a MIDI keyboard that didn't have a pedal.

Figure 5-6:
Don't be fooled: When the line is up, the sustain pedal is down, and vice versa. In the world of MIDI software, this particular graph is upside-down from the physical control—the foot pedal—that generates its data. That is, up is "on," and down is "off."

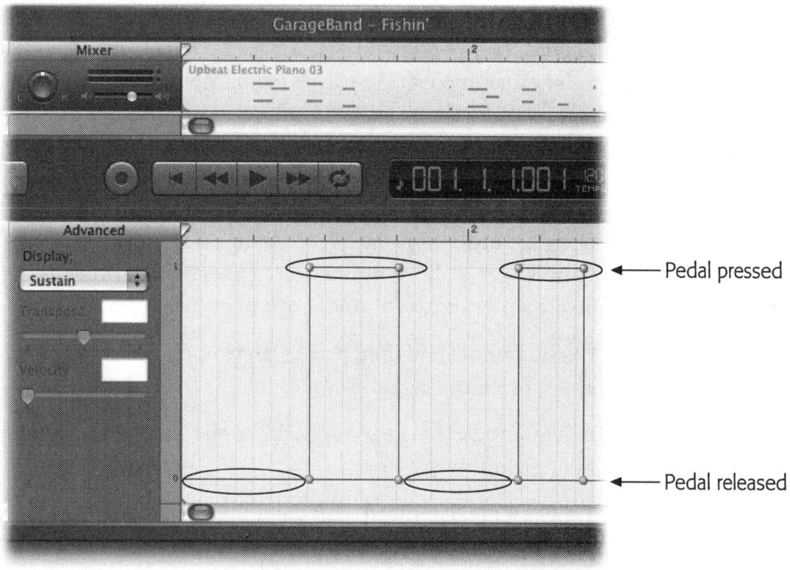

Pedal pressed ◄—

Pedal released ◄—

Pedaling step by step

Either way, the steps are the same. (If you'd like to follow along, create a new document and insert the loop called Upbeat Electric Piano 03. Its notes are short and sharp, so you'll hear a clear difference when you start adding the sustain pedal.)

1. **Open the Advanced panel of the Track Editor.**

   You can see the little triangle to click for the Advanced panel in Figure 5-5.

2. **From the Display pop-up menu, choose Sustain.**

   You've just told GarageBand which kind of invisible MIDI data you want to change.

3. **While pressing the ⌘ key, click a spot along the light gray, top line (labeled 1 in Figure 5-6).**

   GarageBand creates a round handle at the point you clicked. You've just created a "sustain pedal down" event where none existed. (Technically, you can click anywhere in the upper half of the Track Editor window, since GarageBand "rounds off" your click to the top line to indicate a full press of the foot pedal.)

   If you play back your region at this point, you'll hear all the notes get "stuck on" at the point where you created the pedal-down event. Unless you enjoy the cumulative, mushy, clashing sound of every note in the piece being held down forever, find a spot to *release* the sustain pedal:

4. **Move the cursor to the right, and then ⌘-click a spot on the bottom gray line.**

   Another round handle appears, this time indicating where your virtual player should take his foot off the pedal. A quick playback will prove the point.

Editing existing pedaling

If you've ever edited volume levels of an iMovie video soundtrack, these round handles should seem familiar. They're audio control points, which you can slide around to fine-tune where they appear.

For example, here's what you can do with pedaling points:

- **Drag a handle right or left** to change *when* the pedaling takes place. The control point directly above or below it, if there is one, goes along for the ride, because it takes two to represent one movement of the pedal.

- **Click a handle and then press Delete** to eliminate that handle *and* the one directly above or below it.

   As you'll quickly discover, clicking *one* handle also highlights the one vertically in line with it.

   For example, if your pedaling map now looks like Figure 5-6, deleting the second pair of vertically aligned points will merge the first pedal press "mountain" with the second one. You'll be left with a single, but longer, pedal-press.

- **⌘-click the top or bottom line** to introduce a new control point.

Editing Control Wheel Data

Many MIDI keyboards—including the $100 M-Audio keyboard that Apple sells as a companion for GarageBand—have one or two *control wheels* at the left side. The pitch wheel lets you bend a note higher or lower in pitch (like a blues harmonica). Its sibling, the modulation wheel, can do a variety of things, like add a sweet vibrato to the sound, change its character, or do nothing at all, depending on which instrument sound you've selected. See page 83 for more on using control wheels.

Here again, the Track Editor lets you edit any pitch wheel or mod wheel information you generated while recording. It even lets you "turn" one of those wheels after the fact, even if you don't even have a keyboard with control wheels.

To inspect your control wheel data, open the region in the Track Editor, open the Advanced panel (Figure 5-5), and from the Display pop-up menu, choose either Pitchbend or Modulation. If pitch wheel or mod wheel information is already a part of the recording, you'll see something like Figure 5-7.

Note: As shown in Figure 5-7, pitch wheel effects usually involve turning the wheel *in between* notes, getting into ready position, and then releasing it, so that it returns to its spring-loaded "at rest" position *during* a note. Or you can do the opposite: Press a key, turn the pitch wheel up or down, and then release both together. Either way, don't be fooled by the up-down and down-up "hills" graphed in Figure 5-7; half of each "hill" actually takes place during the silence between notes.

Most people turn the mod wheel, the other hand, both up and down during a single note (to make the vibrato gradually begin and end, for example).

Figure 5-7:
When you're viewing pitch wheel information, as shown here, the ruler scale goes both upward and downward from 0, because a pitch wheel's "at rest" position is in the middle (see Figure 4-9). You can turn it either up or down. A mod wheel's "at rest" position, though, is turned all the way down, and you turn it only upward, so its scale goes from 0 (at rest) to 127 (all the way up).

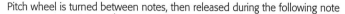
Pitch wheel is turned between notes, then released during the following note

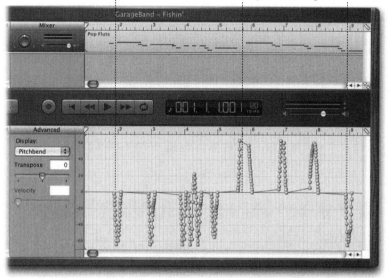

Pitch wheel data is represented on a scale of 0 (when you're not touching the wheel) to positive or negative 63 (when you've turned the wheel as far as it will go); the mod wheel's scale goes from 0 (at rest) to 127 (turned all the way).

In the case of the pitch wheel, each notch (from 0 to 1, for example) represents one half-step, which is one adjacent key on a piano keyboard. That's useful to remember if you're inclined to add pitch wheel data to a recording manually (because your keyboard doesn't have wheels, for example).

Once you've got that fact in mind, the techniques for adjusting or creating wheel control points are very similar to the methods for working with sustain pedal data:

- ⌘-click in the Track Editor to create a new round control handle. This is how you'd start "turning" the wheel during a note even if you don't actually have a keyboard with wheels.

• **Drag a control handle** horizontally to change its timing, or vertically to adjust the intensity of its effect. (Again, 0 means "wheel is at rest.")

• **Select a group of control handles** to move them all at once; drag any *one* of them as a handle.

This tactic is especially useful when you want to edit pitch bend or mod wheel data in a track that you recorded live. As shown in Figure 5-7, using a control wheel during a live performance generates a *torrent* of control handles. Turning the wheel smoothly and gradually, as you would in a live performance, spits out dozens of control points (0-3-5-11-22-24, and so on). By dragging a whole batch of points at once, you can adjust the timing or intensity of a wheel turn with a single drag. The selected points retain their spatial relationship as you drag them.

• **Delete a turn of the wheel** by selecting all of the representative control points and then pressing the Delete key.

Control wheels: do-it-yourself

If you'd like to experiment with control wheel data, create a new GarageBand project. Double-click the icon of the Grand Piano starter track, scroll down to Woodwinds, click Pop Flute, and then close the dialog box. (A flute is a great sound for testing control wheels, because its notes are long and sustained so that you can hear the effects over time.)

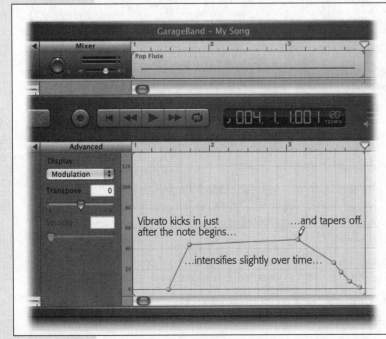

Figure 5-8:
Most instruments' vibratos sound most realistic with the mod wheel turned up only part way—about 50 or so. For added realism, make the vibrato begin and end gradually, and don't begin the wheel turn until a moment after the note has been struck.

Now open the miniature GarageBand onscreen keyboard (choose Window→Keyboard, or press ⌘-K). Press the letter R key on your keyboard to begin recording, and hold down a long note—C4, for example—on the little onscreen keyboard. Press the Space bar to stop recording after a few seconds of that note.

Now double-click the new green region to open the Track Editor. Make sure the Display pop-up menu says Notes. Zoom in until the note bar you recorded stretches across most of the screen.

Change the Display pop-up menu to say Pitchbend. Now, starting at the 0 midline, go nuts ⌘-clicking control points into a hilly shape, as shown in Figure 5-7. When you play this back, you'll hear the gradual bending of the note over time.

You can repeat the same experiment with the modulation wheel. But this time, start your "hill" from the 0 line at the bottom of the graph, as shown in Figure 5-8. You'll hear your virtual flutist add a gradual vibrato to the note as the "hill" of your mod wheel graph gets higher.

Recording and Editing Live Audio

W hen you get right down to it, GarageBand is actually three programs in
one. It's a loop-building program that lets anyone build great-sounding
compositions, even with no musical training. It's a MIDI sequencing
program that records whatever you play on a MIDI-compatible keyboard, guitar,
or drum set. And now, as you're about to find out, it's also a digital multi-track tape
recorder that can record live sound.

That's an important feature, because plenty of musical sources don't have MIDI
jacks—including your own voice, not to mention mandolins, harps, violins, castanets,
and eight-year-olds burping.

The beauty of GarageBand is that lets you layer these recordings *on top of* tracks that
you've built using its other tools (like loops and MIDI performances), and can play
all of it back together at once. The creative possibilities that result are mind-blowing—and make possible a world where Joe Nobody, a guy with a great voice but no
money, can produce a studio-caliber demo CD in his living room.

But using GarageBand for *nothing* but its audio-recording features is also perfectly
legitimate. Forget the loops, forget MIDI, just use it as a tape recorder with a lot of
tracks. You'll still enjoy the freedom to edit your recordings, stack up tracks to create
harmony, process them with special sound effects, and mix the whole thing down to
a polished, single track.

The Setup

GarageBand can record live audio from two kinds of sound inputs: microphones, and direct line inputs (from electronic instruments like guitars and keyboards, audio interface boxes, and mixers).

The Microphone

To record singing, acoustic instruments, or the world around you, you'll need a microphone.

Note: Some acoustic guitars have built-in pickups. If yours does, you don't need a microphone; you can plug the guitar straight into an audio interface, as described next.

This mike can take any of several forms:

- **The built-in microphone on Mac laptops, iMacs, and eMacs.** The drawback of this approach is that you might also pick up the Mac's own fan sounds, and the quality isn't quite studio caliber. But it's cheap, it's built-in, and it works fine for everyday recordings.

- **A cheapo USB microphone.** At Amazon.com or Buy.com, you can pick up a microphone that plugs directly into your Mac's USB port for under $20. They come

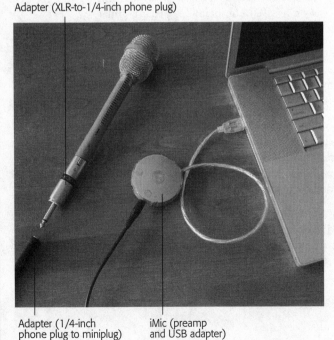

Adapter (XLR-to-1/4-inch phone plug)

Adapter (1/4-inch phone plug to miniplug)

iMic (preamp and USB adapter)

Figure 6-1:
Adapting your microphone to the Mac may require more than one adapter. Here, a professional microphone (with an XLR connector on the end) connects to a plug adapter, which goes into a Griffin iMic for signal boosting. The iMic then plugs into the Mac's USB jack.

in two forms: Headset mikes, designed for use with speech-recognition software, and desktop mikes, which stick up, stalk-like, from a little stand on your desk. Both work great for recording vocals and—if you position them close to the sound source—acoustic instruments.

- **A regular microphone.** If you have access to a more professional microphone, then by all means, use it. You might run into two problems, though.

First, there's the little matter of fitting the microphone's cable into the Mac's tiny, one-eighth-inch, Walkman-headphones miniplug microphone input (see Figure 6-1). If your microphone's cable ends in a quarter-inch phono plug instead, or even a professional, nickel-sized XLR connector, the cheerful staff at your local Radio Shack will be happy to sell you an adapter. (At Apple's Web site and others, you can buy this adapter in the form of the $20 Monster iStudioLink.)

Second, many microphones (and other sound sources, like record players and tape decks) don't put out enough signal for the Mac's microphone jack. You'll probably need a *preamp* to boost the signal to audible levels.

The most inexpensive option is the $40 Griffin iMic (*www.griffintechnology.com*), which offers not only a built-in preamp but also cleaner sound circuitry than what's built into the Mac. (It, too, is shown in Figure 6-1.)

For even more flexibility, you can use an *audio interface* box like the M-Audio MobilePre USB, which you can also find on the Apple Web site ($150). This more professional box offers three different kinds of input jacks for various microphones and instruments, including both microphone preamp inputs and high-impedance instrument inputs for guitars and basses.

Both the iMic and the MobilePre draw their power from the USB jack, so you don't even have to carry along a power adapter.

Line Inputs

If you have an electric guitar, electric violin, or synthesizer keyboard whose built-in sounds you want to capture, don't bother with the microphone. Instead, connect the instrument's line output cable (which would otherwise go into an amplifier) into an audio interface, like the iMic or M-Audio MobilePre described above. The audio interface then plugs into your Mac's USB port.

In more elaborate setups, you can even connect the outputs from a standalone mixing console. You'd do that if, for example, you wanted to record the playing from several live instruments at once into a single GarageBand track. (Of course, using a very basic program like GarageBand to record from thousands of dollars' worth of recording equipment in this way is a little like using iMovie to edit "Lord of the Rings," but hey—whatever floats your boat.)

Because this cable is coming directly from a sound source and not from a microphone, it's called a *line input*.

Introducing the Mac

As you're starting to realize, the Mac is capable of recording sound from a number of different sources: its own built-in mike, an external mike, a line input, and so on. When the moment comes to click the Record button in GarageBand, how will the Mac know what to listen to?

You'll tell it ahead of time, that's how. Figure 6-2 shows the two-step procedure.

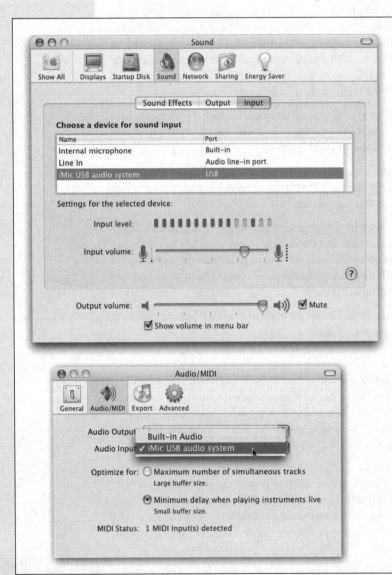

Figure 6-2:
Top: From the menu, choose System Preferences. Click the Sound icon; then click the Input tab. Specify which sound source you want to record (in this case, a microphone connected to the iMic adapter). Before you close this window, drag the slider to adjust the general volume level for your singing or playing. Ideally, the loudest notes should illuminate the rightmost dancing bars briefly. (The highest level bar "sticks on" for about a second to make it easier for you to spot your volume peaks, as shown here.)

Bottom: Now return to Garage-Band. Choose GarageBand→ Preferences, and click the Audio/MIDI tab. Using the Audio Input pop-up menu, check to make sure that the correct input is selected—that, in effect, GarageBand is prepared to listen using the correct "ear."

Recording a Live Audio Track

Once you're hooked up, recording a voice or electronic instrument is a lot like recording from a MIDI instrument as described in Chapter 4. In general, though, you'll spend a lot more time in the New Track (or Track Info) dialog box, telling GarageBand about the nature of the sound you're about to record.

Phase 1: Create the Track

What you want is a track that turns bluish when you click it. That's a *Real Instrument* track, as opposed to the green Software Instrument tracks described so far in this book.

Note: When you record digital audio, you create *purple* regions in the timeline. They're the same digital audio as GarageBand's blue, digital-audio *loops,* and you work with them the same way; a single track can contain both blue and purple regions.

Still, the color-coding is a handy means of helping you tell *your* creations apart from Apple's canned ones. (Yours can't be transposed, sped up, or slowed down, for example.)

If you don't already have a digital-audio track ready to record, there's a short way and a long way to go about creating one.

The short way is to choose Track→New Basic Track. You get a new, empty Real Instrument track that comes with no effects, monitoring off, and stereo recording on. (You can read about these settings in the following paragraphs.) *Basic* is right.

If you'd like more control over your new track, though, choose Track→New Track instead. This way, the New Track dialog box appears (Figure 6-3).

Figure 6-3:
The instruments listed here aren't instrument sounds. They're effect presets that audio engineers consider ideal for the listed instrument types. To use it, click an instrument name in the left column, then an individual effect preset in the right-side list.

Click the Real Instrument tab, and then work through the options as follows:

- **Bass, Drums, Guitars, etc.** It's important to realize that the names listed here don't represent instrument *sounds;* you're going to supply the sound yourself.

  Instead, these are canned sets of *effects,* like reverb and echo, that, in the opinions of GarageBand's creators, are especially well suited to these instrument types. If you plan to sing, for example, you'll find that Live Vocals (in the Vocals category at left) gives your singing sound just a gentle touch of pro-sounding reverb; Male Dance Vocals makes it sound like you're singing in a deserted alley; Ambiente Vox sounds like you're at the bottom of the Grand Canyon; and so on.

  Technically, though, there's nothing to stop you from selecting the "wrong" instrument type, choosing one of the Horns effects to apply to your guitar playing, for example. Your guitar won't sound like a brass instrument in the least—you're just adding certain processing effects to it—and you might even come up with a strange, spooky sound that's just right for the effect you seek.

Tip: It's a great idea to "walk" through these various effect presets with the up and down arrow keys on your Mac keyboard, listening to each as you play or sing a few notes. Eventually, you'll begin to associate the specific sounds of each preset with its name, and you'll identify your favorites for use in subsequent hit singles.

  You can read much more about GarageBand's effects in Chapter 7. For now, though, note that you don't have to make a decision before you record; you can change the effects applied to your live-audio track at any time, before or after the recording session.

  To sing without any help from GarageBand's studio-engineer elves, for example, just click the Vocals category, and then click Unprocessed. (On the other hand, a little reverb tends to smooth out the rough edges of the sound, making it sound more professional. As a result, you may feel more comfortable and confident in your singing or playing. That's a psychological by-product technically called the Singing in the Shower Effect.)

- **Mono or Stereo.** GarageBand can record both the left and right channels of sound from a stereo signal—a stereo microphone, for example, or the left and right outputs from a mixing board. If your sound source does, indeed, produce both left- and right-channel sound, turning on Stereo here tells GarageBand to record them simultaneously. Later, you can use GarageBand's mixing tools to emphasize or de-emphasize one channel or the other, if you like.

  Plenty of instruments, however, produce only a single stream of sound. These are *monophonic,* or mono, sound sources: an electric guitar, for example, or a cheap USB desktop microphone. If that's what you're using, click Mono instead. You'll save a lot of disk space. (Stereo recordings, of course, use up twice as much disk space as mono.)

- **Input.** Even though this pop-up menu appears *above* the Mono/Stereo switch, you'll generally use it *after* making your Mono/Stereo choice. If you've selected

Stereo, this pop-up menu is irrelevant; it always says Channel 1/2 (meaning that it will record from both left and right channels).

This pop-up menu is useful when, for example, you've indicated that you want to record a Mono track, but you've connected a stereo sound source. In that case, this pop-up menu lets you specify *which* channel you want to record: the left (Channel 1) or the right (Channel 2).

The Input pop-up menu is also important when you've connected an audio interface that has enough input jacks for several mikes or instruments at once. Suppose you have an eight-channel box connected, with different microphones or instruments connected to each pair of inputs. In that case, with the Stereo button turned on, you would use the Input pop-up menu to specify which channels you want to record: "Channel 1/2 ," "Channel 3/4," "Channel 5/6," or "Channel 7/8."

- **Monitor: Off/On.** "Monitor," in this case, means "play what I'm playing through the speaker, so that I can hear it."

Now, your first reaction to this option might well be, "Well, DUH! Of *course* I want to hear myself. It's called an electric guitar, hello! It doesn't make any sound at all unless it's hooked up to an amp or some speakers!"

And sure enough, if you're playing an electronic instrument like a synthesizer or electric guitar, you'll want Monitor to be On. That way, you'll be able to hear your own playing in the context of any other tracks you've already recorded. (You'll also be able to hear yourself when you're *not* recording, so you can rehearse parts before recording them.)

But if you're recording from a microphone, the situation is slightly more complicated. In that case, you can already hear what you're playing or singing. Furthermore, if Monitor is turned on during the recording, your microphone will also pick up *that* sound, coming out of the Mac's speakers.

Unfortunately, that kind of setup produces the ear-splitting, high-pitched whine known as *feedback* (a staple of the standard teen-movie scene in which the doofus principal first steps up to the microphone at the school assembly).

So how do you avoid feedback? Your first instinct might be to turn *off* the Monitor feature. Now you'll hear only the *existing* GarageBand tracks playing as you sing or play—no feedback. Trouble is, GarageBand may then wind up recording both your voice *and* any previously recorded tracks as they play along with you—an ugly situation, because their sound will become a permanent part of your vocal track once you're done.

Fortunately, there's a simple solution to both problems: If you're recording from a microphone, *listen through headphones*. Leave the Monitor feature On, so you can hear yourself as you play or sing.

Tip: Turn Monitor off when you're finished recording. That way, you won't reopen this GarageBand project next week without headphones connected—and get a blast of feedback in your ears.

• **Icon pop-up menu.** Use this pop-up menu, if you like, to choose a little picture to represent the recording you're about to make. (It's purely cosmetic, and has no audible link to the instrument sound.) Apple gives you 68 little graphics to choose from—every instrument in GarageBand, plus silhouettes of singers.

Tip: To open this palette of icons, you don't have to click the tiny, down-pointing triangle, as you might expect. Instead, click squarely on the icon itself. That broader target means quicker access.

When you're finished setting up your new Real Instrument track, click OK. You return to the main GarageBand window, where your new, blue track appears, ready for recording.

Phase 2: Prepare the Studio

From here, recording live audio is a lot like the MIDI-recording procedure described in Chapter 4. For most people, the routine goes like this:

1. **Turn on the metronome, if you like.**

   Use the Control→Metronome command, or the ⌘-U keystroke, to turn the metronome clicker on or off. (See page 75.)

2. **Choose a tempo.**

   When you record from a MIDI instrument (Chapter 4), the tempo (speed) of the music during your recording makes no difference. During *recording,* you can set the piece so slow, your part is pathetically easy to play. You can stumble along, playing one note per second, like a first-time piano student—and then during *playback,* you can crank up the tempo to make yourself sound like you're some kind of fleet-fingered prodigy. The pop stars do it all the time.

   When you record live playing or singing, however, *you lose this advantage.* It's very important to set GarageBand to the final, finished tempo *before* you record. That's because when you change the tempo of a piece, audio regions that you've recorded yourself don't expand or contract to stay aligned with the rest of the music, as GarageBand loops do. Every track in your piece will therefore change tempo *except* what you've recorded, which will remain locked in its own independent tempo track, sounding clueless, clashy, and out of step when you play it back with the other tracks.

   Take this moment, therefore, to play back your piece, or at least the hard parts, a few different times at different tempos. (See page 76 for details on using the Tempo control.) Settle on the speed that will suit the finished product. Ask yourself: "Is this your final answer?" because you can't change your mind later without having to rerecord your live performance.

3. **Choose a key.**

   This, too, is an important, last-chance decision that you must make *before* you sing or play. Go through the piece a couple of times to make sure it's not too high or too low for your singing voice, or—if you're playing an instrument—to make sure it's in a comfortable key for playing.

If the tracks you've already created are made of Apple loops or your own MIDI performances (Chapter 4), it's no big deal to shift their key higher or lower before you record. (See page 92 for details on transposing.)

But once you've recorded a digital audio track, you're stuck. If you sing in the key of D, the vocal track will have to stay in the key of D forevermore; you can't transpose digital audio.

Note: Yes, OK, fine, you *can* if they're GarageBand's blue-tinted audio loops. But they've been blessed by some kind of secret Apple audio-transposing mojo—and *your* digital-audio regions don't have it.

---

4. Put the Playhead where you want recording to begin.

To start at the beginning, press the letter Z key or the Home key. To start anywhere else, click in the beat ruler or use the keyboard shortcuts (page 15) to put the Playhead there. Of course, you may find it best to put the Playhead a few measures to

---

FREQUENTLY ASKED QUESTION

Real-Instrument Delay

I've got my synthesizer's outputs connected to the Mac. I'm lovin' this thing! The only trouble is, there's a fraction-of-a-second delay between the time I press a key and the time I hear the sound. The response times are killin' me. What's up with that?

When you press a key, it's taking that much time for the signal to go down the cord to your Mac, undergo processing by GarageBand's effects, and emerge through your Mac's speakers. (In the music biz, this frustrating delay is called latency.)

Most people don't have to contend with latency problems. The issue crops up only on certain Macs and with certain equipment setups.

In any case, GarageBand comes equipped with a latency-reducing feature, right there in the GarageBand→Prefer-

ences dialog box. Click the Audio/MIDI button to reveal the controls shown here.

If you click "Minimum delay when playing instruments live," the latency problem should clear up, or at least shrink dramatically.

As you can read right in the dialog box, though, there's some fine print: "Small buffer size." In English, that means, "You've just diverted some of GarageBand's horsepower to solving this latency thing. The program therefore has less power available for playing back your piece.

If you're using a slow Mac, or if you've got a lot of tracks, GarageBand may have trouble keeping up."

In that case, see Chapter 10 for some GarageBand speed tricks.

---

the *left* of the part where you want to begin singing or playing, so you'll be able to get into the groove of the music before you begin.

5. **Set up a countoff.**

   As noted on page 76, GarageBand can "count you in" with a measure full of clicks at the proper tempo so you'll know when to come in. To turn on the countoff, choose Control→Count In, so that the command bears a checkmark in the menu.

6. **Put on your headphones, if you're using them. Get ready to play or sing, and then click the red, round Record button.**

   Or just press the letter R key on your Mac keyboard.

   Either way, you hear the countoff measure, if you've requested one, and then GarageBand begins to record.

7. **When you come to the end of the section you hoped to record, tap the Space bar (or click the Play button) to stop recording.**

   On the screen, you'll see the new purple region you recorded.

Tip: Instead of stopping altogether, you can also tap the R key on your keyboard to stop recording but *keep playing.* You can then listen for a while, and then tap R again to record a later section.

In fact, you can tap R as often as you like during recording. Each time, GarageBand seamlessly kicks in to, or out of, Record mode as it plays.

---

8. **Play back your recording to hear how you did.**

   Rewind to the spot where you started recording. Tap the Space bar to hear your performance played back.

Multiple Takes

As long as you've got yourself a high-quality software studio, you may as well avail yourself of the various cheats that professional recording artists use—and that means mixing and matching the best parts of each "take."

One strategy involves recording your live audio part for the entire song, start to finish. If you mess up, just keep going.

Then prepare for a second attempt like this:

1. **Mute the first track.**

   That is, click it and press the letter M key on your keyboard, or click the little speaker icon in its track header.

2. **Create a second Real Instrument track with the same settings.**

   As it turns out, GarageBand offers a handy shortcut for this step: Choose Track→ Duplicate Track (⌘-D). GarageBand gives you a perfect duplicate of the track— empty of notes or regions, but with its settings and effects intact.

3. Rerecord.

Repeat these three steps until you've got yourself a number of alternate takes to choose from.

Figure 6-4:
Top: In this example, you've recorded two different attempts at the same vocal track. The first take was superior in almost every way—except for the middle part.

Middle: Click the first track and Shift-click the second, so that they're both selected. Position the Playhead just before the messed-up portion and press ⌘-T (the Split command). Then position the Playhead just after that section and press ⌘-T again. You've just chopped up both takes.

Bottom: Drag the middle segment of the bottom track (the good one) upward so that it replaces the bad portion of the first take. Now you have a single, unified track containing the best of both attempts. Delete the second-take track.

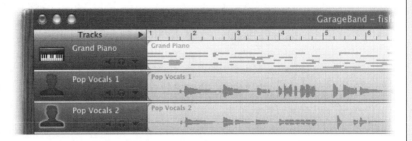

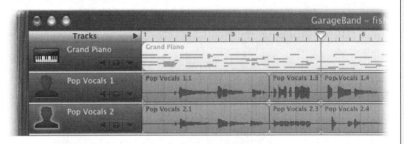

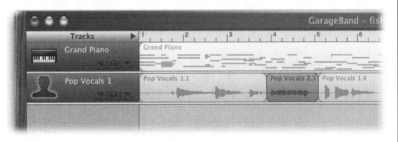

Now it's a simple—and, frankly, enjoyable—matter to chop up these various takes, deleting the bad portions and leaving only the good ones, as shown in Figure 6-4. (Of course, you can also copy and paste successful parts—the chorus, for example—without having to redo them.) For a discussion of splitting, recombining, and otherwise editing Real Instrument regions, see Chapter 5.

Punching In and Out

If *most* of the first take was good, but you flubbed a shorter section somewhere in the middle, you may want to record right over the bad spot. That's where *punching in* comes in.

As you can read on page 79, punching in and out is when the software switches from Play mode to Record mode automatically during a segment of the music that you've bracketed in advance (in GarageBand's case, using the yellow Cycle stripe at the top of the window).

Using punch in/punch out for a Real Instrument track is *almost* exactly the same as for a Software Instrument track. Once again, the idea is to turn on cycling (press the letter C key on your keyboard), adjust the yellow Cycle stripe so that it highlights the music you want to rerecord, turn on the Control→Count In command, and then press the letter R key (or click the round red Record button) and get ready to play. (See Figure 6-5 for the rest of the story.)

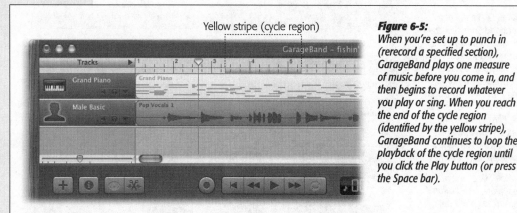

Yellow stripe (cycle region)

Figure 6-5:
When you're set up to punch in (rerecord a specified section), GarageBand plays one measure of music before you come in, and then begins to record whatever you play or sing. When you reach the end of the cycle region (identified by the yellow stripe), GarageBand continues to loop the playback of the cycle region until you click the Play button (or press the Space bar).

There is, however, one big difference between punching into Real Instrument and punching into a Software Instrument. With a Real track, GarageBand records only what you sing or play the *first time through* the cycle region. Then, when the playhead reaches the end of the yellow cycle stripe, GarageBand instantly stops recording and switches to playback-only mode. (In other words, you can't keep playing or singing to build up a cumulative take, one pass at a time, as you can when playing a MIDI instrument.)

The nice part is that if even your punched-in recording wasn't quite right, taking another stab at it is supremely easy. Just tap the letter R key again. GarageBand automatically plays the measure before the yellow stripe, and once again auto-records whatever you play when the playhead reaches the punch-in region. You can repeat this exercise as many times as you need to get the passage perfect.

Editing Real Instrument Regions

When it comes to editing, Real Instrument regions don't offer nearly as much flexibility as Software Instruments. Real Instrument regions are digital recordings of live performances; you can't very well correct a wrong note, boost the emphasis of a sung word, shift the performance in pitch, draw in new notes, or have any of the kind of fun described in Chapter 5.

Still, as Chapter 3 makes clear, you can massage *any* kind of region—Real or not—in a number of useful ways. You can chop them up, rejoin them, drag them around in time, copy and paste them, and so on.

If you double-click a blue or purple region, in fact, you behold the sight in Figure 6-6: actual audio waveforms that make it very easy to isolate certain notes or syllables. You've just opened the Track Editor for a Real Instrument region. (If you've clicked a blue track to select it, you can open the corresponding Track Editor in any of three other ways: Choose Control→Show Editor, press ⌘-E, or click the ✳ button below the track headers.)

The "mountains" on display in the Track Editor for a Real Instrument region show the bursts of volume in the track—individual notes of an instrument, for example, or words in a vocal track. (A flat straight line means silence.)

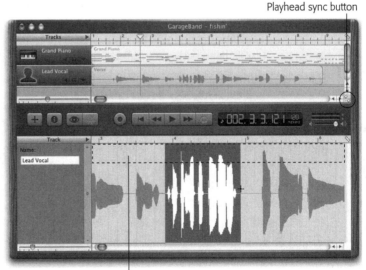

Figure 6-6:
By zooming in, you gain incredible precision in selecting portions that you intend to cut or copy.

Note, however, that if you can't use this zoomed-in view for the purpose of positioning the Playhead to split a region unless you've turned on Playhead synchronization. To do that, make sure that the button circled here shows two aligned Playheads; if not, click there!

Playhead sync button

Area where dragging moves the region
instead of making a selection

There are a few tricks worth noting here:

• The top edge of a region in the Track Editor—maybe about the top eighth of it (Figure 6-6)—is a special zone. Inside it, the cursor changes to this ◂▸ shape. You can now *move* the region by dragging it from side to side.

Tip: When your cursor has that shape, you can also select an *entire* region with a single click. (Yes, that's easy to do in the *timeline,* but it wouldn't otherwise seem possible in the *Track Editor.*)

If you click any lower, your cursor becomes a simple cross ✛, and you actually wind up dragging across waveforms and highlighting them. Learning to know how high to position your cursor for these two different purposes is just part of the game.

- If you drag the upper-right corner of a Real Instrument region *in the Track Editor,* your cursor takes on the curly Loop shape, and you wind up *looping* the region—that is, making it repeat. In other words, it behaves exactly as though you're dragging the upper-right corner of the *un*magnified region up in the timeline, as described in Chapter 3.

- If you drag leftward on the *lower*-right corner of a region in the Track Editor, the cursor changes to this ⊩ shape, and you wind up *trimming* the region—essentially hiding the outer notes. It's just like dragging the trailing edge of a region in the timeline (except that you must use only the lower-right corner as a handle—not the entire right edge, as in the timeline).

- If you paste Real region B on top of Real region A, the pasted region wipes out whatever was underneath, just as you'd expect. But suppose you change your mind.

If you then move or cut away the pasted region, you can tug outward on the end of original region A. The wiped-out soundwaves *grow right back*, revealing that GarageBand was only hiding them, not forgetting them.

Which gives you a great trivia question for your next bar bet: How is a GarageBand region like the leg of a starfish?

Multitrack Recording—In One Pass

I'm mucho confused. A sales guy told me that GarageBand can record multiple tracks. But I can't find any way to record both my guitar playing and my singing at the same time!

Some confusion is understandable. GarageBand does let you record multiple tracks—but only one at a time! So it is a multitrack *recorder,* but it doesn't do multitrack *recording.*

GarageBand does, however, record each track in stereo. If you're determined, therefore, here's a little secret: You can record two instruments simultaneously as long as only one is on each stereo channel.

For example, if you have a mixer, pan your microphone all the way to the left channel, and your guitar all the way to the right.

Or, if you don't have a mixer, buy a Y adapter from Radio Shack: two mono jacks connected to a single stereo plug.

Add whatever adapters you need so that you can plug your microphone and your guitar into this Y adapter simultaneously. The separation between the two instruments won't be total—there will be some "bleed" between the channels—and you'll have to fiddle with the volume levels afterward, but it's a start.

Then, if you want to split this stereo channel into two independent tracks, export your GarageBand song to iTunes. From there, drag it to the desktop. Open it in Amadeus (a sound-editing program that you can download from the "Missing CD" page at *www.missingmanuals.com*).

Choose File→Export Dual Mono, which saves each channel of stereo as an independent, monophonic AIFF file. Drag the two resulting files back into GarageBand, and you've got two separate tracks!

It's work, but it works.

Effects, Guitar Amps, and Instrument Modules

GarageBand is more than a MIDI sequencer, more than a loop-based music construction set, even more than a multitrack tape recorder. It's also the equivalent of a six-foot-tall, $100,000 rack of studio processing equipment and a room full of guitar amplifiers.

The point is to give you exactly the same professional edge that recording artists have. If your singing sounds a little dry, you can "sweeten" the track with a little reverb. If you're looking for a distinctive keyboard sound for the indie post-grunge trash music you're trying to record, you can bleach out all of the low frequencies and add some stereo tremolo. And if you're a guitarist, GarageBand is pleased to offer you a music store's worth of amplifiers from every decade since 1960.

You can apply these effects to both Real and Software Instruments. You can also apply them on a track-by-track basis (when you're trying to fine-tune one instrument's sound) or to the entire mix at once (when you want to tweak the acoustics of your "garage" space).

Either way, you'll soon discover that the simple, idiotproof face of GarageBand gradually disappears as you begin drilling down into the intricacies of its effects and instrument modules. They offer some of the world's most advanced recreations of real-world, rack-mounted recording machines ever written—and they offer the technical complexity to match.

Instrument-Named Presets

Whenever you double-click a track's header, its Track Info dialog box appears. At the top of it, GarageBand presents a list of what appear to be instrument names (Figure 7-1).

At first glance, these instrument names may seem to have completely different functions for the two kinds of tracks in GarageBand:

- If you've opened a blue Real Instrument track, these instrument names don't refer to instrument sounds; they identify *effects presets*. Each is a carefully adjusted combination of studio processing effects—reverb, EQ (equalization), and so on—that, in the opinion of a professional recording engineer, is well suited to the instrument named in the list.

These effect presets...

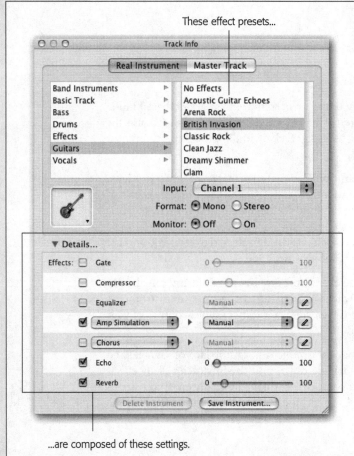

Figure 7-1:
The Track Info dialog box is a lot like the New Track dialog box. But when you click Details, some important controls appear at the bottom. These are the building-block effects generators that make up the instrument-named presets in the top list. (And the two pop-up menus in the Details panel list the building blocks of those building blocks. It's possible to burrow down very deeply into GarageBand's effects-processing underworld.)

...are composed of these settings.

- If you've opened a green Software Instrument track, you might assume that the instrument names here—Grand Piano, Orchestral Strings, and so on—*are* instrument sounds. After all, selecting a different instrument in the list changes the sound of whatever's in the track.

  But as you'll find out in this chapter, these instrument names also include custom-tailored effects. These are, in other words, instrument-and-effect presets.

  For each one, you can modify not only the effect Apple has assigned, but even the sounds themselves, which GarageBand generates from 18 built-in modules—Piano, Strings, Guitar, and so on. For a given instrument named in the list, you can even substitute a different sound module altogether.

When you click an instrument category in the left-side list, the presets are listed in the right-side list. Apple has tried to name them helpfully, to suggest their sonic effect: for example, Edgy Drums, Punk Bass, or (in the Vocals category) Epic Diva. In the Guitar category, most of these presets incorporate the famous GarageBand *guitar-amplifier simulations* (page 132).

Whatever effect preset you choose becomes part of the track. Any sound in that track is affected the same way by those effects.

Save Instrument, Delete Instrument

For want of a better term, Apple calls the effects presets in this dialog box *Instruments*.

In the following pages, you'll learn how to operate the knobs and dials of the individual effect processors (Compressor, Reverb, and so on) that make up each Instrument. The process begins by clicking the Details triangle to expand the dialog box, as shown in Figure 7-1.

It's comforting to know, though, that once you've spent some time tweaking the effects settings for a certain "instrument" (effects preset), you can save your work for use with other tracks and in other GarageBand projects. All you have to do is click the Save Instrument button at the bottom of the dialog box. GarageBand invites you to name your new effect preset. Thereafter, it will appear in the right-side list (see "Giggly Baritone" shown in Figure 7-2).

In fact, GarageBand is so concerned that you might lose hours effects fiddling that, if you try to close the dialog box or select a different "instrument" *without* clicking Save Instrument, it shows you the warning box in Figure 7-2.

So yes, it's very easy to create *new* effect presets. Fortunately, it's also easy to prune the list, throwing away any that you've created that, in the cold light of day, you decide really aren't such masterpieces. Just highlight its name in the right-side list and then click Delete Instrument at the bottom of the dialog box.

Note: You can't use the Delete Instrument button to delete any of *Apple's* effect presets—only your own misbegotten attempts.

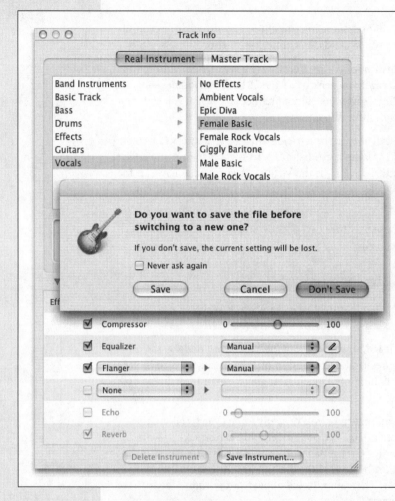

Figure 7-2:
"Save file?" What file? Turns out GarageBand means, "Save this instrument-named effect preset?" In other words, you've made some changes to the effects associated with, in this case, Female Basic, and GarageBand wants to know if you want them permanently stored as part of the Female Basic preset.

(If you turn on "Never ask again," GarageBand won't just never ask again—it will never save your preset changes, either. If you miss seeing this warning box, choose GarageBand→Preferences, click General, and turn on "Ask before discarding unsaved changes."

Effect Modules

See the flippy triangle next to Details? As noted earlier, clicking it makes the Track Info dialog box expand. You've just revealed a set of building-block effects like Gate, Compressor, Reverb, and so on (Figure 7-3). These are the components of the instrument-named presets in the lists above.

Now, if you've spent the prime years of your life hanging around recording studios, terms like *Gate, Compressor,* and *Equalizer* may already be familiar to you.

If you're anyone else, well, resign yourself to the fact that *reading* about effects is not a very good way to learn about them. The fact is, their names are little more than puny human attempts to describe sounds that are, in many cases, other-worldly and indescribable.

Still, the prose that follows may be helpful if you read it *while* performing any of these three self-guided exercises:

- Play with the tutorial file called "06—Effects" (on the GarageBand Examples CD described on page 13). It's a project whose tracks are already set up with various processing effects. To compare them, all you have to do is solo one track at a time (click it and type the letter S key) and play it back.

- As a convenient software quirk, the Track Info dialog box behaves more like a separate program than a true dialog box. That is, even when it's in front of the main GarageBand window, you have full access to GarageBand's controls. You can start and stop playback, add loops, edit notes, and so on.

Figure 7-3:
The instruments named in the top part of the dialog box refer to combinations of effects that Apple engineers set up using the Details panel. Yet even these components have components. As you can see here, the true effects aficionado can work this dialog box from the bottom up, first creating a sub-preset for each effect, then naming the collection of presets for the list at top.

To edit one of these sub-presets, click the adjacent pencil button.

Tip: You can even click a different track without first closing the Track Info dialog box. You'll see the dialog box update itself instantly to reflect the effects of the currently selected track.

If you've already recorded a live performance onto a track, therefore, one great way to experiment with effects is to turn on *cycling playback* for some of it (page 12). Now, in the Track Info dialog box, expand the Details section if necessary, and start the music playing. (You can just tap the Space bar to start and stop the music.)

The music continues to play, looping over and over again, as you tweak its sound with the GarageBand effects controls.

- You can also listen to how each effect changes the sound *while* you play—that is, before you've actually recorded anything. Just connect your microphone or instrument output to the Mac. Play or sing, listening with headphones, as you fiddle with the controls in the dialog box.

In any case, here's a summary of what you'll find in the Details panel. (For a deeper analysis of what these common studio effects do, visit *www.harmony-central.com/ Effects/effects-explained.html.*)

To apply a certain effect to the track you're editing, turn on the checkbox next to its name, and then explore the pop-up menu to its right.

Note: Before you go nuts adding effects to an individual *track,* remember that you can also apply any of these effects to the *entire song,* using the Master Track feature described in the next chapter. Part of the art of mixing is knowing when to process just one instrument, and when to tweak the entire overall mix.

Generator (Software Instruments Only)

This pop-up menu appears only in the Track Info dialog box for Software Instrument tracks. Most people, most of the time, are content to let GarageBand's piano be a piano, its guitar be a guitar, and so on.

You can, however, delve into the sophisticated modeling software that GarageBand uses to produce these sounds, either to subtly tweak the built-in sounds or to radically remake them. In fact, using the Save Instrument button described earlier, you can even create an entirely new Software Instrument, named whatever you please. (You also use this pop-up menu to load new sounds that you've found online; see Chapter 9.)

The first step is to choose the basic instrument sound you want from the pop-up menu. Most of them are just what they sound like: Piano, Strings, Horns, Woodwind, Guitar, Bass, Drum Kits. The remaining ten modules are software versions of synthesizers, capable of generating a wild variety of sounds—and not just musical notes (see Figure 7-4).

Familiar instrument names

When you select a traditional instrument name from the Generator pop-up menu, the pop-up menu to its right comes to life. It lists sub-species of the instrument's type: Alto Sax, Tenor Sax, and so on.

If you now click the pencil button, you see a dialog box like the one shown in Figure 7-4. Here's where you can adjust several parameters of the underlying sound. For most instrument sounds, you get three sliders:

- **Volume.** You guessed it: How loud the sound is.

- **Cutoff.** This slider adjusts cutoff frequency for a *lowpass filter*, whose effect is to filter out high frequencies. If you try it on the Grand Piano, for example, dragging the Cutoff slider to the left muffles the sound, as though you're turning down the treble control on a stereo.

- **Release.** This slider governs how long a note "rings" after you've struck the key. In the real world, a piano note, for example, falls silent the instant you take your

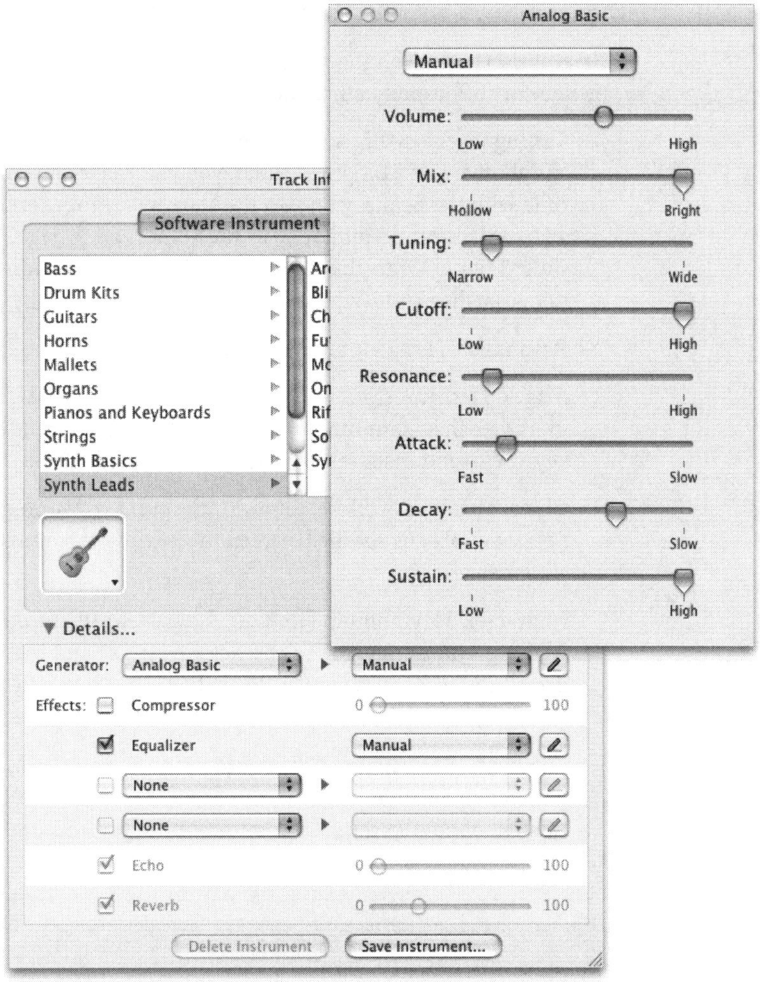

Figure 7-4:
You can adjust the quality of GarageBand's built-in instrument sound generators by clicking the little pencil button. Sometimes you're offered only a few options; sometimes, as with the synthesizers (like the one shown here), you can adjust as many as eight different sliders. In combination, they offer you a nearly infinite number of different sound possibilities.

finger off the key (unless you're pressing the sustain pedal, of course). But by dragging this slider toward Slow, you can make the notes hang in the air longer before fading away.

Note: The Manual dialog box for electric pianos is slightly different. It also offers two options for the underlying Tone: Tines (a bell-like sound, like the classic Fender-Rhodes electric piano of the '80s), and Reeds (a more nasal, oboe-like sound).

Synthesizer generators

When you choose one of the synthesizer modules from the first pop-up menu, however, your options multiply considerably. Now when you click the pencil button, the manual-settings dialog box contains a full arsenal of synth controls—and learning what they all do could take you years. In the real world, synth programming is a full-time hobby, if not a full-time job.

In addition to the Volume, Cutoff, and Release parameters described above, the synth generators offer many other sliders. They vary by module, but here's a taste:

- **Tuning.** Some synth sounds are actually composed of multiple "voices" playing simultaneously. Using this slider, you can make the secondary voices play out of tune with the primary one. At the Narrow setting, detuning the voices in this way adds only a subtle piquancy to the sound, an intriguing twang; as you drag the slider toward Wide, the secondary voices begin to sound like completely different notes, farther and farther from the one you're actually playing.

- **Resonance.** Has a lot to do with how rich and full-bodied the synth sounds.

- **Attack, Decay.** A slow *attack* means that when you strike the key, the sound eases in, rather than sounding instantly. A slow *decay* means that after you release the key, the sound eases out instead of cutting off sharply.

- **Glide.** This wacky effect, found in the Analog Mono generator, connects all the notes you play by sliding between the pitches. It sounds like a slide-whistle player gone berserk.

- **Character, Harmonics, Timbre.** These controls, found primarily in the Digital synth modules, change the character of the sound in ways that are impossible to describe in words. Set your Software Instrument track a-playing (or even a-cycling) and drag these sliders to hear for yourself.

- **Drawbars, Percussion Time, Percussion Level, Click, Distortion.** These are all parameters unique to the Tonewheel Organ generator. In combination, they're capable of simulating a huge variety of organ sounds. Choose a preset from the pop-up menu at the top of the dialog box to see some of the possibilities.

Tip: You can add new instrument generators to this pop-up menu. See Chapter 9.

Gate (Real Instruments Only)

The *gating* function (often called a *noise gate* by recording geeks) simply eliminates all sound that's quieter than a certain level, which you specify by dragging this slider. The result: total silence in the quieter sections of a track.

In the recording industry, gating can be useful to eliminate hiss from the silent parts of, for example, an old recording. Very few of the GarageBand presets use gating, but you can apply it to your own recordings—for example, when you're trying to get rid of the hum from a microphone or other component.

Compressor

Imagine a graph of your song's volume level over time. A studio *compressor* limits this volume graph so that it doesn't vary so wildly. There's less difference between the loudest and softest parts.

Because compressors can bring out the "highlights" of a track without making the background so low as to be inaudible, they're among the most frequently used effects in today's pop music. A compressor adds punch to a solo or—if you apply it to the Master Track—the overall song. It also helps the music sound better on cheap speakers—like boombox speakers, portable iPod speakers, or your Mac's speakers.

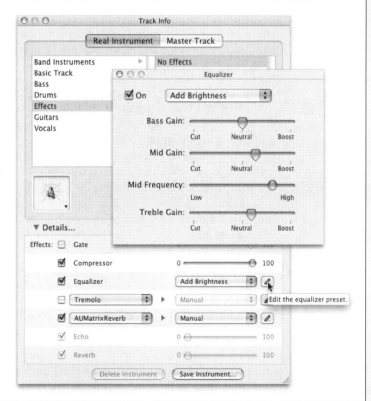

Figure 7-5:
When you click GarageBand's pencil button (indicated by the cursor), you open the Equalizer dialog box (lower right). Adjust the sliders to boost or reduce the corresponding sound frequencies. If you like, you can then save your settings by choosing Make Preset from the pop-up menu (where it now says Add Brightness). You'll be asked to name the settings, which will thereafter appear in the pop-up menu along with Apple's own presets. (Figure 7-6 shows this process in more detail.)

To try out this effect, turn on its checkbox and then drag the slider. 0 means no compression; 100 means maximum compression.

Equalizer

If you've ever fiddled with the *graphic equalizer* on a stereo, or even the software one that's built into iTunes, you already know about these controls. An equalizer lets you boost or repress certain frequencies—like the bass or the treble—to suit different kinds of music. A "graph" for classical music, for example, might slightly boost the low and high frequencies for more sparkle, letting the middle ones "sag"; a pop-rock setting might boost instead the middle frequencies, to bring out the vocal parts.

When you turn on GarageBand's Equalizer checkbox, the pop-up menu to its right offers 21 canned equalizer setups bearing self-explanatory names like Bass Boost, Brighten Strings, and Reduce "S." In the unlikely event that none of these presets is quite what you want, you can click the pencil button to its right to adjust the various frequencies yourself (Figure 7-5).

The truth is, many of the Equalizer presets might make more sense when applied to a finished composition than just one instrument track. But now and again, they can be useful in giving a recording just the right nuance. For example, in the guitar preset called Summer Sounds, the "EQ" of the midrange has been boosted to give your guitar more of a Beach Boys sound.

Tip: If you'd prefer finer control over the various frequencies, don't bother with this user-friendly, quick-and-dirty option. The AUGraphicEq function described in the box on page 134 offers 31 individual sliders for extremely precise adjustment of various sound frequencies.

"Additional Effects" Pop-Up Menus

These two unlabeled pop-up menus, near the middle of the Details panel, are complex and deep enough to merit a book of their own. These are fantastically sophisticated software controls that emulate racks full of studio equipment. You can spend hours in here, fiddling with the sliders and checkboxes, in an effort to find the perfect tweak for your vocal or instrumental line.

Note: The two pop-up menus are identical. Apple has given you two of them so that you can apply two effects simultaneously.

Actually, there are a total of *four* pop-up menus. Each time you choose an effect category from a *left-side* pop-up menu, the pop-up menu to its *right* comes to life, pre-stocked with useful presets. (As you're beginning to notice, GarageBand offers presets for the component effects that make up the *instrument-named* presets listed at the top of the dialog box. Presets within presets.)

You may find only three presets in this second pop-up menu (Soft, Medium, Hard) or as many as 20 (Birdish, Club at Next Door, Slow and Deep, and so on). You can add your own presets to this second pop-up menu, too, as shown in Figure 7-6.

Note: Once you've used the pencil button *once,* GarageBand leaves you stuck in "I Want to Adjust This Effect Manually" mode until you quit and reopen it. That is, *every* time you choose from the first effect pop-up menu, its underlying manual-adjustment dialog box pops up automatically, without your having to click the pencil button.

On the other hand, you don't have to *close* this manual-settings dialog box before choosing a different effect from the first pop-up menu. You can feel free to experiment, choosing different effect names and admiring the way the manual-settings dialog box changes before your eyes each time.

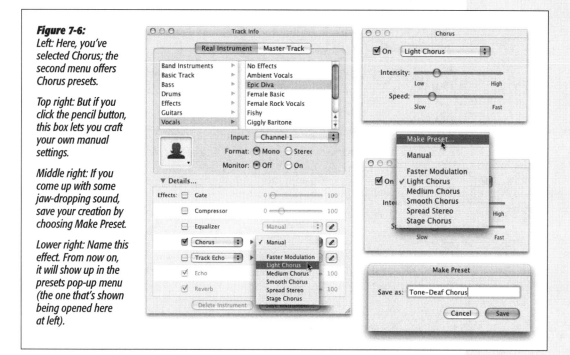

Figure 7-6:

Left: Here, you've selected Chorus; the second menu offers Chorus presets.

Top right: But if you click the pencil button, this box lets you craft your own manual settings.

Middle right: If you come up with some jaw-dropping sound, save your creation by choosing Make Preset.

Lower right: Name this effect. From now on, it will show up in the presets pop-up menu (the one that's shown being opened here at left).

Now that you understand the basic ritual—choose an effect generator from the first pop-up menu, choose a preset from the second, and adjust manually if you like—here's a list of the primary effect generators as they appear in the first pop-up menu.

Note: After each description, you'll find a brief account of what the manual-settings dialog box offers (the one that appears when you click the pencil button).

Treble Reduction, Bass Reduction

As you might expect, these effects crank down the high or low frequencies of this track's music, respectively. Use Treble Reduction if the source material is too hissy; use Bass Reduction if it's too boomy. (The equalizing options perform much the same function, but with more precision.)

Manual options: Frequency (Low—High).

Distortion

Most musicians go out of their way to make sure that the *input volume* of their microphone or instrument isn't up too high. (That's why you opened System Preferences and adjusted the level slider as described on page 108.) If the input is too "hot," the level meters go off the scale, resulting in the screechy, garbled sound known as *distortion* or *clipping.*

In some musical circles, however—especially heavy-metal ones—distortion is the whole point. It's the trademark sound of guitarists who turn their amplifiers "up to 11," as the cast of *This is Spinal Tap* might say.

Using this option, you can drive *any* musical material into distortion-land, even if the levels were perfectly fine in the original recording.

Manual options: Drive (Low—High), Tone (Dark—Bright), Output Level (Low—High).

Overdrive

This effect, also common in electric guitar music, is related to distortion. It simulates the sound of an overdriven tube amplifier, adding the intensity of distortion without quite as much "trashiness."

Manual options: Drive (Low—High), Tone (Dark—Bright), Output Level (Low—High).

Bitcrusher

GarageBand generally strives to preserve the maximum sound quality of your instruments. It's capable of CD quality, meaning sound that's described by 44.1 kilobits of data per second.

It wasn't always this way. Primitive computers like the very first Macintosh and the Atari, not to mention AM radios, use far less data. As a result, they sound tinny and flat next to, say, the typical GarageBand instrument.

The Bitcrusher effect is designed to throw away musical data *on purpose,* giving your track a retro, played-over-the-phone-line sound. Its presets include AM Radio, Classic 8-Bit (that is, like the oldest Macs), Meet Atari, and others. Some, like Other World, reduce lyrics to unintelligibility; others, like SR Crush, give vocal lines a buzzing, robotic, Vocoder quality. All of the presets do a real number on the sound quality of your track, blasting it into awfulness for use only in special circumstances. (Ever heard the beginning of the Electric Light Orchestra's "Telephone Line?" The opening verse is meant to sound as though it's sung over the phone—and now you can perform the same processing in the privacy of your own home.)

Manual options: Resolution (Low—High), Sample Rate Reduction (Small—Huge).

Automatic Filter

This pop-up menu unleashes a wide spectrum of truly wild and severe effects. Most introduce some form of pulsing, tremolo, or wobbling. A few highlights among the others:

- **Birdish** adds a high-frequency sweep to the sound, as though your composition were so good, aliens were trying to beam you up.

- **Club at Next Door** is truly hilarious. It removes all frequencies except the very lowest, so that only the throbbing bass remains. It's pretty much exactly what you'd hear of your next door neighbor's stereo through an apartment wall, or, as the name suggests, if a dance club were across the street.

- **Slow Shutter** sounds exactly as though an older brother is covering up your mouth with his hand, then flapping it open and closed while you try to speak or sing. It has an extreme "wah-wah" sound to it.

Manual options: Frequency (Low—High), Resonance (Low—High), Intensity (Down—Up & Down), Speed (Slow—Fast).

Chorus

Chorusing is a famous and frequently used effect in pop music (ever heard Abba?). The fundamental idea is that the computer duplicates your track and offsets the copy by just a millisecond or two, so that you sound like there's two (or more) of you singing or playing together. It also makes the two copies slightly out of tune with each other, which helps with the illusion of multiple voices singing at once.

The presets here are primarily designed to let you control how *much* chorusing you want. Among them, Spread Stereo is among the most interesting, because it attempts to place you and your clones in different spots along the left-to-right stereo "soundstage."

Manual options: Intensity (Low—High), Speed (Slow—Fast).

Flanger

Here's another classic rock processor, frequently applied to guitars and keyboards by a little foot switch-operated box on the stage floor. And now it's yours, at no extra charge.

You'll recognize it when you hear it: a sweeping, side-to-side, filtery effect. It's something like chorusing described above, but the duplicates of the sound are played back much more out of tune from the original. (Hint: It's most effective in stereo. Go dig out your iPod headphones.)

Manual options: Intensity (Low—High), Speed (Slow—Fast), Feedback (Low—High).

Phaser

Sometimes called a *phase shifter,* this flanger-like whooshing effect should also strike you as familiar from the pop world. It, too, sounds like somebody is cyclically rotating the dials on some selective-frequency machine, and it, too, sounds especially good on guitars, keyboards, and vocals.

Manual options: Intensity (Low—High), Speed (Slow—Fast), Feedback (Low—High).

Tremolo

Tremolo is a close relative of *vibrato.* On paper, you might describe it as a subtle up-and-down wobble, either in pitch or in volume—but in the real world of solo voice or solo instruments, you'd describe it as a beautiful, professional sound. It's also a characteristic sound of guitar amps from the '50s and '60s (think The Ventures).

The GarageBand Tremolo effect won't turn a tone-deaf screecher into Pavarotti, though. You can't apply it selectively just to the ends of longer notes, as musicians tend to do in live performance. Many of the presets sound just a hair machine-generated, especially because many of them create the vibrato effect not by subtle waves of *pitch* but by whipping back and forth from left to right in stereo. (Here's another effect that sounds best with headphones on.)

Still, several of these presets can lend interest and magic to a track, especially to a solo line with sustained notes. (If you're a singer and don't have a natural vibrato, try the preset called Soft and Fast, for example. Especially if you've also dialed up a little reverb, as described below.)

Manual options: Intensity (Low—High), Speed (Slow—Fast).

Auto Wah

"Wah" here refers to the *wah-wah pedal,* a staple of electric guitar players. The name, as you can probably guess, is an onomatopoeia—the name describes the sound of the effect.

Onstage, guitar players traditionally control the timing and intensity of the "wah" by riding a pedal with one foot. In GarageBand, you can't actually control either the timing or intensity, except in your selection of preset.

Even so, you have an entire music store's worth of wah-wah pedal simulators here, with names like Wow, Duck, and CryBaby. Some of them distort the music beyond recognition; others make you sound like you're playing live from outer space. All of them take the range of sounds you can make with your guitar alone (or whatever your instrument) far beyond what you can play without GarageBand's assistance.

Manual options: Sound (Dark—Bright), Reaction (Light—Strong), Mode (Thick, Thin, Peak, Classic 1/2/3).

Amp Simulation

If you're an electric guitarist, and you've slogged along this far, here's what you've been waiting for, the gem of GarageBand for guitarists: the amp simulators. These are the effects Steve Jobs and pop artist John Mayer demonstrated onstage when GarageBand was first unveiled at a Macworld Expo; this is the feature that gets true garage-band musicians drooling.

As it turns out, the sound an electric guitar makes is profoundly affected by the amplifier it's plugged into. Various bands of the last 40 years have put both themselves and certain amps on the map by creating trademark guitar sounds.

Unfortunately, amplifiers are expensive, heavy, and impractical to transport in big numbers. To have a single software program on, say, a laptop, that can deliver perfect impersonations of 17 classic amplifiers—with names like Grunge, Scorching Solo, British Invasion, and Seventies Rhythm—is, for guitarists, quite a treat.

(For anyone else, it may be no more than a big yawn. That's an OK reaction, too.)

As you can guess, these amp simulations work best if you have an electric guitar connected to your Mac. (Run its line output into one of the audio interface boxes described on page 107, for example.) Listen on headphones as you experiment and noodle.

Manual options: See Figure 7-7.

Figure 7-7:
These core effects lie at the heart of the amplifier simulations for guitars. The manual options here are the most elaborate of any GarageBand effect. Beginning with the type of guitar you're playing, these controls let you specify everything about the amp, from its gain (the strength of the incoming signal) to output (the strength of the post-processed signal).

You can tweak the controls to your heart's delight—just as guitarists love to do with their real amps.

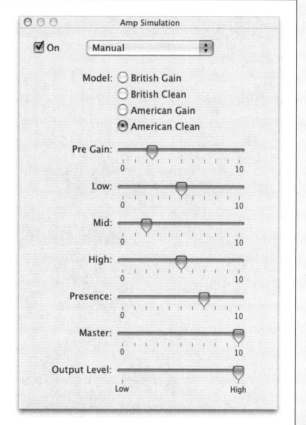

Echo, Reverb

You might suppose that *echo* and *reverb* are the same thing: the nice echoey sound of, for example, your shower.

Audio Unit Effects

Audio Units are plug-ins, in a format created by Apple (but embraced by many other companies) that exploits Mac OS X's sophisticated audio "plumbing." Because GarageBand (and Logic, Final Cut, and Soundtrack) understands Audio Units plug-ins, you've got yourself a quick, easy way to expand its arsenal of pro-quality sounds and effects.

The first mention you're likely to see of Audio Units is at the bottom of each component-effect pop-up menu, where you'll find a long list of effects beginning with the letters AU: AUBandpass, AUDynamicsProcessor, AUDelay, and so on.

These controls give you direct access to some of

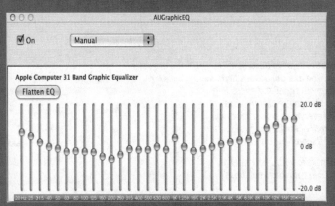

the Audio Units that come with GarageBand. As you'll soon discover, these controls can be a good bit more technical than what you've encountered so far. Once you start drilling down into the AU labyrinth, you may wish you had the assistance of seasoned studio wonks even to figure out what you're looking at. (And you can get that help, too, by visiting Web sites like *www.osxaudio.com, www.audio-units. com,* and the GarageBand discussion board at *http://discuss search.info.apple.com.*)

You don't get any presets for most AU effects, as you do with the GarageBand Effects listed above them. For these babies, the right-side pop-up menu usually says Manual, and the only way to adjust them is to click the pencil (if necessary) to

bring up the corresponding manual-control dialog box.

As you can see here, these dialog boxes don't even look the same as the others in GarageBand. They're in another realm of tweaky complexity.

Still, some of these options are good to have. Remember, for example, the Equalizer described on page 128? It's nice to have, but it's not a full-blown graphic equalizer like the one in iTunes.

Choosing AU-GraphicEQ, however, you get the dialog box shown here, complete with sliders for 31 individual sound frequencies.

Another AU effect that could, in a pinch, be useful is AUDelay. It's something like an echo effect on steroids: the reverberations can continue indefinitely, building and accumulating, until a single spoken sentence turns into the cacophony of 50 drunken people at a frat-house party.

If you do decide to explore the arcane audio settings of the AU set, note that you don't have to do without canned presets altogether. You're perfectly welcome to populate the pop-up menu with your own presets. Just fiddle around in the manual-settings dialog box (like the graphic equalizer pictured here) until you're satisfied, and then choose Make Preset from the pop-up menu at the top of the box. Name your preset, and be AUfully proud of yourself.

Actually, in studio terms, they're different. *Echo,* sometimes called *delay,* is literally an echo, giving you fainter and fainter distinct repetitions of each sound, each separated by a fraction of a second (think Grand Canyon). *Reverb* is a sweet, subtle, professional-sounding reverberation that smoothes the rough edges of a musical performance (think shower stall, empty alley, or concert hall).

You'll probably use Echo only rarely, for special effects. Reverb, on the other hand, is useful for practically any kind of solo. There's not a pop star alive, for example, whose recordings aren't "sweetened" with a little reverb. The audience may not be able to pinpoint why your singing or playing sounds so great, but they'll definitely hear the difference.

Each of these effects has its own on/off checkbox and slider, which goes from 0 to 100 percent.

Note: If the Echo and Reverb checkboxes are dimmed, it's because these effects are turned off in the Master Track (see Chapter 8).

The fix: In the Track Info dialog box, click the Master Track tab, and then turn on the Echo and/or Reverb checkboxes. When you return to the Software Instrument or Real Instrument tab, you'll see these checkboxes come back to life.

The explanation: As it turns out, the individual tracks' Echo and Reverb sliders simply govern how much of these effects are sent to the Echo and Reverb in the Master Track. Studio musician call these *send effects.* (The Track Echo effect in the two unnamed pop-up menus are different; it gives you a truly track-independent echo.) So if Echo and Reverb are turned off for the entire song, they're also turned off for every individual track.

Part Two:
Beyond the Garage

2

Mixing and Publishing

By this time, you may have mastered GarageBand. Perhaps you've dialed up your own effects, masterfully combined loops with live audio, honed your mastery of musical arrangements and orchestration, and even added a little mod-wheel tweak here and there. At this point, you may even have the next "Oops, I Did It Again" right there on your screen.

But it's not doing anyone much good sitting in GarageBand. For most people, the whole point of making music is sharing it with others.

This chapter describes how to wrap up your workflow in GarageBand and present it to a wider audience. It's all about fine-tuning your piece, mixing the tracks (adjusting their relative volume levels), and finally handing the whole thing off to iTunes. From there, you can convert the song to any common music file format (like MP3), burn it to a CD, load it onto an iPod, or post it online for your screaming fans to discover.

Mixing Tracks

Next time you listen to the radio, notice how each song ends. A few of them end with a dramatic climactic stopping chord, but most gradually fade out.

GarageBand not only lets you create convincing fadeouts for your songs, but even lets you adjust the volume graph for individual tracks along their lengths. For example, you can make the piano part loud during the introduction of the piece, and then pull back to a softer level when your singing begins.

This business of adjusting the relative volume levels of a song's tracks is called *mixing*. It's both an art and a science; two different people mixing the same song can create totally different psycho-musical effects. You're no longer wearing the composer's hat, or even the rock star's hat; you're now assuming the engineer's and producer's roles.

Here are the tools at your disposal, as described in the following pages:

- You can adjust the relative overall volume levels of the tracks.

- You can create volume fluctuations *within* a track.

- You can adjust the left-to-right positions of your track instruments in the stereo "soundstage."

- You can make overall volume changes—to all tracks at once—to create, for example, a fadeout at the end of the song.

Overall Track Volume

The most basic mixing skill is knowing how to adjust track volumes relative to each other. That is, you might want to make the drum track a little quieter, the vocals a little louder, and so on.

The key to this basic mixing feature is the *track mixer*, a little panel that sprouts when you click the small triangle identified by the arrow cursor in Figure 8-1.

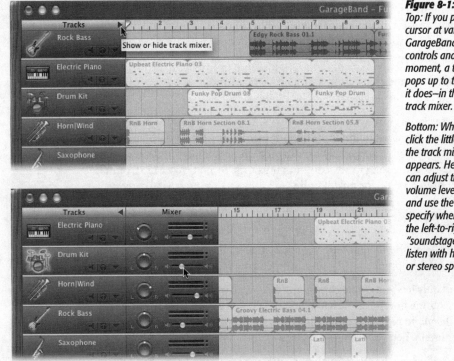

Figure 8-1:
Top: If you point your cursor at various GarageBand screen controls and wait a moment, a tiny balloon pops up to tell you what it does—in this case, the track mixer.

Bottom: When you click the little triangle, the track mixer panel appears. Here, you can adjust the overall volume level of a track and use the knob to specify where it sits in the left-to-right stereo "soundstage" when you listen with headphones or stereo speakers.

Using the volume slider that you find here is simple enough:

- Drag the tiny, white, round handle to decrease or increase the track volume.

- Click inside the slider to make the volume handle jump to that spot, without having to drag.

- Option-click one of the tiny speaker icons, or anywhere along the slider's length, to restore the track volume to its original factory-set volume level. (Note to studio veterans: technically, you're setting the track to 0 decibels. Note to everyone else: And why is "normal" zero? It's a long story with its origins in the world of recording-studio equipment, but the bottom line is that on this kind of meter, 0 dB means, "anything higher will distort." Absolute silence, incidentally, is represented on these meters as –96 dB.)

Tip: If you can't seem to adjust the slider at all, it's because you've programmed in volume changes using the Track Volume track described next. The track mixer slider is "live" only if you've never fiddled with the track's volume track.

GEM IN THE ROUGH

Check One, Check Two...

You can use the track volume slider shown in Figure 8-1 even while the song is playing back.

Why is that so useful? Because the two tiny graphs just above the volume slider illustrate the volume level of the left and right stereo channels in real time. They light up with tiny bars, as illustrated here, resembling the digital LED level meters on modern studio equipment.

When you're preparing your song for release to the masses, observe these meters while the song plays back. You want to adjust the volume so that they dance primarily in the green area, slipping into the yellow area only during the loudest passages.

What you don't want is for the graph to extend into the red bars, or, worse, for the two tiny dots at the right end—the *clipping* indicators—to illuminate. That's a sign that the volume is so loud, distortion may result. You'll be pumping out too much signal for the speakers on the

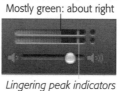

Mostly green: about right

Lingering peak indicators

In the red zone: too much

Red clipping indicators

other end, resulting in a garbled, overblown sound.

(Once the two clipping-indicator dots have turned red, they stay red to get your attention. They return to black only when you click them, telling them, in effect, "OK, OK, I get it—I've got a clipping problem. I'll fix it.")

As the music plays, you'll notice that while these volume meters are bouncing around, every so often, one graph bar will remain illuminated for a second. That's your peak volume meter. It remains illuminated for a moment to help you spot the high points of your track volume.

You can boost or reduce the volume of green Software Instrument tracks whenever you feel like it. But when it comes to Real Instrument recordings, the time to pay attention to these level meters is while you're recording. If the microphone or line input setting was too loud or too soft, adjusting the track volume slider may not rescue the recording.

Volume Adjustments Within a Track

All this time, GarageBand has been concealing a little secret from you. Each track can, at your command, sprout a real-time graph of its volume over time. By dragging this "rubber band" line up or down, you can program in gradual (or sudden) volume changes that GarageBand will incorporate into the playback.

To reveal this graph, use one of these techniques:

• Select a track and then press the letter A key.

• Click the tiny triangle identified in Figure 8-2.

To hide the volume track, repeat the same procedure.

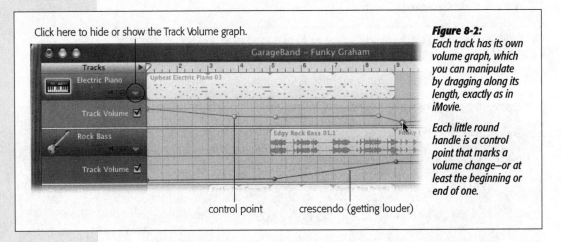

Click here to hide or show the Track Volume graph.

Figure 8-2:
Each track has its own volume graph, which you can manipulate by dragging along its length, exactly as in iMovie.

Each little round handle is a control point that marks a volume change—or at least the beginning or end of one.

control point   crescendo (getting louder)

This graph of track volume comes in handy in many ways. For example, you can begin the piece with its instrumental introduction at full volume, and then pull back the band so that you can hear the singing. You can also create professional sounding fadeins and fadeouts at the beginnings and ends of your songs.

The key to turning on this feature is the Track Volume in the track header. When you turn it on, a horizontal line appears in the volume track, stretching from edge to edge. This line is a graph of the track's volume, which you can manipulate it like a rubber band. Here's how it works:

• If you've also opened the track mixer panel (Figure 8-1), adjusting the overall track volume makes this horizontal volume graph float up or down accordingly.

• Click directly on the line and drag upward or downward. The original click produces a small spherical handle, while the drag produces a slant in the line from its original volume level. Simultaneously drag left or right to adjust the timing of this fluctuation.

- To make the volume take another dip or swoop, click elsewhere on the volume line and drag again. You've just created a second round orange handle, which you can now position independently.

- To remove a volume fluctuation, click the orange handle to select it, and then press the Delete key. (Alternatively, drag an orange handle so far to the right or left that it overlaps the adjacent one.) The orange ball disappears, and the "rubber band" of the volume graph snaps back to the previous round orange handle, stretched tight.

- To make a sudden volume change, zoom way in, then drag an orange handle carefully until it's *almost* directly below the previous or next one. (Don't drag it directly underneath—if you do that, the other handle will disappear. In that case, use the Edit→Undo command to restore it.)

- Consider making your volume adjustments *while* the music plays back. GarageBand dutifully changes the mix in real time as you fiddle.

- You can drag a group of handles higher or lower—thus proportionally boosting or decreasing the volume for an entire stretch of music—by selecting them en masse first. You can also drag a group of control points sideways, making the volume fluctuation take place sooner or later. Figure 8-3 has the details.

Tip: In fact, you can use that same trick to drag the *entire* volume graph up or down for the length of the song. To select all of the handles in the entire volume track, click the volume track *header* (marked by the words "Track Volume" at the left edge of the window).

Figure 8-3:
Top: You can select a group of control points either by Shift-clicking the ones you want, or, as shown here, by dragging horizontally through them.

Bottom: Then, you can drag the group either horizontally (to change the timing) or vertically (to change the overall level of the volume change), using one of them as a handle.

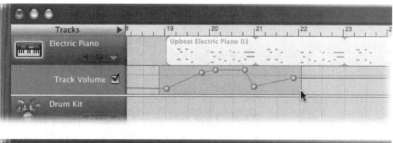
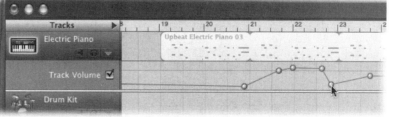

• To restore the original, straight-line condition of a clip's volume, select all of the orange handles (see the previous Tip) and press Delete. (Of course, you can also delete only a subset of them by first dragging a selection, as shown on Figure 8-3, at top.)

Tip: When you're finished editing volume fluctuations, you can turn off the Track Volume checkbox again. GarageBand will remember all of the changes that you've made—you'll still hear the volume changes on playback—but it dims all of the handles and rubber-band graph lines, so you won't drag something out of alignment by accident.

Pan Position

The beauty of stereo is that there are *two* speakers or headphones, which happens to correspond very nicely with the number of ears on your head. When you listen to music in stereo, part of the realism stems from the instruments' varied placement in the stereo *sound field* or *soundstage*. In other words, some instruments seem to be coming from the left side of the room, some from the right, and some from directly in front of you, almost as though you were listening to them live.

Over the ages, record producers have become very skilled at exploiting this phenomenon. When they mix the song, they use knobs or software to specify where each track should sound like it's coming from—left, right, center, or anywhere along the scale. In short, they spend a lot of time thinking about the *pan position* of each instrument (that is, its position along the sonic *panorama* before you).

As it turns out, GarageBand provides this flexibility, too. All you have to do is to open the track mixer panel, as described in Figure 8-1.

Unless you intervene, every instrument starts out sounding like it's coming out of both speakers—left and right—with equal volume. Every instrument starts out with a *center* pan position; accordingly, every track's pan knob starts out with the little white notch pointing straight up to the center position.

Here's how to work this knob (Figure 8-4):

Figure 8-4:
You can't really gauge the effects of the pan control unless you're listening with headphones, or sitting between two stereo speakers. And it probably goes without saying that you should keep the music playing while you make these adjustments.

- Don't even bother grabbing the tiny rim of the knob and then dragging the mouse along it. This will effectively turn the knob, but it requires the precision of a neurosurgeon.

  Instead, click one of the tiny white dots around the *outside* of the knob (or, for extreme panning, click the letter L or R). Instantly, the white notch on the knob turns to face your click.

- Option-click anywhere on the knob to reset it to center, making its little white notch point straight up again.

Leaving everything set to the center is fine if people are going to be in mono anyway—from a Power Mac speaker, say, or over the Internet in a file that you've distilled down to a single mono track to make it a quicker download.

Most professionally recorded songs, however, feature instruments that are carefully spread out across the stereo field. In general, the most important instruments—the soloist, the drummer, bass player, and maybe the guitars—stick with center positions, but the "flavor" instruments might be spread out to the left and right sides.

You can inject some fun into the process by introducing variations on this formula. If you're singing a duet—maybe even a duet with yourself—you could put the two voices on opposite channels, so it sounds like they're really facing each other. (The more you turn the pan knob, for example, the farther to the left or right you place that instrument.)

Using volume, pan, and reverb together, in fact, you can dial up a pretty convincing sonic impression of a track's position in three-dimensional space.

The Master Track

It's nice that you can control the volume of individual tracks, and of individual sections of music along their lengths. But as a final step before unveiling your masterpiece to the world, you'll want to look over the master volume for the entire mix and set up any master effects, like reverb, that you want to apply to the entire garage band.

Tip: Perform the following adjustments *after* adjusting the mix of your individual tracks.

You apply most of these all-track changes using the *Master Track*. It's an additional horizontal track that appears at the bottom of the track list, as shown in Figure 8-5.

To make it appear, choose Track→Show Master Track, or press ⌘-B. (To hide the Master Track once again, choose Track→Hide Master Track, or press ⌘-B a second time.)

If you've learned to manipulate the effects, overall volume, and volume graphs for individual tracks, you already know how to operate them for the Master Track. The only difference is that you're now affecting all tracks simultaneously. For example:

• **Set the overall volume level for your song** using the master volume slider identified in Figure 8-5. Play back the entire song, watching the volume-level meters
just above the slider to make sure that they don't cross into the red zone during
the loudest portions of the music, and that the two little clipping indicators don't
light up. (See the box on page 141 for more detail on using these meters.)

The point is to make sure the music will sound good when other people play it on
their computers, iPods, or CD players. Volume that's too low to hear the detail, or
so high that you're introducing distortion, will seriously hinder your chances of
getting picked for *American Idol.*

Tip: Don't get into the habit of using this master slider to adjust GarageBand's playback volume while
you're working on your compositions. For that purpose, use the speaker-volume keys on the top row of
your keyboard. Or, if you don't see them on your keyboard, use the speaker-volume mini-menu in your
menu bar. (And if you don't see *that,* choose →System Preferences, click Sound, and turn on "Show
volume in menu bar.")

Use the master output volume slider only to determine the final volume level for your piece, as it will be
when you export it to iTunes, post it online, and so on.

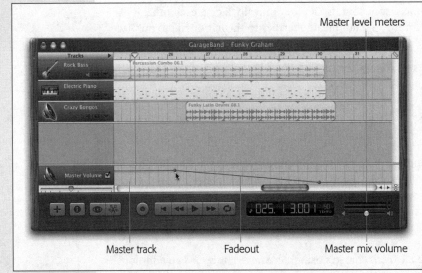

Master level meters

Figure 8-5:
*This track is probably
hidden most of the time
that you're working in
GarageBand. It's espe-
cially useful, however,
at the end of the com-
positional process, just
before you "publish."
In this illustration, the
song ends with a nice
fadeout, courtesy of the
master-track volume
graph.*

Master track   Fadeout   Master mix volume

• **Create fade-ins, fadeouts, and other whole-song volume fluctuations** by turning
on the Master Volume checkbox and then manipulating the horizontal master-
volume graph, exactly the way you would adjust an individual track's graph.

• **Set up reverb, compression, and any other whole-song processing effects** by
double-clicking the Master Track's header (where it says Master Volume at the left
edge of the window). Doing so produces the Track Info dialog box for the Master
Track, as shown in Figure 8-6.

In this dialog box, you can specify a degree of echo, reverb, equalization, or compression. You can also apply any of the GarageBand "additional effects" like Bitcrusher, Chorus, Flanger, and so on, using the pop-up menu in the middle of the Details panel. All of these effects are described at length in Chapter 8.

Tip: If you create a combination of effects that sounds particularly appropriate for your style of music, and you think you might use them later for subsequent compositions, click the Save Master button shown in Figure 8-6. You're asked to type a name for this effects preset, and then click Save. From now on, you'll see your new Master Track preset listed in the right-side list of the Track Info dialog box—or at least until you use the Delete Master button to remove it.

Figure 8-6:
You can get to this dialog box either by double-clicking the Master Track header, or by double-clicking any other track's header and then, in the Track Info dialog box, clicking the Master Track tab. Either way, this is where you set up processing effects for the entire mix. This is also, incidentally, the only place where you can change the time signature or key signature of the piece once you've created the file.

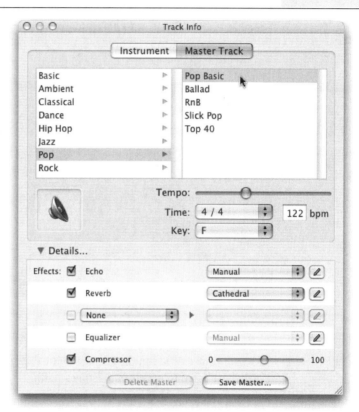

Publishing the Song

Suppose, that the music sounds great, the mix is on target, and everybody who hears the song playing in GarageBand is blown away. This is the moment you've been waiting for. You're about to liberate your tune, freeing it from GarageBand and getting it into a program that's far better at playing and distributing digital music—iTunes.

From there, you can burn it to a CD, convert it to an MP3 file, use it as background music for iPhoto, iMovie, or iDVD, and so on.

Here's how the process works.

1. **Choose GarageBand→Preferences.**

   The GarageBand Preferences dialog box appears.

   The music you create in GarageBand will wind up in one iTunes *playlist* (a subset of your music collection that you've built for a certain purpose). Unless you specify otherwise, iTunes will name it "Casey's Playlist" (or whatever your account name is, as identified on the Accounts panel of System Preferences in Mac OS X). Here's your opportunity to assign your collected GarageBand works a more resonant title.

2. **Click the Export tab. Edit the iTunes Playlist, Composer Name, and Album Name boxes (Figure 8-7).**

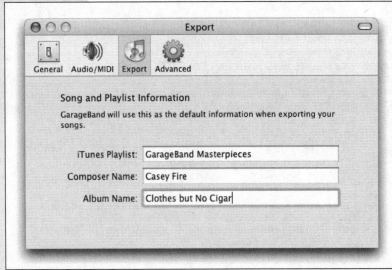

Figure 8-7:
In iTunes, almost every song displays labeling information: composer name, album name, and so on. All right, maybe you're not much of a composer, and you probably don't yet have an album out—but at least you can pretend by filling in the boxes here.

   Once you've filled out the last line of the dialog box, click once in another one of the text boxes to make your changes "take."

3. **Close the Preferences box.**

   The only information you didn't have to fill in is the name of the song. But of course, iTunes already knows that information—it's whatever name you gave your GarageBand project when you created it.

4. **Specify which tracks you want to export.**

   Most of the time, you'll want to export *all* of the tracks. In certain situations, though, you may not want some tracks to be a part of the finished mix. If you really *do* have a garage band, for example, you might want to make yourself a track that includes the backup band but omits your part, so that you can practice by playing along with it.

Note: You may be too young to remember the Music Minus One albums, but they were really cool. Each record was intended to help you learn to play a certain instrument. A full orchestra played on the left stereo channel, and your solo part was recorded on the right. As you got better at playing, you could gradually turn down the right channel until only the accompaniment remained audible—and you, the soloist, provided the missing part.

Maybe, too, your intention is to create a karaoke album of your own greatest hits—that is, minus the vocals.

Or maybe you just want to send a record company's talent scout a couple of different mixes, each with a different instrumentation. (Some people, for example, like to try out a couple of different drum loops for the same song. Each one lends a different flavor to the piece. So for comparison, you can export the song twice, one with each drum track playing.)

FREQUENTLY ASKED QUESTION

Real-time Automated Mixing?

Hey, I was at my buddy's place the other day. He paid $600 for his mixing software, but it does something cool. He can adjust the pan control, or adjust the processing effects for a track, while the music is playing—and the software memorizes it and recreates it automatically the next time the piece plays back. Is there any way to make GarageBand automate the mix like this?

Can GarageBand memorize the movement of its knobs and sliders for fully automated mixes? No.

Can you simulate this effect with a tricky workaround? Yes.

As you can read in Chapter 12, it's possible to export a partial or finished GarageBand mix and then bring it right back into GarageBand as a frozen, but full-quality, unified track. All you have to do is find a piece of software that can record the playback as you fiddle with panning and effects, thus

capturing your real-time adjustments for posterity.

Fortunately, exactly such a program exists. It's Audio Hijack, a handy little $16 shareware utility that can capture virtually any sound that's passing through the Mac. Most people use Audio Hijack for things like capturing Internet radio broadcasts, but you can put it to another use entirely. (You can download it from the "Missing CD" page at *www.missing manuals.com*.)

All you have to do is set up Audio Hijack to record the output from GarageBand, as shown here. Play your piece, making any panning or effects adjustments you like during the playback. When it's over, you'll find an AIFF file on your desktop, named after GarageBand.

Drag this icon right back into an empty Real Instrument track in GarageBand. From here, follow the procedure described on page 183.

Either way, silence the tracks you want omitted by clicking each one and then pressing the letter M key (or clicking the little speaker in the track header). Doing so mutes the track. Now when you export your song to iTunes, they won't be part of the mix.

5. **Specify how much of the song you want to export.**

In most cases, you'll want to export the entire song, which is fine. In that case, skip this step.

But selecting a specific part of the song can be useful now and then. Maybe you've got a shorter version that you want to keep distinct from the extended mix, for example.

Maybe, too, you want to export a region that's *longer* than the song. You might want to incorporate a few seconds of silence at the end, so that your listeners can reflect thoughtfully on the impact of what they just heard. Or, more practically, maybe you've discovered that GarageBand exports only up to the end of the last region, and is therefore chopping off a little bit of reverb that rings past that moment.

In any case, the trick to specifying how much of the song you want to export lies in the cycle region. Figure 8-8 explains.

6. **Give the piece one last listen.**

Yellow bar: Only this much will be exported

Cycle button

Figure 8-8:
Press the letter C key, or click the cycle button, to make the yellow highlighting bar appear at the top of the GarageBand window. Zoom out as much as necessary, and then drag the edges of this yellow bar until it brackets the portion of the song you want to include. GarageBand will export only as much of the song as you've indicated with this cycle region.

Put on headphones if possible, press the letter Z key to rewind, press the Space bar to play, and watch the output-level meters at the lower-right corner of the GarageBand window to make sure that the two little clipping dots are turning red—or that your piece isn't so quiet that the dancing meter bars never even touch the yellow region. (See the box on page 141.)

7. **Choose File→Export to iTunes.**

   GarageBand takes a moment to create your final mix, merging all those tracks down to just two channels: left and right stereo. In a moment, the iTunes window appears automatically.

   As shown in Figure 8-9, a new playlist has joined the others in the Source list at the left side of the window. This is where you'll find your exported GarageBand masterpieces.

Tip: Of course, you can always change the playlist name in the GarageBand→Preferences dialog box. Doing so will build a second playlist in iTunes, containing all your GarageBand exports henceforth.

To hear your opus now that it's been freed from the protective walls of GarageBand, click the playlist name and then double-click the name of the song displayed to its right.

Figure 8-9:
Your GarageBand creations ultimately land in iTunes, which also came on your iLife DVD. (You can find it in your Applications folder.) Many of the keyboard shortcuts are exactly the same as in GarageBand: Press the Space bar to start and stop a selected song, press ⌘-up arrow and ⌘-down arrow to adjust the volume during playback, and so on.

Your GarageBand playlist   Songs you've exported

Having your finished GarageBand pieces stored in iTunes, rather than GarageBand, is a wonderful convenience. iTunes starts up faster than GarageBand, it's easier to search and sort, you can't accidentally mess up your piece by clicking in the wrong place, and the actual music file is much smaller than your original GarageBand project.

Tip: Behind the scenes, your exported GarageBand song is saved as an AIFF file in your Home→Music→iTunes→iTunes Music→Import folder. Back up this folder if you want to make safety copies of your finished projects.

Converting to MP3, AAC, WAV, or Apple Lossless

When it arrives in iTunes, your GarageBand masterpiece has been frozen into what's called an AIFF file (Audio Interchange File Format). AIFF files truly sound spectacular. In fact, they're what the record companies put onto commercial music CDs.

These are not, however, what you'd call petite files. A typical pop song occupies 40 or 50 MB on your hard drive, Web site, or iPod. That's a shame, because not many people will tolerate a 50 MB download just to hear your work.

Fortunately, iTunes makes it very easy to convert your songs to other formats, most of which take up far less space. MP3 files, AAC files, WAV files, and Apple Lossless files are all examples of formats you can use. Here's an introduction to each one:

- **MP3 files.** The most popular music files online are MP3 files, which you can find on the Web by the hundreds of thousands. (MP3 is short for MPEG Audio, Layer 3. And MPEG stands for Moving Pictures Experts Group, the association of engineers that also defined the specifications for DVD video, among other formats.)

  And why is it so popular? Well, suppose you copy a song from an Outkast CD directly onto your computer, where it takes up 47.3 MB of hard disk space. Sure, you could now play that song without the CD in your CD drive, but you'd also be out 47.3 megs of precious hard drive real estate.

  If you let iTunes convert it into an MP3 file instead, it will still sound really good, but now only takes up about 4.8 MB of space on your hard drive—roughly 10 percent of the original

  MP3 files are so small because they omit frequencies that are too high for humans to hear, along with any sounds that are blotted out by louder sounds. All of this compression helps produce a smaller file without overly diminishing the overall sound quality of the music.

- **AAC files.** The Advanced Audio Coding format may be relatively new (it became official in 1997), but it has a fine pedigree. Scientists at Dolby, Sony, Nokia, AT&T, and Fraunhofer collaborated to come up with a method of squeezing multimedia files of the highest possible quality into the smallest possible space—at least small enough to fit through a modem line. During listening tests, many people couldn't distinguish between a compressed high-quality AAC file and an original recording.

  What's so great about AAC? For starters, this format can do the Big Sound/Small File Size trick even better than MP3. Due to its tighter compression technique, a song encoded in the AAC format sounds better (to most ears, anyway) and occupies less space on the computer than if it were encoded with the same quality settings as an MP3 file. Encoding your files in the AAC format is how Apple says you can stuff 10,000 songs onto a 40 GB iPod.

  The AAC format can also be copy protected (unlike MP3), which is why Apple uses it on the iTunes Music Store. (The record companies would never have permitted Apple to distribute their property without copy protection.)

- **WAV files.** WAV is a standard Windows sound format, although Macs can play these files, too. Windows fans download WAV recordings for everything from TV-show snippets to system-alert noises. A WAV song usually sounds better than the same song in MP3 but takes up more room on your hard drive or iPod.

- **Apple Lossless Encoder files.** As you now know, programs like iTunes create MP3 and AAC files by throwing away some of the audio data (mostly stuff you can't hear anyway). Geeks call these *lossy* formats. But for true audiophiles with impeccable taste and bionic ears, lossy formats make music sound thin, tinny, and screeching.

Of course, WAV and AIFF are lossless—no audio data is lost—but these files take up a huge amount of hard-drive space.

In iTunes 4.5 or later, you can use the Apple Lossless Encoder instead. It offers great-sounding files that take up about half the space of an uncompressed CD track. (This format requires not only iTunes 4.5, but also QuickTime 6.5.1. or later.)

How to convert your files

All right, suppose you're now sold on the benefits of converting your GarageBand masterpieces into smaller files. Here's how to proceed:

1. **In iTunes, choose iTunes→Preferences. In the dialog box, click Importing.**

   You see the dialog box shown in Figure 8-10.

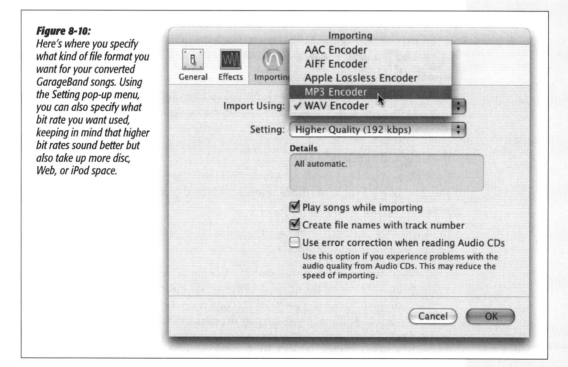

Figure 8-10:
Here's where you specify what kind of file format you want for your converted GarageBand songs. Using the Setting pop-up menu, you can also specify what bit rate you want used, keeping in mind that higher bit rates sound better but also take up more disc, Web, or iPod space.

2. **From the Import Using pop-up menu, choose the file format you want.**

   Choose AAC, Apple Lossless, MP3, or WAV. Also specify a Setting, if you like (see Figure 8-10).

Tip: If you intend to post this masterpiece online or send it by email, consider using MP3. It's the most widely compatible format.

---

3. **Click OK. In your GarageBand playlist, select the song or songs you want to convert.**

   To select one song, just click it. To select all of them in the list, choose Edit→Select All (or press ⌘-A). To select a consecutive subset of the songs, click the first one, and then Shift-click the last one. To select a random assortment, click the first, and then ⌘-click each additional song.

4. **Choose Advanced→Convert Selection to MP3.**

   Beware: The menu command changes according to your selection in step 2. For example, it might say Convert Selection to AAC instead.

   iTunes flies into action, simultaneously playing your song and converting it.

5. **To look at the finished product, click the Library icon at the top of the Source list.**

   You'll find your song mixed in with all of your other iTunes files, in alphabetical order (assuming you're sorting your list by song name).

   Of course, the original AIFF version is here, too. One way to tell which is which: Highlight the song's name and press ⌘-I (or choose File→Get Info). The resulting dialog box identifies the file format.

At this point, you can turn the new file into a bona fide, independent file icon by dragging its name out of the list to any visible spot on your desktop. It's now ready to send by email, post on the Web, copy across the network, and so on.

Burning GarageBand CDs

Controlling your own private recording studio isn't the only traditional function that you're whisking away from the big corporate record companies. You're in charge of your own CD-pressing plant, too.

In fact, iTunes can burn your GarageBand hits—or any songs in your iTunes Library—into three kinds of discs:

- **Standard audio CDs.** If your Mac has a CD burner, it can record selected sets of songs, no matter what the original sources, onto a blank CD. (For maximum CD-player compatibility, leave your GarageBand projects in AIFF format for this kind of CD.) When it's all over, you can play the burned CD on any standard CD player, just like the ones from Tower Records. This time, however, you hear only the songs you like, in the order you like, with all of the annoying ones eliminated.

Tip: Use CD-R discs. CD-RW discs are not only more expensive, but may not work in some standard CD players. (Not all players recognize CD-R discs either, but the odds are better.)

- **MP3 CDs.** A standard audio compact disc contains high-quality, enormous song files in the AIFF format. An MP3 compact disc, by contrast, is a data CD that contains music files in the MP3 format.

  Since MP3 songs are much smaller than the AIFF files, many more of them fit in the standard 650 or 700 MB of space on a recordable CD. Instead of 74 or 80 minutes of music, a CD-R full of MP3 files can store *10 to 12 hours* of tunes.

  Just about any computer can play an MP3 CD. But if you want to take the disc on the road or even out to the living room, you'll need a CD player designed to read both standard CDs and discs containing MP3 files. Many modern players can play both CDs and MP3 CDs, and the prices are not much higher than that of a standard CD player. Some DVD players and home-audio sound systems can also play MP3 CDs.

- **Backup DVDs.** If your Mac has Mac OS X 10.1 or later and an Apple SuperDrive (that is, it can play and record both CDs and DVDs), you have another option. iTunes 4 can back up 4.7 GB of your music collection at a time by copying it to a blank DVD. (You can't play this disc no matter what kind of player you have; it's merely a glorified backup disk for restoration when something goes wrong with your hard drive.)

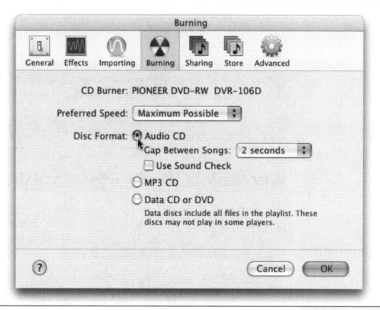

Figure 8-11:
Choose iTunes→Preferences, and then click Burning. Here, you select the recorder you wish to use, as well as what kind of CD to make: a standard disc (Audio CD) that will play in just about any CD player, an MP3 CD that will play in the computer's CD drive (and some newer home decks), or a backup just for safekeeping.

Select the type of disc you desire in the Preferences dialog box (Figure 8-11). Then proceed as follows:

1. **Select the playlist you want to burn.**

   To ensure that all of the playlist's songs will fit on a CD, consult the readout at the bottom of the window. It tells you how much playing time is represented by the songs in the playlist.

Note: If it runs out of room on the first CD, iTunes will ask you to insert another disc and then pick up where it left off.

---

2. **When you're ready to roll, click the Burn Disc button at the top-right corner of the iTunes window.**

   The icon changes into a yellow-and-black graphic that resembles the symbol used for fallout shelters in the 1950s.

3. **Insert a blank CD into your computer's drive when prompted. Click the Burn Disc button again after the program acknowledges the disc.**

   iTunes prepares to record the CD, which may take a few minutes.

   Once iTunes has taken care of business, it lets you know that it's now burning the CD. Again, depending on the speed of your computer and CD burner, as well as the size of your playlist, the recording process could take several minutes.

   When the disc is done, iTunes pipes up with a musical flourish. Eject the CD (by pressing the Eject key found in the upper-right corner of the Mac keyboard) and label the top of the newly minted music storehouse with a magic marker (or your favorite method).

Tip: You can set up your computer to auto-eject the CD when it's finished ripping—ideal if you plan to copy a bunch of CDs to your hard drive, assembly line–style.

In iTunes, choose iTunes→Preferences (Mac). Click the General icon or tab. Where it says, "On CD Insert," choose "Import Songs and Eject." From now on, each CD spits out automatically when it's done.

Your Music in iMovie, iPhoto, and iDVD

One absolutely fantastic use of GarageBand is applying professional-sounding background music to the movies, slideshows, and DVDs that you can make using the other programs in the iLife suite. Music you create yourself has a number of advantages over music cribbed from other sources:

- **It's completely royalty-free.** Even if your iMovie film becomes a hit at the Sundance Film Festival, no lawyers will come a-calling for payment.

- **It's perfect for the part.** You don't have to settle for a piece of music that's only quasi-appropriate for your movie or slideshow, or waste precious dollars buying songs from the iTunes Music Store only to discover that they don't quite work in the context of your project. With GarageBand, you can make music with *exactly* the tempo, feeling, lyrics, and instrumentation your movie or slideshow requires.

- **It's the right length.** You can create GarageBand compositions that begin and end at precisely the right times for their task.

- **It's flexible.** If you one day decide to create a director's cut of your iMovie project, or even a 30-second theatrical preview, you can easily pop back into GarageBand to adjust the original song accordingly. If you use somebody else's music, you can't adjust the tempo, or rearrange the sections, or eliminate the bridge—but if it's your own music, you're free to do what you like, quickly and easily.

Suppose, then, that you've created a few GarageBand works of art and exported them to iTunes. Here's how to incorporate them into your movies, slideshows, and DVD projects.

iMovie

In iMovie, click the Audio button on the right side of the screen. As shown in Figure 8-12, iMovie now displays a complete listing of what's in your iTunes Library.

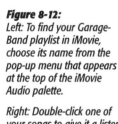

Figure 8-12:
Left: To find your Garage-Band playlist in iMovie, choose its name from the pop-up menu that appears at the top of the iMovie Audio palette.

Right: Double-click one of your songs to give it a listen. If you think it's right for the piece, drag it directly downward into one of the two audio tracks of the iMovie timeline.

Choose the name of your GarageBand playlist from the pop-up menu. At this point, you can operate as though you have a mini-iTunes right there in iMovie. For example:

- To listen to a song before committing to it as a soundtrack, click its name in the list and then click the triangular Play button. (Click the same button, now shaped like a square Stop button, when you've heard enough.)

- Click one of the three headers—Artist, Song, or Time—to sort the iTunes music list alphabetically by that header.

- Change the arrangement of the three columns by grabbing the headers and dragging them into a different order.

- Rather than scroll through a huge list, you can locate the tracks you want by using the capsule-shaped Search field near the bottom of the window. Click in the Search field, and then type a word (or part of a word) to filter your list. iPhoto searches the Artist, Song, and Album fields of the iTunes Library and then displays the matching entries. To clear the search and view your whole list again, click the X in the search field.

To install one of your GarageBand tracks in your movie, drag its name downward into one of the two parallel audio tracks, as shown at right in Figure 8-12. iMovie imports the song, turning it into a horizontal purple stripe, which you can drag from side to side to adjust its placement in your video.

You can also edit its overall volume, or even drag control points to make its volume fluctuate along its length, exactly as in a GarageBand volume track. Just remember to turn on the Edit Volume checkbox at the very bottom of the iMovie window first.

iPhoto

Perhaps more than any other single element, *music* transforms a slideshow, turning your ordinary photos into a cinematic event. When you pair the right music with the right pictures, you do more than just show off your photos; you create a mood that can stir the emotions of your audience.

Your first iPhoto slideshow is born with a ready-to-use soundtrack—J. S. Bach's Minuet in G. In fact, Apple sends iPhoto to you equipped with *two* Bach classics—the Minuet in G and *Jesu, Joy of Man's Desiring*.

Not to knock Bach, but it's fortunate that you're not limited to his music only. To choose a soundtrack of your own creation, start by clicking the name of the album that contains the pictures you want (in the Source list at the left side of the window). Then click the Slideshow button at the bottom of the screen.

The Slideshow dialog box appears. When you click the Music tab, as shown in Figure 8-13, you should feel as though you're in familiar territory; the dialog box displays your iTunes Library and playlists, exactly as described earlier.

This time, though, you can choose between an individual song and the entire playlist:

- **To use the entire GarageBand playlist** as a soundtrack for your slideshow, you don't have to do anything special at this point. At slideshow time, iPhoto will continue through all the songs in the playlist before starting over.

- **To use just one GarageBand song** as a soundtrack, click its name in the list. The song will loop continuously for the duration of the slideshow.

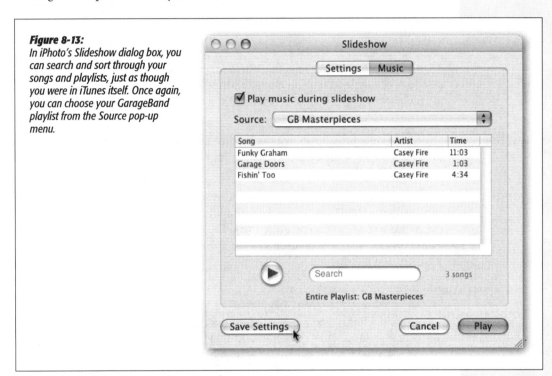

Figure 8-13:
In iPhoto's Slideshow dialog box, you can search and sort through your songs and playlists, just as though you were in iTunes itself. Once again, you can choose your GarageBand playlist from the Source pop-up menu.

Once you've settled on an appropriate musical soundtrack for the currently selected album, click Save Settings (to memorize that choice without starting the slideshow) or Play (to begin the slideshow immediately). From now on, that song or playlist will play whenever you run a slideshow from that album. It also becomes the *proposed* soundtrack for any new slideshows you create.

Alternatively, if you decide you don't want any music to play, turn off the "Play music during slideshow" checkbox on the Music panel of the Slideshow dialog box.

Note: You can't select multiple songs from the song list in the Slideshow dialog box. If you want to use only a subset of your GarageBand playlist as the audio backdrop for your slideshow, you must return to iTunes and create a new playlist. Drag into it the desired songs from your GarageBand playlist, in the order that you want them to play. Switch back to iPhoto, and choose that playlist from the pop-up menu in the Slideshow dialog box.

---

iDVD

Rounding out Apple's "ordinary mortals can do creative work that's just as good as the pros" campaign, iDVD lets you create your own, Blockbuster-style DVDs, containing either movies you've created in iMovie or slideshows of your digital photographs. (Of course, this feat requires that your Mac have a SuperDrive, a drive that both plays and records both CDs and DVDs.)

You can use your GarageBand compositions in two ways: as background music for a slideshow, and as the looping background music for a *menu screen* (say, the scene-selection screen that first appears when the DVD is inserted).

Music for slideshows

A DVD is a perfect delivery mechanism for digital photos. Instead of passing around a tiny pile of fragile 4 x 6 prints, your audience sits comfortably on the couch, watching the photos at gigantic size—on the TV screen—accompanied by your musical genius.

To create a slideshow, begin by clicking the Customize button at the bottom of the iDVD screen. The Customize "drawer" opens up at the side of the window, as shown in Figure 8-14.

Click the Media button at the top of this drawer. If you choose Photos from the pop-up menu, iDVD presents your entire iPhoto picture collection, complete with the albums you've used to organize them. Drag an album's name directly onto your main DVD menu screen to install it there as a button.

Customize drawer

Menu screen

Customize button

Figure 8-14:
To add a new slideshow, drag any album (from the top pane of the Photos palette) onto your iDVD menu screen. You can also select more than one album and drag them en masse. (The usual multiple-selection tricks apply: ⌘-click several albums consecutively to select all of them, for example.)

When your fans insert this DVD into their DVD players, clicking that button with the remote control will begin the slideshow.

Once you've installed a slideshow button on your main menu screen, you can double-click it to open the Slideshow Editor. Here you can drag photos into any order you like (Figure 8-15).

Figure 8-15:
The iDVD Slideshow Editor lets you build and customize your slideshows. Each slide appears in order, with its number, a thumbnail, and the name of the source file (that is, the original graphics file on your hard drive). Click Return to go back to iDVD's menu-editing mode.

Mini-iTunes

Audio well

Of greater interest to you at this point, however, is the Audio "well" identified in Figure 8-15. Back on the Customize drawer, choose Audio from the pop-up menu. Once again, iDVD shows your entire iTunes music collection, complete with your GarageBand playlist. You can search and sort this list exactly as you can in iPhoto.

To use your entire GarageBand playlist, drag its name onto the Audio well, again as shown in Figure 8-15. To use a single song, drag only its name.

Tip: When it's empty, the Audio well looks like a small speaker. When it's occupied, its icon identifies the kind of audio file you've installed, as shown in Figure 8-15.

To try out a different piece of background music, drag a new song or playlist into the Audio well. Should you decide that you don't want music at all, drag the file icon directly out of the Audio well and onto any other part of the screen. An animated puff of smoke confirms your decision.

Tip: An option called Fit to Audio appears in the Slide Duration pop-up menu after you've added a sound file to your slideshow (Figure 8-15). If you choose it, iDVD will determine the timing of your slides automatically—by dividing the length of the soundtrack by the number of slides in your show. If the song is 60 seconds long, and you've got 20 slides in the show, each slide will sit on the screen for three seconds.

To return to iDVD's menu editor, click the Return button at the bottom right of the Slideshow Editor.

Music for menu screens

You can also use one of your GarageBand pieces as the music that plays in the background while your audience surveys its choices on the main menu screen (or one of your submenu screens, for that matter).

Here again, you open the Customize drawer, click the Media button at the top, and then choose Audio from the pop-up menu. Now you can drag the name of either your GarageBand playlist or one of its individual songs onto the mockup of your menu screen. You'll hear it begin playing immediately. (The Motion button at the bottom of the iDVD window is designed to simulate the way the menu screen will look when it's actually playing on somebody's TV. Click it to start and stop the music and animation.)

Now, if you click the Preview button to test your DVD design, the music plays automatically whenever this menu screen appears.

If you change your mind, simply drag a different song out of the mini-iTunes list onto the menu screen. Or, to leave the menu screen with no music at all, click the Settings button in the Customize drawer. Finally, drag the icon out of the Audio well, so that it disappears in a puff of smoke.

Tip: Ordinarily, iDVD will play your entire piece or playlist, up to 15 minutes long. (After all, if your fans really need 15 minutes to decide which scene of your DVD to play, they're probably too clueless to notice that the music has begun to repeat itself.)

If you like, though, you can limit the amount of music that plays. Click the Settings button in the Customize drawer, confirm that the Motion button is illuminated so that your music is playing, and drag the Duration slider to specify how much of the music will play before looping.

Advanced GarageBand

Most people have their hands full with the basic GarageBand tools—at least for the first few weeks. The world is full, however, of a special species known as the Power User: the Mac aficionado who digs a little deeper, spends time reading Web sites, and has the time to experiment in the quest for greater knowledge and cool hacks.

This chapter is for you, Power User.

It might just as well have been called Miscellaneous GarageBand, because the hacks and tricks in this chapter don't fall neatly into any one category. Still, there's enough here to occupy those rare stretches when you feel no musical inspiration but still want to fool around with GarageBand.

More Free Software Instruments (SoundFonts)

A *SoundFont,* as any happy computer-based musician can tell you, is a sampled instrument sound, a snippet of recorded audio, that you can trigger with the keys of a MIDI instrument, like the MIDI controllers described in Chapter 4.

If this sounds an awful lot like GarageBand's Software Instruments...well, you're right. The difference is that SoundFonts are available by the thousands, mostly for free, all over the Web. Wouldn't it be awesome if you could expand GarageBand's sound library by installing industry-standard SoundFonts?

You can. It's easy to do, you'll be the first on your block to do it, and it's a cheap and thrilling way to expand GarageBand's instrument repertoire.

1. Download some promising-sounding SoundFonts.

A quick Google search for *free soundfonts* will unearth dozens of Web sites filled with them. If you're in a hurry, you might start at, for example, *www.hammersound. net*. Download as many as you like.

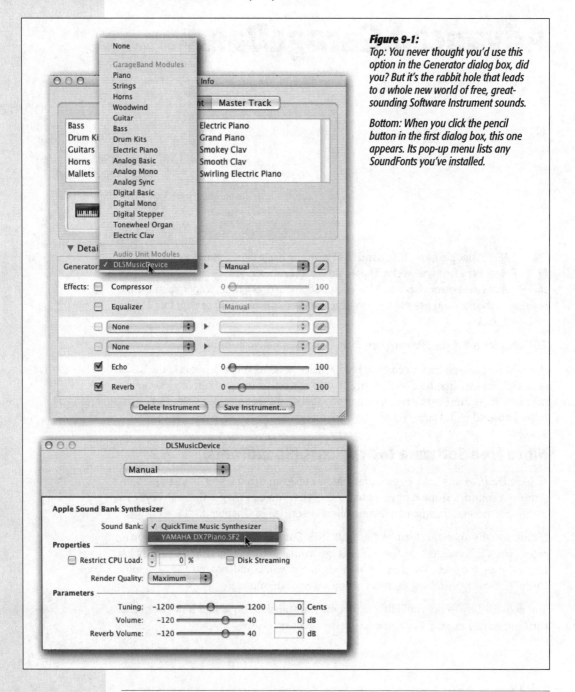

Figure 9-1:
Top: You never thought you'd use this option in the Generator dialog box, did you? But it's the rabbit hole that leads to a whole new world of free, great-sounding Software Instrument sounds.

Bottom: When you click the pencil button in the first dialog box, this one appears. Its pop-up menu lists any SoundFonts you've installed.

Tip: The SoundFonts from Hammersound require the latest version of StuffIt Expander to decompress them after downloading. You can get it from *www.stuffit.com*.

2. **Once you've downloaded the SoundFont, drag its icon into your hard drive→ Library→Audio→Sounds→Banks folder.**

   This is where your SoundFont collection will live. To remove a SoundFont file, drag it out of here; to rename one, rename it here.

3. **Open GarageBand. Create a green Software Instrument track, and then double-click its header.**

   The Track Info dialog box appears.

4. **Expand the Details panel, as shown in Figure 9-1 at top. Then, from the Generator pop-up menu, choose DLSMusicDevice.**

   If this doesn't sound like the sort of friendly name that Apple would give an instrument, you're absolutely right. This is *not* an Apple sound; instead, it refers to the kind of file you've downloaded.

5. **Click the pencil button to open the second dialog box (Figure 9-1, bottom). From the Sound Bank pop-up menu, choose the name of the SoundFile you want.**

   Close the little dialog box when you're finished.

   At this point, you can play some notes on your MIDI keyboard and hear the new sound in action. But to make selecting your new instrument easier the next time, take one more step:

6. **Click Save Instrument. Type a name for the instrument you've just added, and then click OK.**

   From now on, you'll be able to call up your SoundFont-based sound just by choosing its name from the right side of the Track Info dialog box, where it appears alongside all the standard GarageBand sounds.

Note: SoundFonts are only one category of plug-in samples that GarageBand can accept. The broader category is called Audio Units, and they're for sale all over the Web. *Electronic Musician* magazine (*www. emusician.com*) regularly reviews them.

Making Your Own Apple Loops

Stuffing your hard drive with GarageBand-ready loops you've bought from companies on the Web is just fine and dandy, as long as you're willing to limit yourself to *other* people's canned creativity. It turns out, though, that with a bit of effort, you can turn your own sonic eruptions into full-fledged Apple Loops, ready for use in your compositions or even for selling online. This advanced technique is also ideal for converting loops originally designed for other music software into official Apple Loops that appear in the GarageBand Loop browser.

All you need is a free program called the Soundtrack Loop Utility. It's part of the Apple-Loops SDK (software development kit), which you can download from the "Missing CD" page of *www.missingmanuals.com.* (You can also find it at *http://developer.apple. com/sdk;* click the link for AppleLoops SDK.)

When you're finished downloading, you'll find a disk-image icon on your desktop called Apple Loops SDK. Inside, double-click the icon called Install Apple Loops SDK, and install the software just like any other program.

After the installation, open your Applications folder. There you'll find the object of this quest: the Soundtrack Loop Utility. You're now only moments away from creating a full-blown Apple Loop:

1. **Open Soundtrack Loop Utility.**

   If an Open File dialog box appears, click Cancel. Edit the information in this window, as shown in Figure 9-2.

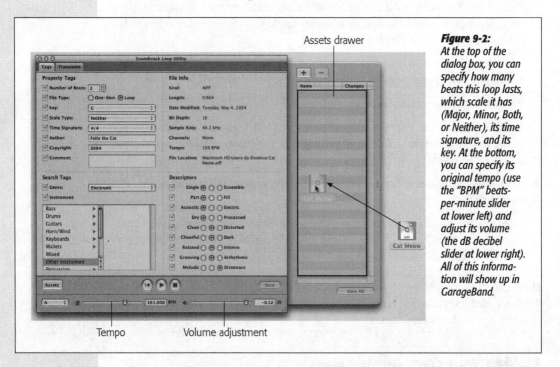

Assets drawer

Tempo   Volume adjustment

Figure 9-2:
At the top of the dialog box, you can specify how many beats this loop lasts, which scale it has (Major, Minor, Both, or Neither), its time signature, and its key. At the bottom, you can specify its original tempo (use the "BPM" beats-per-minute slider at lower left) and adjust its volume (the dB decibel slider at lower right). All of this informa-tion will show up in GarageBand.

2. **Switch to the Finder. Locate the AIFF or WAV file that you want turned into a loop. Drag it into the Assets drawer (Figure 9-2).**

   You can drag a whole batch of them at once, or even a folder full. Either way, your raw sound files now appear in the Assets drawer.

3. **Click the first sound you want to loop-ize. On the Tags tab, specify its category, key, and other characteristics.**

You may recognize a lot of the terms on this screen—they're the various category buttons in the GarageBand Loop browser. For example, the Genre pop-up menu controls the primary category this loop will occupy: Electronic, Jazz, World, or whatever. The Descriptors list lets you specify additional categories for this loop: Acoustic, Cheerful, Intense, and so on.

Finally, use the Instrument list to identify which instrument produced this sound, or if it's just a sound effect, choose Other Instrument.

4. **Click the Transients tab, and make sure that the beats fall where you think they should fall.**

Remember how GarageBand can adjust a loop's tempo to perfectly fit the existing music in your piece? Well, you're about to find out how it can be so musically smart. Turns out you can *show* a loop where its beats fall, so that later, GarageBand can make it play slightly slower or faster. See Figure 9-3.

Figure 9-3:
To show this loop where its own beats fall, click to place the little handles at the top of the screen. Drag them sideways, if necessary, so that their vertical lines fall at the right places in your sound wave-form. Click a handle and press the Delete key to get rid of one.

5. **When you're finished preparing your loop, click Save.**

Your AIFF or WAV file has now been converted into a living, breathing Apple Loop. Repeat with the next sound, if you've imported more than one.

When you're finished, install your new loops into GarageBand by dragging their icons into the Loop browser, exactly as described on page 41.

Moving Your Loops to Another Drive

Those GarageBand loops are great—but lordy, they're big. The 1,100 of them that come with a basic GarageBand installation take up 1.1 GB of hard drive space and the Jam Pack, if you install it, scarfs down another 3 gigs.

That's all fine if you sit all day in front of your Power Mac G5 with its 160 GB hard drive. But if you're using a laptop, that's a lot of real estate for a program that may (ahem) not be the software that earns you your living.

The question inevitably arises: "How can I move those loops to another drive to save space?"

For example, maybe you have an iPod that, when you're home, you use as an external hard drive for that PowerBook. And maybe you want to store your loops there. (Let's assume that when you're *traveling* with the PowerBook, you don't use GarageBand and therefore have no need for its loops.)

1. **Open your hard drive→Library→Application Support→GarageBand folder. Copy the Apple Loops folder to your second drive.**

Figure 9-4:
It might feel a little odd dragging a copy of your Apple Loops folder into the Loop browser, so that GarageBand can recognize the exact same Apple loops it had in the first place. But this is the official routine for moving loops to a different hard drive.

A hard drive, please. Anything slower (like a DVD) will slow down GarageBand too much.

Moving Your Loops to Another Drive

2. **Open the Apple Loops folder. Throw away everything inside.**

   For example, choose Edit→Select All (⌘-A), and then File→Move to Trash (Shift-⌘-Delete).

   You're not throwing away the *folder*—only what's inside it.

3. **Now open the Apple Loops Index folder. Throw away everything inside it.**

   Once again, leave the folder—just discard what's in it.

4. **Open GarageBand again. Click the eyeball icon to open the Loop browser.**

   GarageBand warns you that it can't find the loops. Click OK.

5. **Find the copy of the Apple Loops folder on the second hard drive, and drag it directly into the Loop browser, as shown in Figure 9-4.**

   GarageBand briskly indexes your loops (takes note of their new location)—and then is ready to roll.

   Ta-da! Reclaimed space.

The iSight as Microphone

Every 5.6 seconds, somebody in the world exclaims: "Hey, how come I can't use my Apple iSight video cam/microphone as a microphone for singing into GarageBand? My PowerBook's fan is too noisy for me to sing into the built-in mike."

The answer: GarageBand, like Apple, is something of a quality diva. It won't tolerate audio coming from a source that provides anything less than CD quality (44.1 kilohertz sampling). In fact, if you choose GarageBand→Preferences and click the Audio/MIDI button, you'll see, in the Audio Input pop-up menu, the dimmed-out text "iSight (not 44.1)."

You can work around this limitation, however, by recording the audio in *iMovie*, which works perfectly well with the iSight. The whole procedure takes a lot longer to read than it actually is:

1. **Create a new iMovie project. At the lower-left corner of the iMovie window, slide the switch to the silhouetted camcorder icon, and from the icon's pop-up menu), choose iSight.**

   You've just told iMovie to record sound from the iSight camera.

2. **Duck back into GarageBand, and start it playing.**

   These steps assume that you've got some instrumental tracks already in there, to which you want to add vocals. (These steps also assume that you're wearing headphones, so that you don't record the accompaniment along with your singing.)

3. Return to iMovie. Click the "Record with iSight" button below the preview monitor—and sing your heart out.

Click the "Record with iSight" button again to stop.

4. Drag the clip you've just recorded into the timeline at the bottom of the iMovie screen. Now, still in iMovie, choose File→Share.

The Share dialog box appears.

5. At the top of the Share dialog box, click QuickTime. From the "Compress movie for" pop-up menu, choose Expert Settings. Click Share.

The dialog box shown at top in Figure 9-5 appears.

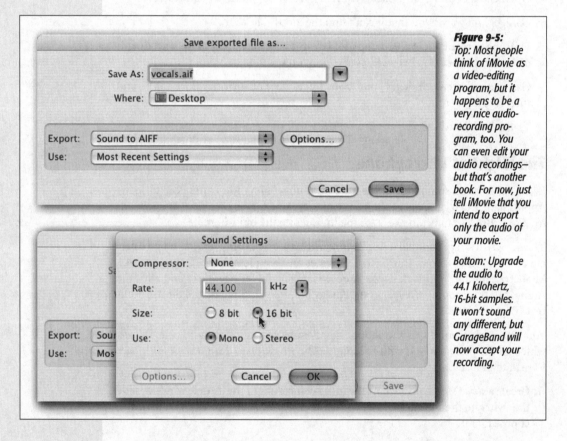

Figure 9-5:
Top: Most people think of iMovie as a video-editing program, but it happens to be a very nice audio-recording program, too. You can even edit your audio recordings—but that's another book. For now, just tell iMovie that you intend to export only the audio of your movie.

Bottom: Upgrade the audio to 44.1 kilohertz, 16-bit samples. It won't sound any different, but GarageBand will now accept your recording.

6. From the Export pop-up menu, choose Sound to AIFF. Then click Options.

Now the second dialog box in Figure 9-5 appears.

7. From the Rate pop-up menu, choose 44.100. Also click "16 Bit."

You've just converted your audio into a format that will make GarageBand happy.

8. **Click OK, choose a name and folder location, and then click Save.**

   The result is a new AIFF sound file on your desktop (or wherever you saved it).

9. **Return to GarageBand. (Stop playback, if it's driving you crazy.) Drag the AIFF file into a Real Instrument track, or into a blank area of the timeline to create a new track.**

   Presto: Great-sounding audio from your iSight!

"Save as Archive"

As noted in the box on page 24, a GarageBand document isn't much of a *document* at all. It's actually a Mac OS X *package*, a folder disguised to work like a document icon.

As long as you use *only* the built-in Apple loops in your composition, you can freely exchange your GarageBand "document" with any agents, producers, or groupies who also have GarageBand. They'll be able to open the project and hear it exactly the way you did. After all, your composition is made exclusively of:

- Built-in Apple Loops, the same ones your audience also has on their Macs.

- Vocal lines and other Real Instrument recordings that you made, which are embedded inside the GarageBand package icon. (They're stored as AIFF files there.)

But what about *other* loops? What about Jam Pack loops, or loops you've made yourself, or loops bought from other companies?

Your audience does *not* have these on hand. They will *not* hear your masterpiece as it exists on your Mac.

The solution is the File→Save as Archive command. It creates what *looks* like a standard GarageBand document icon—but inside, it actually stores copies of all the loops you've used in your piece.

Needless to say, the resulting file takes up a lot more disk space than a regular GarageBand document. In fact, it can be huge. But at least it's self-contained and ready for glitch-free distribution.

ReWire

ReWire is a music-synchronization technology that lets music programs running on the same machine control *each other*. As its developer, Propellerhead Software, puts it, ReWire is an invisible cable that streams audio from one computer program into another.

How is this useful? Because not all music programs have every feature in the world. The software called Reason (also from Propellerhead), for example, is wildly popular among Mac musicians who've tried it. Reason beautifully simulates the controls—and the sounds—of a sophisticated real-world synthesizer, complete stacks of recording-studio processing modules. It can't, however, record live audio (like singing), and it doesn't offer looping.

But GarageBand does, of course. Thanks to ReWire, you can create a little musical ecosystem of programs that work well together.

Suppose, for example, that you have Reason (or you've downloaded the free demo version just to fool around with it). All you have to do is:

- Open GarageBand.

- Then open Reason.

You've just established GarageBand as the *master,* the software that will control all *other* ReWire-compatible programs (the slaves). If you now click Play in GarageBand, you'll hear whatever music is in Reason begin playing in perfect sync. Change the tempo in GarageBand, and Reason's tempo changes too. The volume slider, Cycle controls, time display, and other GarageBand controls work, too, controlling both programs simultaneously. (To make the slave program louder or quieter relative to GarageBand, go into that program and adjust the output volume manually.)

Figure 9-6:
Go ahead and add vocal tracks, throw in some loops, record some MIDI keyboard performances, and otherwise use GarageBand as you normally would. The only difference is that you've got a whole orchestra of synthesizers—in the form of Reason, or whatever other ReWire-comptible programs are running—playing along.

The mind-blowing thing is that when your work is finished, you can use File→Export to iTunes command as usual. GarageBand will incorporate both its own tracks and those from Reason into the finished product.

In short, the slave program (Reason, in this example) behaves exactly as though it's a set of tracks right in GarageBand (Figure 9-6).

Tip: One chief advantage of using Reason (or another ReWire program) as a slave backup band for Garage-Band is that it doesn't require nearly as much memory and processor horsepower as GarageBand. You can build up a number of tracks in Reason, then use GarageBand only for recording a few live-instrument tracks, like voice and acoustic guitar.

You can read a lot more about ReWire at *www.propellerheads.se.* There you'll find not only a step-by-step mini-tutorial, but also a list of pro music programs that work with ReWire. They include Digital Performer (Mark of the Unicorn), Live (Ableton), Pro Tools (Digidesign), Logic (Apple), Cubase (Steinberg), and others.

The Speed Chapter

G arageBand, as you may recall from Chapter 1 (or as you may have discovered on your own), is a power hog. It thrives on memory and processor speed, eternally craving more, more, and more. Even a handful of tracks is enough to redline your system, turning the Playhead orange, then red, and finally summoning the dreaded dialog box shown in Figure 10-1 as playback grinds to a halt.

Tip: The Playhead changes color, turning orange and finally red, as you approach the system-overload point. It's your early-warning system that your piece is approaching GarageBand BogDown.

Figure 10-1:
When GarageBand can't keep up with everything going on in your tracks, you'll see this message, or one that says, in the smaller type, "This song has too many real instrument tracks to be played in real-time. To maximize performance, look in Garage-Band Help under Performance."

Part of the song was not played

This song has too many tracks, effects, or notes to be played in real-time.
To optimize performance, see the 'Optimizing GarageBand performance' page in GarageBand Help.

Continue

There's no cause for panic, though. In the end, it's you who's made GarageBand gasp for air, by overextending your Mac—and therefore it's you who can undo the damage, too. This chapter presents the accumulated wisdom of thousands of online GarageBand fans sharing their workarounds, plus Apple's own suggestions. They're presented here in decreasing order of importance and urgency. (Or better yet, try the first steps first!)

Set the Stage

You can avoid many overburdened-Mac situations just by taking the time to set up your GarageBand environment smartly. For example:

- Quit as many other programs as possible. GarageBand needs all the memory it can get.

- Every PowerBook, iBook, and Power Mac G5 lets you switch your computer's brain into a slower, reduced-power mode to save heat and battery charge. But for GarageBand, that's just asking for trouble; it needs every hair of horsepower it can get.

  So choose $\bullet$→System Preferences, click Energy Saver, then click the Options tab. Now from the pop-up menu, choose Highest. Close the window.

  Your laptop battery won't last quite as long, and your G5's fan might spin up a little more, but at least you'll be able to get some meaningful work done in GarageBand.

- Don't try to play a song, loop, or audio file that's on a CD or DVD. Copy it to your hard drive first.

- Turn off FileVault, if you're using it, by choosing $\bullet$→System Preferences, clicking Security, and clicking Turn FileVault Off. (FileVault is a Mac OS X security feature that encrypts your entire Home folder; you'd remember turning it on.) It slows down data transfer from your Home folder dramatically.

WORKAROUND WORKSHOP

Delayed Gratification

Yes, it's easy to overwhelm the Mac by using a lot of tracks and effects during playback and recording. But keep in mind that when GarageBand exports your song to iTunes at the end of the compositional process, it has all the time in the world. At that point, it doesn't have to keep up with real-time playback, and can handle as complex a piece as your imagination can dream up.

Therefore, you can consider all the tips in this chapter to be temporary, simply for use while you construct your piece. Just before exporting the completed masterpiece, you can, if you wish, undo any of the tweaks described in these pages,

confident that the exported song will contain every track and effect you've added.

The only thing to be careful of: If you put together a ten-track song on a Mac that can handle only five tracks—by listening to only five tracks at a time—you may get clipping (distortion) when they're played all together. Because you'll never play all ten at once in GarageBand, you'll never see the clipping indicators (page 141) come on.

After exporting to iTunes, therefore, listen through the song carefully to make sure that the whole thing sounds good.

Alternatively, copy your GarageBand projects to a location outside your Home folder—into the Shared folder, for example. That way, you can leave FileVault turned on without any speed penalty.

Mute Some Tracks

If GarageBand announces that "Some parts were not played," then OK, but at least *you* should be the one determining *which* parts. As you work, you can mute the tracks whose playback you consider expendable for the moment. (Click each track and press the letter M key, or click the little speaker icon in the track header.)

Any track that you silence like this is one more task crossed off the Mac's real-time To Do list. By selectively muting and un-muting tracks, you should be able to get your piece mostly ready. Afterwards, you can either export the thing, convert some Software Instrument tracks to Real Instruments, or even bounce the whole thing into iTunes and back. Both of these radical tactics are described later in this chapter.

Combine Tracks

Playing more tracks makes GarageBand work harder. In many cases, though, you can combine the *material* from several tracks into a single one.

It's especially easy to combine blue Real Instrument tracks. Figure 10-2 shows the procedure.

Figure 10-2:
Top: These three Real Instrument tracks are making this old Power Mac's heart race. There's no good reason for them to occupy different tracks, since their regions aren't playing simultaneously.

Bottom: By dragging all of their regions into a single track, you ease your Mac's burden considerably. The only downside is that you've lost the ability to specify different effect settings for each track.

A reminder: Use this trick only on regions that don't overlap.

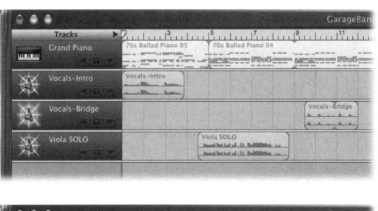
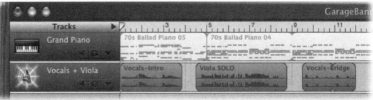

Combining green Software Instrument tracks is more difficult, because dragging a region into a different track usually means that its instrument sound changes. Not to worry: You can always turn a Software Instrument region into a Real Instrument region, as described on page 36, and then merge them.

Temporarily Squelch the Effects

The *effects* described in Chapter 7 (reverb, EQ, and so on) represent the state of the art in software simulators. But it's still quite a feat for the Mac to pass the sound of your various tracks into these software modules, calculate the new, post-processed sound, and then send it back out your speakers—all in real time.

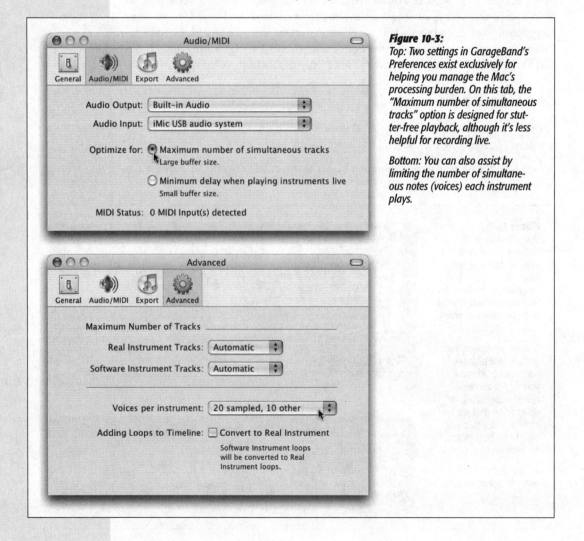

Figure 10-3:
Top: Two settings in GarageBand's Preferences exist exclusively for helping you manage the Mac's processing burden. On this tab, the "Maximum number of simultaneous tracks" option is designed for stutter-free playback, although it's less helpful for recording live.

Bottom: You can also assist by limiting the number of simultaneous notes (voices) each instrument plays.

One of the quickest and easiest ways to alleviate the Mac's speed burden, then, is to turn off some effects. (Double-click a track to open the Track Info dialog box, expand the Details panel, and start turning off checkboxes.) You can always turn them on again before you export the finished piece to iTunes.

Tip: Amp Simulation is among the most processor-intensive effects of all, capable of bringing a G3-based Mac to its knees single-handedly. If you're a guitarist and you ache for the flexibility of having different guitar effects at your fingertips, but your Mac doesn't have the muscle for GarageBand's simulators, consider buying an inexpensive multi-effects box from a company like Digitech or Korg (under $100). A box of this type lets you apply the effects to the sound *before* it reaches GarageBand, so you can leave the Amp Simulations turned off.

It's worth considering, too, whether you'll actually *hear* individual track effects. Once you've added master effects like reverb, not all individual track effects are even audible.

Enlarge Your Buffer

In the GarageBand→Preferences, click the Audio/MIDI button to see the controls shown at top in Figure 10-3. Setting it to "Maximum number of simultaneous tracks" devotes more of the Mac's energies to playing back your piece.

The disadvantage of this setting is that when you record from a MIDI keyboard, you may experience *latency*—a frustrating, fraction-of-a-second delay between each keypress and the playing of its sound.

The trick, then, is knowing when to switch this setting. Leave it on "Minimum delay when playing instruments live" when you're recording, and compensate by turning off some tracks if the Mac begins gasping. After the recording, change the setting to "Maximum."

Lose Some Software Instrument Voices

Some instruments, like flutes and kazoos, can play only one note at a time—in software parlance, one *voice* at a time. A piano, meanwhile, can theoretically play 88 notes at once, although you'd need a few friends to help you press the keys if you wanted to hear more than 10 notes simultaneously.

But the more Software Instrument voices GarageBand must play, the more your Mac sweats. As shown in Figure 10-3 at bottom, a certain pop-up menu in the Garage-Band Preferences dialog box lets you limit the number of voices that get played. In a pinch, you can set a limit on these voices, thus saving GarageBand further effort and sometimes making an unplayable song playable again on your Mac.

The wording of this dialog box is a tad cryptic, in that it refers to "sampled" and "other" voices. To understand this lingo, it helps to understand the two different ways that GarageBand can create Software Instrument sounds:

- **With samples.** A *sampled* instrument sound began life as a recording of a real-world instrument playing one note in a real-world studio. Pressing a key on a MIDI keyboard triggers a playback of that short recording. In the case of woodwind instruments, the sampled sound seamlessly repeats for as long as you press the key.

  In GarageBand, all the woodwind, brass, piano, guitar, bass, strings, and drum sounds are sampled sounds.

- **With synthesis.** The rest of the Software Instrument sounds are created using software algorithms; in essence your Mac becomes a musical synthesizer. GarageBand's clavinet, organ, electric piano, and synthesizer Software Instrument sounds are all created this way.

  Synthesized sounds put a greater strain on your Mac than sampled sounds, since GarageBand must compute these sounds on the fly.

When you inspect the dialog box in Figure 10-4, the options in the lower pop-up menu should make more sense. Suppose, for example, that you choose "10 sampled, 5 other." You've just specified that no Software Instrument will be allowed to play more than 5 notes simultaneously if it's an electronic keyboard sound (organ, electric piano, and so on), or more than 10 notes at once for any other Software Instrument.

Now, you might be aghast at this suggestion. Surely eliminating notes from your chords would eviscerate your harmonies, leaving them sounding hollow and empty.

In truth, though, you might never miss the notes that GarageBand leaves out of a busy orchestration. Meanwhile, thinning out the voices could make all the difference in a GarageBand composition that's too complex for your Mac.

Tip: Speaking of voices: When keyboard players attempt to create guitar parts by playing a MIDI keyboard, they often forget that a guitar has only six strings. If you play freely with both hands on the keyboard, using all 10 fingers, you may inadvertently create a guitar part that would be unplayable on an actual guitar.

Reduce the Track Overhead

Every time you create a new GarageBand project file, the program allots some memory to hold a certain number of tracks. (The exact number depends on the speed of your Mac and how much memory is installed.)

But if you intend to create nothing but a single-line kazoo recording, that's a lot of memory being set aside that could be used for other purposes...like keeping up with playback.

That's why, as soon as you know how many total tracks your piece will have, you should choose GarageBand→Preferences, click the Advanced tab, and change the Maximum Number of Tracks pop-up menus (shown in Figure 10-4 at bottom).

You're telling the program: "I intend to use no more than eight Software Instrument tracks and eight Real Instrument tracks" (or whatever), "so please put whatever additional memory you were holding back into the pot. I could use it right about now."

Convert Software Instrument Loops

As you may have read in Chapter 1, Software Instruments are much more trouble for the Mac to play back than Real Instruments.

Now, at first glance, that statement might seem to be illogical—in fact, reversed. After all, green Software Instrument regions contain very little data—only a list of note triggers ("Play middle C for one beat, then C sharp for two"). MIDI *files* take up only a few kilobytes on the hard drive. They're absolutely minuscule compared with digital recordings like Real Instrument regions, which take up 10 MB per minute. So why isn't it easier for the Mac to play the little files than the big ones?

Because it must also *generate the instrument sounds,* not to mention processing them with effects, as it plays each MIDI note. It's not the triggering that's so much work; it's the synthesizing.

To play a blue or purple Real Instrument region, on the other hand, the Mac just plays back a bunch of sound data that's already fully formed on the hard drive.

In any case, exploiting this little quirk of Software and Real Instruments is an excellent way to reduce the load on your Mac's processor, because GarageBand makes it easy to *convert* the former into the latter.

For example, GarageBand offers at least three ways to convert green loops into blue ones that are easier for the Mac to play:

- If you press the Option key before dragging a green loop out of the Loop browser and into an empty spot on the timeline (and keep the key down), GarageBand creates a blue Real Instrument track. It then converts your loop into the familiar blue soundwaves found in a Real Instrument region.

- If you enjoy that auto-conversion so much that you'd *always* like GarageBand to convert green loops, choose GarageBand→Preferences, click the Advanced tab, and turn on "Convert to Real Instruments." From now on, every loop you drag out of the Loop browser (into a blank spot in the timeline area) creates a blue Real Instrument track and region.

Tip: Pressing the Option key simply reverses this Preferences setting. If "Convert to Real Instruments" is turned on, for example, then Option-dragging a green loop does *not* convert it to a blue one.

- You can drag a green loop that's already *in* a track into a blue Real Instrument track. GarageBand converts it to a Real Instrument region as described on page 36.

Remember, though, that once converted to digital-audio form, a loop loses much of the editing flexibility it once had. You can no longer change individual notes inside it, for example. (Fortunately, you *can* still adjust the tempo of the piece, and even transpose your converted loops, just as you would any blue Apple Loops.)

Convert Software Instrument Recordings

The three green-to-blue conversion tricks described above work only on Software Instrument *loops*. They don't work on MIDI regions that you've recorded yourself (using, for example, a MIDI keyboard controller).

That's a shame, because converting your *own* Software Instrument regions into Real Instrument regions would take even more pressure off your Mac's processor.

Still, you *can* convert this kind of region—just not quite as easily. You'll export the region (or its whole track, if you like) to iTunes, which turns it into an AIFF recording in the process—and then reimport it into GarageBand.

Here's the drill:

1. **Isolate the green Software Instrument track you want to convert.**

   That is, make sure it's the only track that plays back. The quickest way might be to turn on its Solo button (the tiny pair of headphones in its track header), as shown at top in Figure 10-4.

2. **Choose File→Export to iTunes.**

   As described in Chapter 8, GarageBand takes a moment to convert the file and lodge it in iTunes, filed in the playlist that you named in the GarageBand→Preferences dialog box.

3. **In GarageBand, figure out where you're going to reimport the track.**

   This time, of course, it will be a digital audio file—a Real Instrument track. You can choose Track→New Basic Track to create an empty track to hold it, or you can drag it into an existing blue Real Instrument track.

4. **Position the iTunes window so that you can see both it and the GarageBand window.**

   Figure 10-4 at middle shows the setup.

5. **Drag the converted file back into GarageBand (Figure 10-4, middle).**

   That is, drag it into the Real Instrument track you identified in step 3. Drag it sideways to position it, if you like.

6. Delete or mute the original Software Instrument track (Figure 10-4, bottom).

That, after all, was the whole point of this exercise.

Your piece should sound exactly the way it did before you performed this little operation. The only differences:

- The Macintosh doesn't have to work nearly as hard to play it.

- You can no longer change the tempo of the piece without leaving your converted track out of sync with the rest of the piece. Your converted track is locked forever at the original tempo. (You can't transpose it or edit its notes, either.)

Tip: Want the best of both worlds? Then keep the original, green Software Instrument tracks around, but mute them. If you ever want to make changes, you can modify the original, editable tracks and then re-convert them.

Figure 10-4:
Top: Isolate the Software Instrument track by turning on its Solo button, the tiny headphones button (circled). Send the track to iTunes.

Middle: You can reimport the converted music by dragging it from iTunes into an available Real Instrument track in GarageBand. Or, if screen space is very tight, you can also drag the file out of iTunes and onto the desktop, where it turns into an icon, and then drag that icon into Garage-Band.

Bottom: The resulting mix sounds exactly the same, but takes up much less processing power.

Software Instrument track to be converted

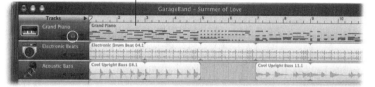

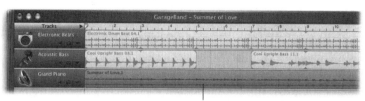

Same music—now in Real Instrument form!

"Bounce Down" Many Tracks into One

And now, one of the most useful and powerful tools in the GarageBand musician's arsenal. It starts with the idea behind the GarageBand→iTunes→GarageBand conversion described earlier and takes it to the logical extreme: exporting *more* than one track, or even *all* of your tracks, and boiling them all down into one!

Suppose, for example, that your Mac can play only five tracks at once before bogging down. But you've got 20 tracks' worth of music in your head! Using the "bounce down" trick, no problem. You could simply proceed like this:

- Export all five tracks to iTunes. Reimport the result into GarageBand as *one* track (it would look something like Figure 10-4 at middle). Delete the original five component tracks, or just mute them. Now you're free to add another four! (Effective total now: nine tracks.)

- Export *these* five tracks (which sound like nine) to iTunes. Reimport into GarageBand as *one* track, delete the original five—and add yet another four. (Effective total: 13.)

The one big caution here is that each time you export your tracks, you're freezing them. You're giving up any ability to adjust their effects, rebalance their volume levels, change the song's tempo, and so on. Take care to finalize each semi-mix as much as possible before exporting.

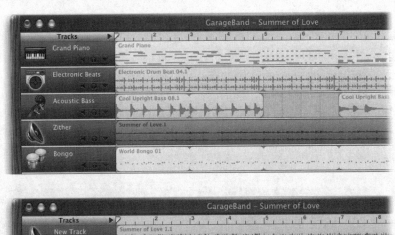

Figure 10-5:
Top: Five tracks, just crackling with music. Finalized and polished to within an inch of its life. And pushing the Mac to its max. How will you gain the headroom necessary to add the four vocal tracks you have in mind?

Bottom: Easy: just export the half-finished mix to iTunes, and then bring it right back in as a single track, shown here. Delete the original five.

Now you've got a nearly empty track canvas in which to add four more tracks.

You've just created what studio musicians call a submix.

And so on. Figure 10-5 shows the basic idea.

Tip: You might also want to use the File→Save As command along the way, preserving each set of exported tracks before you delete them, so you can return to the original GarageBand files if necessary. (Like when you get a dual-processor Power Mac G5 with 1 gig of RAM.)

Turn Monitoring Off

When you're recording live audio from a microphone or electronic instrument, and GarageBand is having trouble keeping up, consider turning off the Monitor option (double-click the track header to see it). In most cases, you can hear your voice or instrument live anyway, and turning off Monitoring eases the Mac's burden because it doesn't have to process and play the sound in real time.

Install More Memory

After a certain point, bending over backward to accommodate all of these work-arounds, settings, and cheats just isn't worth it. If you're still getting "Parts were not played" messages after following all, or even some, of the steps in this chapter, you should just break down and give your Mac the gift of more memory.

With more RAM, GarageBand can hold more of the sampled audio (blue Real loops, your purple Real recordings, and green, sampled Software Instruments) in memory, and therefore doesn't have to read as much information from your hard drive, which is what slows GarageBand down.

In particular, if your Mac has only 256 or even 512 megabytes of memory, you're living at the edge, as far as GarageBand is concerned. (To find out how much you have, choose →About This Mac.) Hie thee immediately to *www.ramseeker.com,* choose your Mac's model name from the pop-up menu, and see just how inexpensive a memory upgrade can be these days.

Troubleshooting

The truth is, most of the troubleshooting you'll do in GarageBand has to do with accommodating its horsepower demands. You'll know there's a problem when you see the Playhead turn orange or red, get skips in the music, or see a note that "Some parts were not played." In that regard, Chapter 10, the one about speed, is the real troubleshooting chapter.

Still, a few other things can go wrong, or at least can baffle you. Here, for your head-ache-relieving pleasure, are recipes for solving the most common problems.

Trouble with Loops

Loops, as described in Chapter 2, are among the greatest joys of GarageBand. So when they don't work, they're among the biggest disappointments.

Your Loop Browser is Empty

Adding more loops to GarageBand isn't just a matter of stuffing them into a certain folder on your hard drive. You also have to make GarageBand *aware* of them. To do that, you force GarageBand to *index* any new loops, building an internal card catalog of which loops you have and where they're stored.

If anything goes wrong with GarageBand's loop index, you may discover that all of the buttons in the Loop browser are dimmed and no loops appear in its list. Other wackiness can result, too, like loops that exist in name only or simply misbehave.

In all of these situations, the solution is to *rebuild* the GarageBand loop index. You do it like this:

1. **Quit GarageBand. In the Finder, open your hard drive window. Then open the Library→Application Support→GarageBand→Apple Loops folder (see Figure 11-1, top).**

   Inside, you'll see the actual text files that constitute your current index.

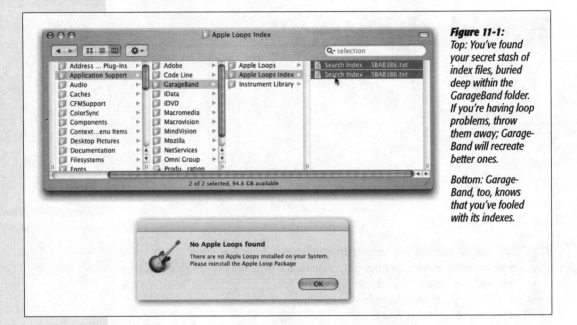

Figure 11-1:
Top: You've found your secret stash of index files, buried deep within the GarageBand folder. If you're having loop problems, throw them away; Garage-Band will recreate better ones.

Bottom: Garage-Band, too, knows that you've fooled with its indexes.

2. **Drag the index files to the Trash.**

   GarageBand will rebuild fresh, healthy ones in just a moment.

3. **Open GarageBand and click the Loop Browser (eyeball) button.**

   GarageBand suddenly realizes that it has no loops, and shows the dialog box at bottom in Figure 11-1.

4. **In the No Apple Loops Found dialog box, click OK.**

   Now return to the Finder.

5. **Open your hard drive→Library→Application Support→GarageBand folder. Drag the Apple Loops folder directly into any visible portion of GarageBand's Loop browser.**

   GarageBand dutifully recreates its loop index, based on the current location and contents of that Loops folder.

Note: If you've installed the Jam Pack, drag *its* folder (also in the Library→Application Support→GarageBand folder) into the Loop browser, too.

New Add-On Loops Don't Show Up

It's a nice perk that GarageBand can accommodate additional loops that were designed for other music-software programs. Note, however, that:

- You should install them by dragging them into GarageBand's Loop browser, *not* by dragging them into a folder in the Finder. Dragging them into the Loop browser ensures that GarageBand indexes the new loops (that is, adds them to its internal database).

- Occasionally, non-Apple loops don't show up in the Loop browser even when you've installed them correctly. In that case, you may have no choice but to drag them from the Finder directly into the GarageBand timeline area, bypassing the Loop browser entirely.

Some Loop Buttons are Dimmed or Missing

Remember that most of the time, GarageBand shows you only a *subset* of the 1,100 loops that it comes with. For example:

- It shows you only the loops that fit your song's time signature, and hides the rest (they wouldn't sound right anyway). If your song is in 7/4 time, for example, you won't see any loops *at all.* The vast majority of Apple loops are in 4/4 time.

- It shows you only the loops that fit your song's *key,* or are close to it. See page 40 for details, and for the workaround.

- Remember that each time you open GarageBand, you see only 30 loop buttons. But you can drag upward the prominent, dark gray, brushed-metal divider bar, using the spot on either side of the time display as a handle, to reveal 24 more.

- By Control-clicking individual buttons in the Loop browser, it's possible to choose new identities for the buttons you see here. That's a great feature, because it means that you can put the buttons *you* consider important in more easily reached positions.

  Of course, it also means that you (or some meddlesome interloper) can duplicate buttons, hide buttons, and so on.

  If you suspect that something's amiss, choose GarageBand→Preferences. Click the General button, and then click the Reset button at the bottom of the dialog box. All buttons return to their original Apple factory-set positions.

Recording and Editing Problems

What can go wrong during the main working phase? Let us count the ways.

There's a Delay When Playing Live

On slower Macs, you may experience an annoying lag between the time you press a key on your instrument and the time the sound comes out of the Mac's speakers. That's *latency,* baby, and there's one—and only one—step you can take to solve it.

See page 113 for the details.

Trouble Staying with the Beat

If you're having trouble playing new music in step with the current tempo, consider these techniques:

- **Slow the tempo (page 76).** Later, you can always crank it back up again for final playback.

  This is, alas, a trick you can use only if you're recording Software Instrument tracks (from a MIDI keyboard controller, for example). If you're playing a live instrument or singing, you must record at the final tempo.

- **Eliminate the delay problem.** It may be that what you're experiencing is the *latency* problem described, and solved, on page 113.

- **Mute some tracks.** If you the other tracks, you'll hear nothing but yourself and the metronome.

- **Add a drum part.** Sometimes, making the drum part more prominent (by silencing the other tracks for the moment) makes it easier to hear the beat. You may even want to consider *adding* a drum part for a song that doesn't need one, just for recording purposes. You can always delete the drums later.

Weird, Phase-Shifty Sound During Recording

Mac OS X comes with a program, in the Applications→Utilities folder, called Audio MIDI Setup. You may have other audio setup programs, too.

Most people never even see these programs, and that's fine. But if you, a power user with a lot of gear and a fancy MIDI setup, have used these programs to configure your equipment setup, note that the Playthru feature of Audio MIDI Setup *duplicates* the effect of the Monitor setting in GarageBand. (Double-click a track's header to turn Monitor on or off.)

If both Playthru (in Audio MIDI Setup) and Monitor (in GarageBand) are turned on at once, the Mac tries to play what you're recording *twice*, nearly simultaneously, resulting in the odd phase shift sound you're hearing. Turn one of those two features off.

No Sound from a Microphone or Real Instrument

If GarageBand doesn't seem to be "hearing" anything from your microphone or line input, the problem is usually that the Mac hasn't been taught to "listen" to the right audio source. Review the steps on page 108, including visiting System Preferences and choosing the correct input in the GarageBand→Preferences panel.

Otherwise, double-check these points:

- Make sure that you've clicked a blue Real Instrument track. If a green Software Instrument track is selected, GarageBand ignores your microphone or instrument.

- Also make sure you haven't muted this track, or soloed another one. (The speaker icon in your track's header should be lit up in blue, and no other instrument's headphones icon should be blue.) While you're at it, make sure that the track's volume slider isn't set to zero (page 140).

- It's possible that GarageBand is set up to listen to the wrong channel (mono instruments). Double-click the track header and check the Input pop-up menu and Format (mono/stereo) buttons, as described on page 110.

- Are you getting *any* sound from GarageBand? That is, is your Mac's speaker turned up? Of course, you won't hear anything at all from your real instrument unless you've turned on Monitor in its Track Info dialog box. Check by double-clicking the track header. (But don't turn on monitoring until you've read the discussion on page 111.)

- If you're using a mixer or audio interface, is its volume turned all the way down?

- Are you getting any sound from the instrument? If it's electric, do you have it turned on, with the volume turned up? Make sure all the connections are good—especially if you've incorporated plug adapters into the mix.

Tip: If you're using a Griffin iMic adapter to connect your microphone or instrument to the Mac, you have some additional checking to do. Make sure you've connected the mike or instrument to the iMic's input jack (the one with a microphone symbol). Also make sure to switch the iMic's selector toward the microphone symbol.

Finally, in GarageBand, you have to choose GarageBand→Preferences, click the Audio/MIDI button, and, from the Audio Input pop-up menu, choose "iMic USB audio system." You should be ready to roll.

No Sound from a MIDI Instrument

Are you having trouble getting GarageBand to "hear" an external MIDI instrument, like a keyboard controller or MIDI guitar? In that case, use the MIDI status light identified in Figure 11-2 as an assistant detective.

Figure 11-2:
This handy little light flickers blue whenever GarageBand is receiving note data, either from its own onscreen keyboard, an external MIDI instrument, or an onscreen virtual keyboard like MidiKeys or LoudK.

Flashing MIDI indicator

The status light doesn't flicker when you play

If that little light isn't flashing when you play your MIDI instrument, the MIDI information isn't reaching GarageBand, for some reason. Here are two things to try:

- Make sure the instrument is turned on and connected to the Mac. If a MIDI interface box is involved, pay close attention: It's very easy to get the MIDI In and MIDI Out cables confused. (You want one cable to run from the instrument's MIDI Out jack to the interface's MIDI In jack, and another cable going from In to Out.)

- Choose GarageBand→Preferences. Click the Audio/MIDI button. See the MIDI Status line? It should say "1 MIDI Input(s) detected" (or 2, or whatever number you have).

If not, it's remotely possible that you're using a MIDI interface that requires driver software of its own. Visit the manufacturer's Web site to seek out a Mac OS X-compatible driver. Without this software installed, the MIDI interface may not work at all.

The status light flickers when you play

If that little indicator *does* flicker on and off, then everything is correctly hooked up and working.

In that case, here's your checklist:

- Make sure you've selected a green Software Instrument track. Otherwise, Garage-Band won't produce sound for your MIDI instrument.

- Make sure that you haven't muted this track or soloed another one, or set your track's volume to zero.

- Choose Window -> Keyboard and click a few keys on the onscreen keyboard to make sure that the selected track has a working instrument selected. (Incidentally, playing a few notes will also help you find out whether your Mac's speaker is turned down all the way.)

You might also try double-clicking the track header to open the Track Info dialog box. Make sure you've selected an instrument and effects preset in the top two lists. And in the Details panel, consider turning off some effects until you find the problem. (Believe it or not, it's technically possible to fiddle with the effects so much that no sound emerges.)

TROUBLESHOOTING MOMENT

Sound, but in the Wrong Account

Help! My brother and I both use GarageBand. I've switched into my account using Fast User Switching—and now when I play my MIDI keyboard, the sounds are coming out in his copy of GarageBand, which is still running in his account!

Pretty cool, though, isn't it? You both are logged in at once, and you're both running GarageBand—but anything you play is being intercepted by his copy!

Gotta love being alive to see this kind of thing.

Anyway, GarageBand works fine with Fast User Switching (a feature of Mac OS X 10.3 and later)—but only one person at a time can use a MIDI interface. You have no alternative but to switch into your brother's account and quit GarageBand.

Now your account has the MIDI instrument's full attention.

- Do you, in fact, have any Software Instruments available? (Double-click a track header to see if anything's in the list.) If you or somebody else has been doing some naughty playing in the Library→Application Support→GarageBand folder, the files may be so dismantled that you need to reinstall GarageBand to get it going again.

Transposing Created Cacophonous Chaos

As described on page 92, you can *transpose* (shift in pitch) green Software Instrument loops and blue Real Instrument loops, which is kind of amazing.

You cannot, however, transpose these kinds of regions:

- Your own live recordings (purple Real Instrument regions).

- Non-Apple loops you installed yourself. (If they're called *Apple* Loops, though, they should be transposable.)

No Sound from External Speakers (or Audio Interface)

Ordinarily, GarageBand sends the sound of its own playback through your Mac's audio circuitry, whether that's through your Mac's built-in speakers or speakers connected to its headphone jack.

But what if you've bought fancy external USB speakers? Or what if you've connected an audio interface box that's hooked up to its own sound system?

In those cases, choose GarageBand→Preferences. Click the Audio/MIDI button. Use the Audio Input Driver pop-up menu to choose the name of your external speakers or interface box. (This assumes, of course, that it's *listed* in the pop-up menu, which often means that you've installed some driver software that came with the speakers or audio box.)

Mixing and Publishing Glitches

There's nothing more annoying than something going wrong when your masterpiece is finished. Here's what to do.

Finished Song Is Too Quiet

If your GarageBand masterpiece arrives in iTunes playing far too softly relative to your other tunes, revisit Chapter 8 for tips on setting the master volume level before exporting.

But if the master volume slider is turned all the way up and the music is *still* too soft, you can also:

- **Add the Compression effect before exporting.** (Double-click the track header, turn on Compressor, and then drag the slider to the right.) Doing so boosts the softest passages and flattens the loudest ones, so that the whole thing remains at a more consistent volume level.

• **Use the iTunes preamp after exporting.** Once the song is in iTunes, you can also boost the volume there. Figure 11-3 has the details.

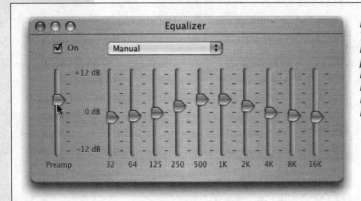

Figure 11-3:
To open this graphic equalizer in iTunes, choose Window→Equalizer, or press ⌘-2, or click the tiny equalizer button in the lower-right corner of the iTunes window. Drag the Preamp slider upward to boost this song's playback level, being careful not to overdo it.

Tracks Panned to One Side Still Play in Both Speakers

Here's a tricky one. Suppose you've used the Pan knob (page 144) to "place" a certain track's instrument all the way to the left side of the stereo field, or all the way to the right. Yet when you listen with headphones, you still hear the darned thing coming out of both speakers!

There are two possibilities:

• Most of the time, the culprit is the Echo or Reverb effect that you've applied to that track. When you turn on these checkboxes for one track, you're actually telling GarageBand how *much* of the *master* track's Echo and Reverb to apply. You're not really applying a *different* echo or reverb to this individual track (see page 135).

   What you're hearing, then, is the sound of your fully panned track reverberating through both speakers, courtesy of the master echo or reverb. And the solution is to turn *off* the track's individual echo or reverb effect. (Double-click its track header and turn off the corresponding checkboxes.)

• Turning on the Compressor effect for the master track also makes all tracks play in both left and right channels. (In this case, though, turning off Compressor for an individual track makes no difference. What matters is the Compressor effect on the *master* track.)

See Chapter 7 for much more detail on these effects, including how to turn them on or off.

Exported Song Won't Appear in iTunes

If a dialog box or alert message is open in iTunes at the moment you export from GarageBand, the handoff won't be successful. Click OK to dismiss whatever's going on in iTunes, and then try exporting again.

Adding On, Moving Up

G arageBand is good for days of fun right out of the box. You can do a lot of great work without ever adding a thing, and without pining for the ability to change the tempo mid-song. Surely 90 percent of all GarageBand fans will be perfectly content with the basic, built-in features.

But if you were content with the mere basics, you wouldn't have picked up a book on the subject, now would you?

Already, the Web is filled with add-on programs that give GarageBand more flexibility and interesting new features—above and beyond the add-on loops described in Chapter 2 and the add-on instrument sounds described in Chapter 9.

This chapter introduces a few of the coolest GarageBand add-ons, suggests where you might go when you decide it's time to graduate to more powerful (and expensive) music software, and points out some Web sites where you can learn more about GarageBand.

Note: All of the programs described in this chapter are available for download from the "Missing CD" page at *www.missingmanuals.com.*

Import MIDI Files (Dent du MIDI)

If you've ever fooled around with music software, you may already have a collection of finished musical masterpieces that you generated with other sequencing programs. You might naturally wonder if you could bring them into GarageBand, where you could dress them up with effects, add GarageBand's great-sounding drum loops, record some live tracks like vocals, and so on.

Your first thought would be: "Hey, I know! I could export my compositions as MIDI files! After all, MIDI files are the universal exchange format for music software!"

Unfortunately, MIDI files are not *quite* universal enough: GarageBand can't import them.

That might seem like a bummer for another reason, too: Hundreds of thousands of MIDI files are all over the Internet, just waiting for you to download. Just go to Google.com, type in *MIDI files "76 Trombones"* or whatever, and in a matter of seconds you've got a list of instrumental versions of that song, arranged and prepared by amateur or professional musicians, ready to download.

Tip: When you click a link to a MIDI file on a Web page, it generally begins to play. Your screen goes blank except for a stray QuickTime scroll bar. That's not really the same as *downloading* the file.

In that situation, hit your browser's Back button. This time, *Option-click* the original link. (Alternatively, Control-click the link and choose from the shortcut menu, "Download Link As" or "Save Link to Disk.")

This time, instead of playing the MIDI file, your browser downloads it to your desktop.

The beauty of downloading MIDI files (apart from their being free) is that you can *work* with them in your music software. Think how great it would be to import a favorite song into GarageBand, substitute high-quality GarageBand Software Instrument sounds for the cheesy QuickTime sounds that you hear when you play them online, redo the orchestration by assigning different instrument sounds altogether to each line, add some live recordings to boost the realism, and so on.

This kind of access to the Web's vast library of ready-to-play music would be ideal for the following:

- **Practicing.** Granted, a lot of these MIDI files are amateur recreations of copyrighted pop tunes. But they make perfect "practice tapes" as you work, in private or in noncommercial gatherings, on your voice, violin, or viola.

- **Karaoke.** So you're having a karaoke party, wedding reception, corporate executive roast, or law-school musical revue, and you need backup tracks for singing funny lyrics. Thanks to the Web, MIDI files, and GarageBand, you can call up almost any song in existence and make it sound great—not to mention adjust it to precisely the length you need—in a matter of minutes.

- **Background tracks.** GarageBand tunes make terrific soundtracks for iMovie movies, iPhoto slide shows, iDVD menu screens, and so on. Building music out of GarageBand loops is easy enough, but now and then you really need a *specific* song in the background. And chances are, you can find it in a MIDI file.

- **Interpretive composition.** You could rework a familiar tune, giving it your own musical spin, as pop artists for generations have done.

That is, you *could* do all of that—if only GarageBand could import MIDI files.

That's where Dent du MIDI comes in. As shown in Figure 12-1, it's a beautifully simple drag-and-drop program that converts a MIDI file into individual, Garage-Band-importable Software Instrument tracks. You can download the program from the "Missing CD" page at *www.missingmanuals.com*.

Note: Don't be fooled. When you run Dent du Midi, it creates what appears to be a folder full of *AIFF* files, which, if you've managed to absorb the teachings of Chapter 1, are destined to become purple, noneditable Real Instrument tracks in GarageBand. That's a fakeout, however, designed to permit GarageBand to import them. (Remember, GarageBand can import AIFF files, but *not* MIDI files.)

Once you drag these files into GarageBand, you'll see bona fide green Software Instrument tracks, filled with deliciously editable piano-roll note bars.

Figure 12-1:
Top: Double-click the Dent du MIDI icon to open this window, complete with a handsome photo of the Swiss mountain of the same name. Drag the MIDI file from the Finder right onto the mountain.

Bottom: In a flash, Dent du MIDI creates a folder full of AIFF files (or what seem to be AIFF files). Drag them into the timeline area of GarageBand to turn them into green Software Instrument tracks filled with MIDI note data (piano-roll note bars) that you can edit, enhance, reassign to other instruments, speed up or slow down, transpose to a different key, and so on.

This feature is useful for converting both your own MIDI files and those you find online.

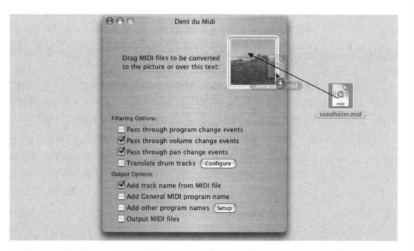

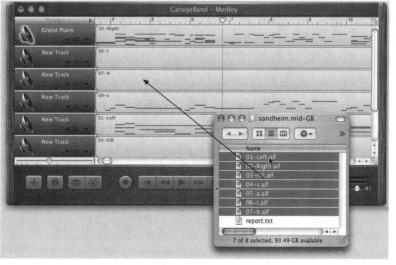

Import iTunes Music Store Songs (Soundflower)

There are any number of reasons why you might want to incorporate songs from your iTunes collection into your GarageBand compositions.

- You want to extract a certain drum hit or a particular orchestral chord for use in your own composition, like generations of rap artists before you.

- There's an "unplugged" guitar-and-voice recording that you'd like, just for practice, to enhance with some other tracks in GarageBand.

- You want to record a vocal line onto a pop song that doesn't have one.

- You yearn to play your own version of *American Idol* and play or sing along with the prerecorded track.

In any case, you're generally free to go. You can drag almost any kind of file right out of iTunes into an empty spot in GarageBand's timeline to install it there as a Real Instrument track—and then layer additional tracks on top of it. The file format doesn't matter: MP3, WAV, AIFF, Apple Lossless, or AAC.

Make that *unprotected* AAC. GarageBand won't accept songs that come with copy protection. Unfortunately, that includes everything you've bought from Apple's $1-a-song iTunes Music Store, which come in protected AAC format.

But if you absolutely, positively want to bring iTunes songs in, you need the free software called Soundflower (a download from the "Missing CD" page of *www.missingmanuals.com*). It's a "virtual cable" that lets you route the audio from any Mac program *into* any Mac program—say, from iTunes into GarageBand.

1. **Install Soundflower.**

   Installing the software requires you to restart your Mac.

FREQUENTLY ASKED QUESTION

What's in a Name

I'm very jazzed by this Dent du Midi thing. But what the heck is going on with its name?

It's named after a mountain.

Better yet, let's let the author of the software answer for himself:

"The name is a bit of a play on words. Dent du Midi is a 10,686 foot (3,257 meter) mountain in the southwest of Switzerland in the west Alps. The name is French and is pronounced something like 'don doo midi,' which I thought sounded like 'don't do MIDI,' which is why it seemed to be an appropriate name, since GarageBand doesn't import MIDI files."

Actually, according to Mac OS X's Sherlock program, which has a translation module, Dent du Midi means "tooth of midday."

And how that relates to GarageBand is a matter of profound contemplation, best left up to you.

---

2. **Open System Preferences. Click the Sound icon. Click the Output tab, and then select "Soundflower (2 ch)" as the output source.**

Figure 12-2 illustrates this step.

Figure 12-2:

Top: In System Preferences, tell your Mac to route all of its audio (including iTunes playback) through the Soundflower virtual cable instead of your built-in speakers. You won't hear anything, but you'll be able to record virtually anything into GarageBand.

Middle: Now, in GarageBand Preferences, you "plug in" the other end of the Soundflower cable—by telling the program to use Soundflower as its input.

Bottom: Finally, you're ready to record. For best results, start GarageBand recording before you switch to iTunes and begin playing, so you won't accidentally chop off the beginning of the song. When it's all over, you can always trim off any "dead air" at the beginning of the track.

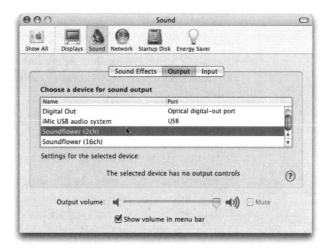

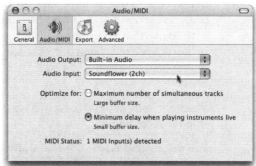

3. **Quit System Preferences. Open GarageBand. Choose GarageBand→Preferences.**

   The Preferences dialog box opens.

4. **Click the Audio/MIDI button. From the Audio Input pop-up menu, choose Soundflower (2 ch).**

   In essence, you've just "plugged in" the other end of the virtual cable.

5. **Close the Preferences window. Select a blue Real Instrument track, position the Playhead where you want to begin recording, and click the round, red Record button (or type the letter R key).**

   GarageBand begins recording. Of course, there's nothing playing at the moment.

6. **Switch into iTunes and double-click the song you want to play.**

   Of course, it doesn't have to be iTunes; you can route the audio from any Mac program into GarageBand at this point. (In fact, you have to be a little careful, since *all* audio will be part of what GarageBand records. So if your Mac happens to beep or say "It's eleven o'clock," that audio will be part of your GarageBand mix, too!)

   In any case, GarageBand is now dutifully recording your iTunes track, copy-protected or not. You can't hear anything, because Soundflower is intercepting all of the signal that would normally be routed to your speakers. But the soundwaves in the GarageBand region in progress, and the bouncing level meters in the track-mixer panel (page 140), should inform you GarageBand is merrily receiving the audio.

7. **When the song appears to be over, click the Play button or tap the Space bar to stop the recording.**

   You've just transferred your music into GarageBand.

Now, at this point, there are a few cleanup maneuvers you might want to make. For example:

- **Trim off any silence at the beginning of the track.** Almost always, there's a little bit of unwanted dead space at the front of the track, which was the time that GarageBand began recording before you switched into iTunes to begin the playback. The easiest way to trim it is to drag the left end of the purple region to the right, until it bumps up against the first soundwaves.

- **Slide the track into place.** Most of the time, you'll want the track to begin at the beginning of the GarageBand project—at 0:00. In that case, after trimming it, drag the whole region to the left as far as it'll go.

- **Match the tempo.** This is a tricky one. If your goal in transferring the song to GarageBand was to edit or embellish it, you may want to make sure that it aligns with GarageBand's beat ruler, so that every "ONE two three four" of the recording aligns with GarageBand's own conception of time.

Note: If the tempo *changes* during the imported song, forget it. GarageBand 1.1 can't handle tempo changes.

Sometimes you get lucky, and the song comes with beats-per-minute information embedded right into the downloaded file. See Figure 12-3.

Otherwise, though, you'll have to resort to trial and error. Choose GarageBand→ Preferences, click the General tab, and turn on "During playback and recording" for the metronome. Then check the Control menu to make sure that the metronome is, in fact, on.

Now start the song playing (or *cycling*—see page 12). As it plays, fiddle with the tempo slider (page 76) until the clicks of the metronome mesh as much as possible with the beats of the song. It may help if you turn down the track volume slightly, so you can hear the metronome better.

Figure 12-3:
To see if your iTunes track was tagged by its creator with certain inalienable beats-per-minute details, click the song in iTunes and then choose File→Get Info (or press ⌘-I). This dialog box appears. On its Info tab, check the BPM box circled here.

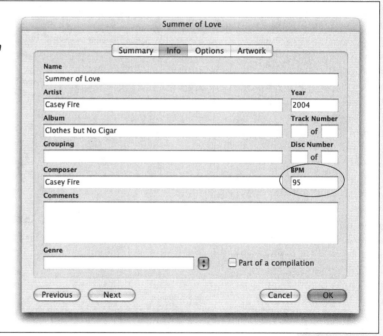

Build Your Own Drum Loops (iDrum)

Nothing defines the character of a pop song quite as much as its drum part. Garage-Band comes with 280 drum loops, but relative to the universe of rock music, that's just dust in the wind.

You can build your own drum parts by recording them with a MIDI keyboard, of course. But what if you're stranded on a desert island with nothing but your laptop and a power outlet (and no MIDI keyboard)? You'll need some other way to build drum loops—like iDrum, a plug-in that installs a full-blown drum pattern editor right into GarageBand.

After installing the software, choose Track→New Track, and proceed as shown in Figure 12-4.

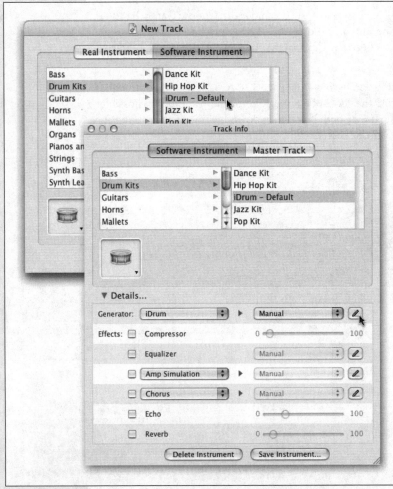

Figure 12-4:
Top left: When iDrum's New Track dialog box appears, click the Software Instrument tab, select Drum Kits from the left-side list, and then click iDrum in the right-side list. Click OK. Now double-click the track header of the track.

Lower right: The dialog box that appears looks very similar, but this time, you can expand the Details panel at the bottom. iDrum should already be selected in the Generator pop-up menu. Click the pencil icon to open the dialog box shown in Figure 12-5.

When you click the pencil icon as described in Figure 12-4, you arrive at the actual iDrum screen shown in Figure 12-5. Here, you've got yourself a mini-GarageBand window, built up of parallel drum tracks. For example:

• Drag these tracks up or down to rearrange them.

• Click the + or – buttons to delete drum tracks.

• Adjust the L–R knob to specify each drum sound's position in the left-to-right stereo sound field.

• Click the M button to mute a drum, or S to solo it.

• Drag the slider to increase or decrease this drum's volume relative to the others.

Building the Drum Pattern

To build a drum pattern, proceed like this, position the iDrum window where you can see both it and the GarageBand window.

Create a new drum track, if necessary, by clicking the + button. Choose a drum sound for this track by clicking directly on the existing drum's name (like Kick 1) and choosing from the pop-up menu.

Note: This pop-up menu reflects whatever sound snippets (AIFF files) are currently in your Home→Library→ Application Support→iDrum→Samples folder.

To create the drum part, drag inside each of the 16 vertical rectangles to the right of the drum header. They represent the sixteenth notes in a 4/4 measure, so to make a drum play on the first and third beats, you'd fill up the first and ninth rectangles. The height of your drag determines how loudly that drum plays on that beat.

Figure 12-5:
Click a drum sound in the left-side column (snare, tom-tom, ride cymbal, and so on), and then "paint" it, by clicking or dragging, onto the proper grid slots. Each drum sound has a different shape and appears in a different vertical location, to help you keep track.

Click to open iDrum main menu   One measure of 16th notes

Click to change drum sound

Tip: Before you spend a lot of time building a handmade pattern, try out some of the samples that come with iDrum. From the iDrum menu identified in Figure 12-5, choose Open. Navigate to your Home→Library→ Application Support→iDrum→Kits folder. There, even if you're just playing with the iDrum demo version, you'll find some useful virtual drum sets to try out.

The full version of iDrum ($50) comes with 200 ready-made drum files, each with several variations.

To check your work, you have two options:

- **Turn off SLAVE TO HOST,** the tiny button at the bottom of the window, so that a black dot no longer appears inside. Then click iDrum's Play button to listen to your drum part by itself.

- **Turn on SLAVE TO HOST,** and then click GarageBand's Play button. This way, you get to hear the drum part played *with* the tracks you've already built in GarageBand. (In fact, if you turn on cycling, you can build your drum part in real time, adding and removing hits as the music plays.)

Finally, one more iDrum control worth noticing: the Song Mode button near the lower-left corner of the window. If it's turned *off*, then iDrum assumes that you're working on a drum part that's only one measure long. It loops that measure, playing it over and over.

If Song Mode is turned *on*, then you can build multi-measure parts. Use the LENGTH indicator to specify the number of measures, and the BAR control to specify which one of those measures is currently displayed in the map. (You change these numbers by dragging upward or downward on them, much like you'd change the GarageBand tempo control [page 76].)

When the loop sounds good, you can proceed in either of two ways: leave the drum pattern as an integral part of your GarageBand project, or export it as a loop.

Option 1: Leave the Drum Pattern in Place

Make sure SLAVE TO HOST is turned on, and then close the iDrum and Track Info dialog boxes. Now, whenever you play your GarageBand piece, you'll hear the drum part played along with it, in perfect sync, even if you change the tempo.

What may be alarming at first is that the Software Instrument part you created for iDrum appears to be *completely empty*. But even when you close iDrum's editor window, it's still running inside GarageBand. It will remain, invisible but active, until you delete the track or change the track's Software Instrument sound.

When you save your GarageBand file, you're also saving iDrum's patterns, loaded drum samples, and the song sequence (if any). The next time you open your song, iDrum will be right where you left it, playing along happily. You can edit the drum part at any time.

Option 2: Export the Pattern as a Loop

Leaving the drum part built into your GarageBand song is very convenient. However, if you're more comfortable editing the drum parts using the standard GarageBand Track Editor, or if it spooks you to *hear* a drum part that you can't actually see, you may prefer to export the drum beat as a loop that you can manipulate as you would any green Software Instrument region.

1. **Click the tiny menu icon at upper-left (see Figure 12-5). From the pop-up menu, choose Save Pattern as MIDI.**

   The Bounce Pattern dialog box appears.

2. **Type a name for your loop, press ⌘-D (to select the desktop for saving this file), turn on "Save in GarageBand-compatible AIFF," and click Save.**

   A new icon appears on your desktop—your saved drum loop. It may look as though it's a digital audio file, thanks to the .aif file name extension. But when you drag it into a green Software Instrument track in step 6, though, you'll find that it is, in fact, a MIDI loop whose individual notes you can edit as described in Chapter 5.

3. **Close the iDrum window and the Track Info window. Drag the new AIFF file off your desktop and into the Software Instrument track you created in step 1.**

   You've successfully installed your own drum creation as a living, breathing Software Instrument loop, one that automatically speeds up and slows down according to the tempo of your GarageBand piece. Feel free to loop it (drag its upper-right corner), copy and paste it, edit its notes in the Track Editor, and so on.

Tip: Once you've exported a drum loop as described here, things get much easier. The next time you want to install an iDrum pattern into your GarageBand track, just position the iDrum window so that you can see the GarageBand track. This time, you can skip the steps above by simply dragging the MIDI DRAG icon (lower-right of the iDrum window) into your GarageBand track.

Remember, by the way, that using the instructions in Chapter 9, you can run your iDrum loops through the Apple Loop Utility to turn them into proper Apple Loops that show up in your Loop browser.

Tip: The preceding instructions show you how to turn an iDrum pattern into a green Software Instrument loop, which has the advantage that you can edit its notes in GarageBand. But if, in step 1, you choose Bounce Pattern to AIFF instead, the Save As dialog box offers an option called Bounce Each Channel to Separate File. It makes iDrum create a separate AIFF file for *each channel* in your drum pattern/song.

That's a very handy feature if want each sound to have its own channel in GarageBand—kick drum, snare drum, and so on—so that you can fiddle with their effect settings independently.

Incidentally, iDrum isn't the only tool for building drum kits and drum loops in GarageBand. You might also want to check out DoggieBox, a less capable but easier to use program, or GarageBand Utilities, a set of three utilities that includes GB Drum Loops. Both of them export GarageBand-ready AIFF files that do nicely as drum loops. You can find both of these, and many other GarageBand utilities, by searching for *GarageBand* at *www.versiontracker.com*.

Add an E-Z Chords™ Feature (ReMIDI)

When you buy a cheapo plastic keyboard for your kids (or for yourself)—perhaps one of those $60 Yamaha or Casio jobbers—one cheesy but highly enjoyable feature is the EZ Chord or 1-Touch Chord feature (or whatever it's called on your model). The basic idea is to help fumbling non-pianists get decent-sounding accompaniments. All you have to do is press one key at a time with your left hand—and the keyboard does the grunt work of playing elaborate full chords, either strummed or *arpeggiated* (broken up into individual notes).

Now your own cheapo MIDI controller (or expensive MIDI synth) can have this feature, even if it's the 49-key M-Audio keyboard that Apple sells as a GarageBand companion. All you need is ReMIDI ($15, shareware).

As you can see from Figure 12-6, ReMIDI offers three ways to trigger each chord:

- **One Finger.** You press a single key on your keyboard, and ReMIDI plays an entire major chord (or minor, or diminished seventh, or whatever chord quality you choose from the pop-up menu) based on that note. Not especially useful for GarageBand purposes, but handy if you're trying to learn to hear the difference between various chord types.

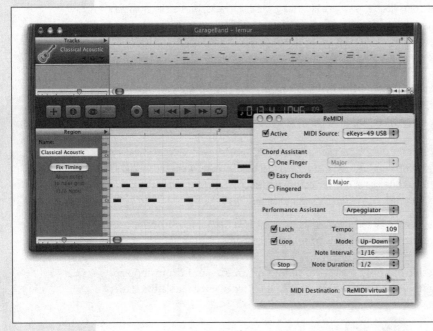

Figure 12-6:
See all those graceful, flowing broken chords? You don't have to learn to play them—let software do the work for you! ReMIDI triggered these notes automatically. All you had to do was show it which chords to play.

- **Easy Chords.** If you press a single note, like D, you get a major chord (D major). But if you simultaneously press any black note below it, you get a minor chord (D minor). Press any lower *white* note simultaneously, and you get a minor seventh chord (Dm7). And press a note along with any *two* lower notes, and you get a major seventh (Dmaj7). (By the way, you can reassign all of these combinations in the ReMIDI→Preferences dialog box.)

- **Fingered.** This option doesn't save you any keyboarding at all—it simply plays whatever chord you play yourself. (You use it primarily in conjunction with the Performance Assistant option described next.)

The real fun begins when you also turn on one of the Performance Assistant options:

- **Strummer** "strums" the chord you've specified using one of the three options described above, as though you're playing it on a guitar, your pick rolling across the strings. Use the Speed slider to indicate how fast ReMIDI strums the notes of the chord. If it's all the way up, you won't hear any strumming at all.

  You can even *vary* the strumming speed in real time during your performance (and no, not by reaching for the mouse and adjusting the Speed slider every third chord). The trick is to use the MIDI Controller pop-up menu to tell ReMIDI what gadget on your keyboard will be the speed controller. If you choose Mod Wheel, for example, then turning the modulation wheel will slow down the strum. (Because the mod wheel also affects many GarageBand sounds, you may want to choose a different MIDI controller from this pop-up menu, if possible.)

Tip: If you're trying to make ReMIDI's strumming sound like a guitar, be sure that (a) you've specified a guitar sound in GarageBand, and (b) you've selected ReMIDI→Preferences and, on the General tab, specified a minimum of 6-note polyphony (that is, six notes in each chord, to match the strings of a guitar).

- **Arpeggiator.** If you choose this item from the Performance Assistant pop-up menu, ReMIDI triggers broken chords for any chord you specify. If you trigger a C chord, for example, ReMIDI plays even eighth notes of that chord—C, E, G; C, E, G—and so on. The Mode pop-up menu specifies whether the chord should be "strummed" upward (C, E, G), downward (G, E, C), Up-Down (C, E, G, E, C), or whatever. And the Note Interval and Note Duration pop-up menus tell the program what note value to use (eighth note, quarter note, or whatever) and how long to hold each one down, respectively.

  You can also turn on Loop to make the running notes keep repeating for as long as you hold down the keys—and/or Latch, which even removes the obligation to hold *down* any keys. The program keeps playing the notes of your previous chord—even when your hand is off the keyboard—until you strike another chord.

ReMIDI + GarageBand

To use ReMIDI, start in GarageBand. Create a green Software Instrument track, and prepare to record (set up the tempo and turn on the metronome, for example). If you plan to use the Arpeggiator option in ReMIDI, set its tempo control to match GarageBand's.

As a last step in GarageBand, click the Record button (or press the letter R key).

Switch into ReMIDI and begin playing your keyboard in time to the GarageBand metronome. When you're finished, return to GarageBand, where you'll see that all your arpeggiated or strummed notes have shown up in your new track. For all GarageBand knows, you played all that fancy stuff yourself!

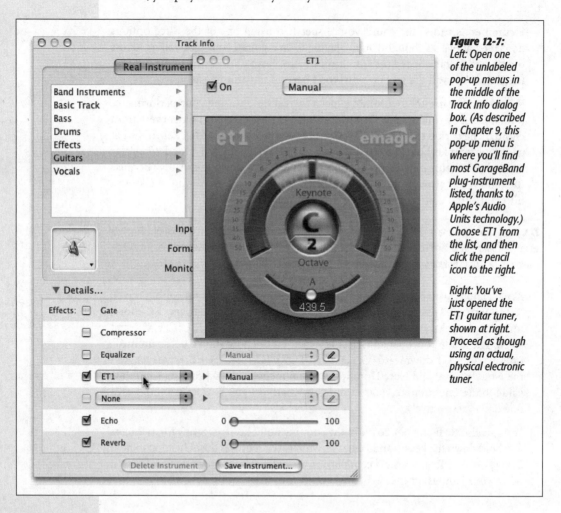

Figure 12-7:
Left: Open one of the unlabeled pop-up menus in the middle of the Track Info dialog box. (As described in Chapter 9, this pop-up menu is where you'll find most GarageBand plug-instrument listed, thanks to Apple's Audio Units technology.) Choose ET1 from the list, and then click the pencil icon to the right.

Right: You've just opened the ET1 guitar tuner, shown at right. Proceed as though using an actual, physical electronic tuner.

Tune Your Instrument (ET1 Guitar Tuner)

GarageBand obviously has a lot of appeal for keyboard players, but its multitrack digital studio features have turned a lot of other instrumentalists' heads, too. If you play a tunable instrument (guitar, violin, flute, or whatever) you may as well add an electronic tuner to your kit. What the heck—it's freeware.

Once you've installed the GarageBand Guitar Tuner software, open GarageBand. Create a new track (Real or Software—doesn't matter). Double-click its header to open the Track Info dialog box. Then click the Details triangle, if necessary, to expand the Details pane, and proceed as shown in Figure 12-7.

Beyond GarageBand

GarageBand is clearly one of easiest-to-use music programs on the planet. In features per dollar, it's also among the least expensive.

GarageBand is not, however, the only music program on earth and—difficult though it may be to believe—some programs do some things better than GarageBand.

When you find that you've outgrown GarageBand and begun to long for more features and flexibility, here are a few programs to consider.

For Loops: Soundtrack

One look at Apple's Soundtrack program, and you'll know where the company got the idea for GarageBand. As you can see in Figure 12-8, Soundtrack is in many ways a professional version of GarageBand's loop-assembly mode.

Of course, GarageBand can do all of that, too. In fact, GarageBand shares much of its design with Soundtrack, including the parallel tracks in the timeline (complete with track headers and beat ruler), a loop browser filled with prerecorded professional Apple Loops, a track-volume track that lets you control volume over time, a set of professional-sounding audio effects, and so on.

But there are some big differences between GarageBand ($50 including four other programs) and Soundtrack ($300):

- Soundtrack comes with 4,000 Apple Loops, almost four times as many as Garage-Band.

- In Soundtrack, you can view a QuickTime movie that's synced up to your music, making it simple to compose—that's right—soundtracks. (You can also import a Final Cut Pro project, complete with scoring markers.)

- Soundtrack can send and receive MIDI time code, an invisible electronic conductor that lets Soundtrack "drive," or be driven by, other music software and external synthesizers and sound modules so that they all play in sync.

- In GarageBand, you're limited to one time signature per song. In Soundtrack, you can change time signatures within the piece.

• You know how GarageBand has a track-volume track that lets you set up prepro-grammed volume changes over time? In Soundtrack, you also get a master *tempo* graph, which you can use to preprogram gradual or sudden tempo changes.

On the other hand, GarageBand offers a few huge features that Soundtrack *doesn't* have, like the ability to record live from a microphone or instrument. Soundtrack is *just* for manipulating loops.

If you do decide to have a look at Soundtrack, you'll be up and running in about ten minutes. That's how similarly the GarageBand and Soundtrack controls are laid out, and how much the central concepts are alike.

Tip: GarageBand and Soundtrack both accept the same Apple Loops, so you can use any set of loops in either program.

The best way to go about it is to drag the Soundtrack loops folder into the GarageBand Loop browser. GarageBand asks whether you want to *copy* all of these loops or just add them to its Loop browser listing without actually copying them. "Index Only" is the option you want, since you probably don't want to use up hard drive space on duplicate loops.

For more on Soundtrack, visit *www.apple.com/track*. For details on its very similar loop-production rival, called Live, visit *www.ableton.com/index.php?main=live.*

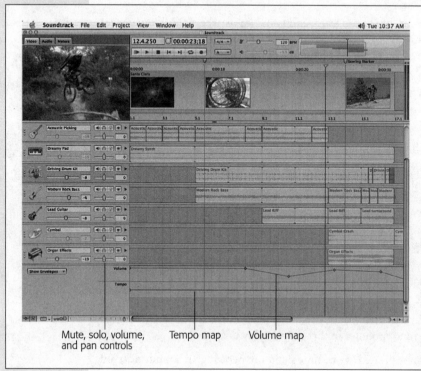

Mute, solo, volume, and pan controls

Tempo map

Volume map

Figure 12-8:
Soundtrack, GarageBand's im-mediate predecessor from Apple, doesn't do live recording. You can't record from a microphone or a MIDI instrument. If all you want to work on is loops, though, this program offers far more power than GarageBand.

The program is tar-geted at people who make DVDs, Web sites, commercials, movies, and so on—anybody who might need very specific pieces of music, of extremely specific lengths, and that don't require royalty payments to anyone.

For Sequencing: Logic Pro, Logic Express, and Rivals

If Soundtrack represents the pro version of GarageBand's loop building personality, then Logic represents the other two-thirds: live recordings from a microphone or instrument (MIDI or analog). In this regard, it has a lot in common with other studio-musician programs like Cubase (*www.steinberg.net*) and Digital Performer (*www.motu.com*).

These are big, expensive, complex programs (Digital Performer's manual is over 1,000 pages long) that require not only a good knowledge of music, but a recessive studio engineer gene as well. Logic comes with dozens of effects and processors; import/export features for every conceivable file format; an editing mode that displays notes in standard sheet music form rather than piano-roll bars; the ability to open, and compose to, a QuickTime movie; a full-blown, onscreen mixing console, complete with sliders and knobs for every track; and much more (Figure 12-9).

Figure 12-9:
Some of Logic's screen design will seem vaguely familiar—a beat ruler, GarageBand-like track headers, and regions containing either MIDI or digital audio are all still there. But the terminology is very different (the Playhead is called the SPL, for Song Position Line), the manual assumes that you're a professional musician or engineer, and the number of options is dizzying.

Both programs can also record the changes you make to volume, tempo, panning, effects, and so on. You just play the piece back, and turn the knobs while it plays, and Logic stores your manipulations so that it can perfectly recreate them later.

Tip: At this writing, you can get a glimpse of the complexity of the modern Mac-based music studio by viewing the QuickTime movie at *www.apple.com/logic/quicktour/gettingstarted.html*.

As in most categories of software, there's an immense amount of power in Logic and its rivals. Indeed, there's scarcely a Grammy-winning producer alive who doesn't use one of these programs, but the learning curve is daunting.

Note: Apple sells two versions of this program: Logic Express ($300) and Logic Pro ($1,000). They're mostly identical, but the Pro offers several virtual synthesizers and samplers, so that you can spend hours dialing up your own sounds; the ability to create surround-sound tracks; and more effects.

GarageBand Online

As with most things Mac, the release of GarageBand triggered the spontaneous formation of a huge, thriving, passionate online community. Web sites and discussion groups appeared almost instantly—and they'll remain a lot more current than a computer book.

Distribute-Your-Music Sites

As noted in the Introduction to this book, GarageBand can, in the right hands, replace one of the record companies' core functions: producing professional, finished-sounding recordings.

The Internet takes care of the other function: Bringing your music to the public.

Web sites like **Soundclick.com, GarageBand.com, Amcast.com, Acidplanet.com, Vitaminic.com,** and **MP3.com** are all dedicated to distributing the music of undiscovered performers (not just GarageBand artists). On Soundclick, for example, you get your own Web page, you can upload an unlimited number of songs, you get your own

---

FOR LA DISC JOCKEYS ONLY

Ableton Live

If you were to poke your head into the trendier LA clubs these days, GarageBand is probably not the program you'll find running on the disc jockeys' PowerBooks. It's more likely to be Ableton's Live ($500).

Like Logic and Digital Performer, this program can record and edit both MIDI performances and live audio recordings. It offers mixing, effects, and automation features, too. It can even stretch or condense any region, MIDI, or digital audio, to make it fit the tempo or the key of your piece

(something like what GarageBand does with only its green and blue loops).

One key difference, though, is Live's orientation toward live, improvisational jamming. As shown here, its Session view looks something like an Excel spreadsheet. You can drag-and-drop sounds, build sequences, and trigger them live, while the music is continuously playing. You can trigger any music clip at any pitch, just by playing the keys on a MIDI keyboard.

---

message board where your fans can talk about your talent, and so on. (The site makes its money by selling promotional services, like featuring you on the home page.)

Your fans can either download or stream (listen to without downloading) your songs, along with those from both signed and unsigned from bands and singers. Most of the songs are free to listen to or download.

GarageBand Help and Discussion

Web sites like **MacJams.com, iCompositions.com,** and **MacIdol.com** have dual functions: First, they're dedicated to helping you share your musical output with other Mac fans—like the Web sites described above, but exclusively for GarageBand compositions. You can also listen to other people's, either by browsing through the musical genres (like Rap or Folk) or by relying on the daily or weekly "most listened to" charts.

Second, these sites also offer news, reviews of GarageBand-related products, tips and how-to articles, discussion boards, and so on (see Figure 12-10).

Figure 12-10:
Back: At MacJams. com and similar sites, you can search a database of GarageBand compositions by name or by category.

Front: Once you click a song to listen to it, you can vote or comment on it. The site shows you the current running scores. Who knows? GarageBand may yet lead to the next American Idol, European Idol, Asian Idol....

Tip: Other sites, like **MacMusic.org, audio-units.com,** and **osxaudio.com,** are dedicated to the wider world of Macintosh music-making. But you'll find a lot of good GarageBand-relevant information and links here, especially if you decide to delve deeper into Audio Units, plug-ins, and other expansion modules.

Loops and Sounds Sites

As you've no doubt realized by now, GarageBand accommodates add-on instruments, add-on sounds, and add-on effects.

A quick search at Google for *free loops, free audio units,* or *free sound effects* will unearth hundreds of Web sites filled with files that you can drag into GarageBand or install as described on page 41, but here are a few to get you started.

Free loops
- *www.loops.net*
- *www.proloops.com/freeloops.htm*
- *freeloops.co.uk*

Free sound effects
- *www.sound-effects-library.com/free/mp3.html*

Free drum loops
- *www.studiopt.com/audio1.html*
- *www.breakbeatsonly.com*

UP TO SPEED

Official Help from Apple

Of course, the ultimate source of GarageBand information and troubleshooting is the mother ship—Apple itself. At *www.apple.com/support/garageband,* you'll find a special Apple Web site dedicated just to helping you with GarageBand. It contains tutorials, lessons, a list of system requirements, and the latest GarageBand updaters.

There's even a Feedback link, so you can send Apple your suggestions for the next version of GarageBand. (No, Apple won't put every feature in. But if enough people seem to be clamoring for the same things, the company may actually respond.)

You'll also find an absolutely enormous treasure trove of questions, answers, gripes, wish lists, and discussion in the official Apple GarageBand discussion forums, which you can also enter from the main GarageBand support page.

If you absolutely, positively must get help by telephone, you can call Apple at 800-275-2273 (that's 800-APL-CARE). For the first 90 days following your purchase of iLife (which, as far as Apple knows, is the date of your first call), the technicians will answer your questions for free.

After that, Apple will charge you on a per-call to answer your questions…and at $45 a call, it ain't cheap.

Free sampled instrument sounds

- *www.mtlc.net/freesamples/freesamples.php* (one free sound sample each day)

- *www.samples4.com/catalog*

Commercial loops

- *www.bigfishaudio.com*

- *www.bitshiftaudio.com*

- *http://mediasoftware.sonypictures.com/loop_libraries*

- *www.drumsondemand.com/apple.htm* (drum loops)

Appendixes

The GarageBand Music Crash Course

As you know from Chapters 2 and 3, it's perfectly possible to glide right through a career in GarageBand without knowing anything at all about music. There's no sheet-music view, so you don't have to know how to read music; the loops come prerecorded, so you don't have to know how to play music; and the automated "players" respond only to dragging and dropping, so you don't even have to know how to talk music.

Here and there, however, you can't avoid at least *seeing* a few musical concepts flash before your eyes. Every time you create a new GarageBand document, you're asked what *key* and *time signature* you want. The *tempo* control is glaring at you from right beside the Play button. And then there's that business of the grid, which helps you (or hinders you) every time you try to drag a region or a note, and whenever you use the Fix Timing button. Unless you have at least some concept of what "1/1 Note" or "1/8 Swing Heavy" means, you'll never be quite in command of even the nonmusical features of GarageBand.

This chapter offers just a few pages of instruction, the most basic initiation to some of the musical concepts you'll encounter in GarageBand. Learning about music properly—with a book, a course, or a teacher—is infinitely more rewarding and thorough, of course. But in the meantime, here's a rudimentary introduction.

Measures

To understand GarageBand's beat ruler, time display, grid system, and other elements, it helps to go back to the dawn of music notation. Giuseppe, or Gustav, or whoever came up with the precursor of modern-day sheet music, began with a set of horizontal parallel lines. It's called a *staff*, but it's the same idea as GarageBand's interface: it's a timeline. You read sheet music from left to right along this timeline.

Now, any sort of measuring stick, whether in sheet music, GarageBand, or a yard-stick, isn't very useful unless it's marked up into subdivisions. So Giuseppe divided his timeline into logical units called *measures*. If you saw the sheet music for "Frère Jacques," each of these phrases would occupy its own measure:

Are you sleeping?
Are you sleeping?
Brother John?
Brother John?

See how those just feel like logical break points?

So now you know about *measures*. The numbers along the beat ruler (top of the GarageBand window) count how many measures into the song you are. The time display (the digital blue readout) also measures measures. And the largest you can make the light-gray lines of the GarageBand grid is "1/1 note," which, in most cases, means "one measure."

The Time Signature

The dialog box that appears when you choose File→New in GarageBand appears in Figure A-1. For the Time setting, GarageBand proposes 4/4—but what's that?

Turns out it's closely linked to the concept of measures.

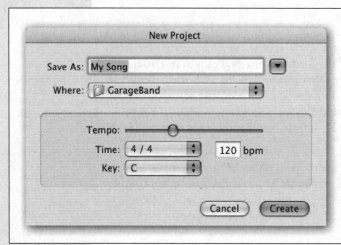

Figure A-1:
The New Track dialog box is the very first thing you see when you create a new GarageBand piece—which is too bad, considering it's one of the few places that could fluster musical newcomers.

In a house, a builder may hold up the roof by installing a beam (a rafter) every eight feet. Music has underlying support structures, too—the beats in a measure. Beats are the clicks of the GarageBand metronome, your foot taps when you're listening to something catchy, and the "One! Two! Three! Four!" that a rock band leader shouts before a song.

Not all songs contain the same number of beats per measure. Waltzes, like "Take Me Out to the Ball Game," "A Natural Woman (You Make Me Feel)," and—of course—"(Once, Twice,) Three Times a Lady" have three beats per measure. In GarageBand, you'd hear the metronome go, *CLICK*-click-click, *CLICK*-click-click, and you'd hear a dancing teacher say, *ONE*-two-three, *ONE*-two-three.

Most pop songs, though, have four beats per measure. In fact, in *most* kinds of music, four-beat measures are the world's most popular type. If you were to chant, "one, two, three, four," rhythmically, over and over again, every song from "Frère Jacques" to "Born in the USA" and "Oops, I Did It Again" will fit your counting.

So how was the inventor of sheet music supposed to tell you how many beats are allowed to fill each measure of music? One attempt may have looked like the top of Figure A-2.

Figure A-2:
Top: Here's one way to tell musicians that there are going to be four beats in each measure of this song. But it's not terribly compact.

Bottom: Over time—possibly about 30 seconds—instrumentalists began to shorten this notation into something more concise. The modern time signature begins to emerge.

Now, one way to fill up the four beats in a measure is to play four *quarter notes,* so called because, obviously, it takes four of them to fill up one measure. A quarter note is one of the world's most popular units of rhythm (see Figure A-3).

Figure A-3:
Top: All of the notes in "Are you sleeping, are you sleeping, Brother John?" are quarter notes. The kick drum of a rock band playing disco is pounding out quarter notes, too. And in the Grid pop-up menu (the little ruler at the upper-right of the GarageBand window), "1/4 Note" is one of the choices—and now you know what it means.

Bottom: It takes two eighth notes to fill up the time of one quarter note, so they often come in pairs. And when they come in pairs, musicians connect them with a beam to make them easier to take in at a glance.

Are you sleep-ing? Are you sleep-ing?

Ma-ry had a   lit-tle lamb,   lit-tle lamb,   lit-tle lamb.

In most songs, your foot naturally taps out quarter notes—but not in all songs. Consider "Jesu, Joy of Man's Desiring," a famous Bach piece that you can hear right now, if you like, by switching into iPhoto and listening to it. (It's one of the preinstalled background music tracks for slide shows.) In this piece, each measure has *nine* beats—but they're not quarter notes. They're notes that last only half as long, so they're called eighth notes. You can see what eighth notes look like in Figure A-3 at bottom.

Back to Giuseppe, the sheet-music-inventing monk. How was he supposed to indicate what *kind* of note (eighth note? quarter note?) gets a beat?

Clearly, the *one* number at the beginning of the song (Figure A-2) wasn't enough information. The next step was to tell players what *kind* of note gets a beat—what kind of note they should tap out with their feet—by adding a second line under the first (Figure A-4).

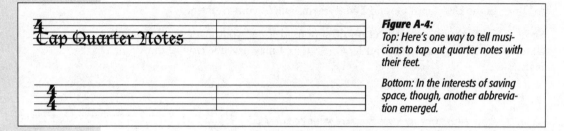

Figure A-4:
Top: Here's one way to tell musicians to tap out quarter notes with their feet.

Bottom: In the interests of saving space, though, another abbreviation emerged.

A *time signature,* then, is the 4/4 at the beginning of a piece of sheet music (or 2/4, or 3/4, or even 6/8) or in the New Project dialog box in GarageBand. It tells you two things. The upper number tells you how many beats each measure has (four beats). The lower one tells you what *kind* of note (quarter note).

Armed with this information, may you have the courage to try *changing* the Time pop-up menu the next time you create a new GarageBand piece. As the old saying goes, all 4/4 and no 6/8 makes Jack a dull boy.

More About Note Values

Music would be pretty boring if it were all written using only quarter-note and eighth-note rhythms. It would be a world of disco.

Fortunately, you can chop up a measure of beats into a world of different rhythms. Some notes ring longer than a quarter note; some are played much faster. Figure A-5 shows five different ways to fill four beats, using different kinds of notes. It should help you understand, if only vaguely, the listings in GarageBand's Grid pop-up menus.

One category in those pop-up menus, however, might puzzle you at first: this business of *swing.* As shown on page 235, for example, you're offered entries like "1/8 Swing Light" and "1/16 Swing Heavy."

Swing is a *feeling,* not a note value. It's a jazz-style way of playing pairs of eighth notes or sixteenth notes so that they, well…swing. Technically, the player is supposed to delay the second note of every pair. But emotionally, it's a whole different feeling.

Trying to explain it in prose is futile, so listen to the GarageBand file called "07—Swing" from the GarageBand Examples CD (see page 13 for instructions on downloading it). You'll hear the same snippet of music played with normal eighth notes, and again with both heavy and light *swing* eighth notes.

The truth, though, is that if you're trying to write any kind of jazz, ragtime, or sultry ballad, you'll be awfully glad that GarageBand even *understands* swing—a lot of less sophisticated music programs don't. Thanks to the Swing commands in the Grid pop-up menu, you can use the Fix Timing button (page 94), for example, to clean up a jazzy performance without losing its swingy feel.

Figure A-5:
Top: A single note that's held for the full four counts of a 4/4 measure is called a whole note, although GarageBand's pop-up menus refer to it as a "1/1 note." (Nobody else calls it that.) It gets all four beats.

Second from top: There's also such a thing as a half note, which gets two beats. (GarageBand calls it a "1/2 note.") It takes two of them to fill up a whole measure.

Third from top: You can fill the same amount of musical time with eight eighth notes, like this...

Second from bottom: ...or even triplets, a funky little rhythm in which you play three eighth notes in the space usually occupied by two regular eighths.

Bottom: Finally, you can fill the same four beats with 16 sixteenth notes.

Key

The other information you're supposed to supply when you create a new GarageBand project is its *key*.

You've probably heard of this business of keys before. In every movie where somebody tries out for a Broadway musical and tells the piano player, "'Somewhere Over the Rainbow' in the key of F, please."

The key of a song specifies its "main" note, the one that it seems to revolve around and land on. In very simple melodies like folk songs, nursery rhymes, and anything by 'N Sync, you can usually figure out the key by looking at the last note of the tune; the song usually ends on the *note* whose name matches the *key*. (Musical notes are named after the letters from A to G. Middle C, for example, is the C in the middle of the piano.)

The key of a song also determines how hard it is for you to sing or play. After all, you can always *transpose* a song (shift it higher or lower into a different key), but after puberty, your voice is pretty much stuck with the range of notes nature gave it. Fortunately, GarageBand can transpose a too-high song down into a lower key to accommodate your voice.

Usually, you choose the key of a GarageBand piece at the moment of creation (Figure A-1). Whatever key you choose here will automatically affect any loops you use in the song, because when you add them to your timeline, they instantly transpose to match your key, no matter what key they were recorded in. (That's one of the most amazing software features of GarageBand.)

Figure A-6:
If you look closely, you'll see that the lower example actually starts one note higher than the upper one. It's been transposed from the original key of C into the higher key of D.

MUSIC CLASS

GarageBand's Idea of a Beat

Technically, "beats per minute" is a vague term; it doesn't tell you what kind of note is getting a click. When you see "120 beats per minute," does that mean "quarter notes per minute?" Or "eighth notes per minute?" Or what?

As you can see by the little tempo notation shown here, real sheet music generally tells you explicitly. In this example, just above the sheet music, a little logo tells you that a quarter note = 120 beats per minute.

To be perfectly correct, GarageBand ought to change the tempo of your piece when you change the time signature to, for example, 6/8. After all, "a beat" is now an eighth note, so the piece ought to play at twice the speed.

But that's not what happens. In short, when GarageBand's tempo controls say "beats per minute," they really mean "quarter notes per minute," regardless of what kind of note is actually getting a beat.

If you're a trained musician, this behavior might throw you. On the other hand, imagine how deeply the prototypical garage band rock musician might care—and maybe you'll cut Apple a little slack.

In fact, you can change the key of your song at any time. Just make sure the Master track is showing (⌘-B); double-click its header; and use the Key pop-up menu again. GarageBand will instantly transpose all of the green and blue loops you've used in your piece, as well as any green MIDI Software Instrument regions you recorded yourself. (See Figure A-6.)

It will not, however, shift the key of any purple Real Instrument recordings you've made (for example, by singing into a microphone). That's why it's important to finalize the key of the song *before* you add the vocals or other live recordings to it.

Tip: Of course, you could always sing *first*, and *then* add the loops. In that case, you'll want to figure out what key you sang in and change the project's key to match, so that any loops you add will fit your key.

Tempo

The *tempo,* the final element of the New Project dialog box, is a measurement of how fast the music plays back. Actually, to be more precise, it's the number of *beats per minute* that go by during playback.

As you now know, those beats usually represent quarter notes. If GarageBand's tempo control says 60 bpm, that's 60 beats per minute, or one foot tap per second. Clock it with your watch right now. Try singing "Twinkle, Twinkle, Little Star" with one syllable per second. That's *dog* slow.

Now try 120 beats per minute, which is what GarageBand proposes for a new song. That's *two* syllables per second for "Twinkle, Twinkle"—and just about right, as you'll hear.

GarageBand, Menu by Menu

Y ou could use GarageBand for years without opening a single menu. But unless you explore its menu commands, you're likely to miss some of the options and controls that make it a surprisingly powerful little recording studio.

Here's a menu-by-menu look at GarageBand's commands.

GarageBand Menu

This first menu, Mac OS X's Application menu, takes on the name of whatever program happens to be running in the foreground. In GarageBand's case, that would be GarageBand.

About GarageBand

This command opens the "About" box containing the requisite Apple copyright, trademark, and version information.

There's really only one good reason to open the About GarageBand window: It's the easiest way to find out exactly which version of GarageBand you have.

GarageBand Hot Tips

Opens a page on Apple's Web site that lists tricks like keyboard shortcuts and provides a brief overview of GarageBand's features—like using loops and recording a live instrument.

Preferences

Opens the Preferences window (Figure B-1), where you can twiddle with four tabs' worth of options.

General

Most of these options are pretty easy to figure out: Do you want the metronome (when it's turned on in the Control menu) to click away only when you're recording, or also when you're playing back the piece? Do you want GarageBand to say, "Save changes?" each time you make a change to an instrument or instrument preset?

"Filter for more relevant results" is a loop browser setting. It hides loops whose original recordings are in distant keys, and might therefore sound a little bit unnatural when transposed to fit your piece (see page 40 for details).

Finally, the Reset button puts all of the loop browser buttons back where they were when you first installed GarageBand. It's mostly useful after you've rearranged the buttons (by Control-clicking them) and then decided that you've made a mess of things.

Audio/MIDI

This panel is primarily useful for telling GarageBand what sound-input source you want it to listen to when recording (Audio Input), and, if your Mac has external speakers attached, which set of speakers you want to use when playing back (Audio Output).

The "Optimize for:" option is designed to offer you a tradeoff. If you turn on "Maximum number of simultaneous tracks," you dedicate more of your Mac's memory and energy to processing tracks—but you may experience a slight delay in hearing the sound when you play a MIDI instrument. "Minimum delay when playing instruments live" takes care of that delay, but may give GarageBand more trouble when you try to play back pieces with a lot of tracks.

Finally, the bottom of this dialog box presents a status line that indicates whether or not GarageBand is "seeing" any MIDI instruments that you've attached. It's a good troubleshooting resource when you're trying to record and aren't getting any response from your keyboard or other MIDI instrument.

Export

Use this panel to specify how you want your exported GarageBand masterpieces to look in iTunes. You can name the playlist that will collect your exports, and what composer and album name you want associated with them.

Advanced

All of the options on this panel involve solving GarageBand speed problems. By limiting the number of tracks using the first two pop-up menus, for example, you make the program set aside less memory for tracks that you have yet to create—memory that might be better used to play back the tracks you *do* have.

"Voices per instrument" is another trick that can help GarageBand play back complex pieces when the Mac is having trouble (see page 179).

Finally, the "Convert to Real Instrument" checkbox tells GarageBand that whenever you drag a green Software Instrument loop from the Loop browser into an empty area of the timeline, you want it converted into an identical sounding blue Real Instrument loop. You lose the ability to edit individual notes in it, but you've turned it into a region that's much easier for the Mac to play without choking.

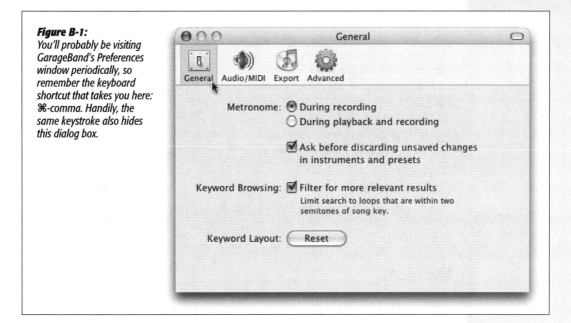

Figure B-1:
You'll probably be visiting GarageBand's Preferences window periodically, so remember the keyboard shortcut that takes you here: ⌘-comma. Handily, the same keystroke also hides this dialog box.

Shop for GarageBand Products

This isn't so much a command as it is a shameless marketing ploy. It opens your Web browser and opens a page on Apple's Web site that sells MIDI keyboards, instrument adapters, audio interface boxes, speakers, headphones, the Jam Pack, and other accessories.

Provide GarageBand Feedback

This command takes you to a Web form on Apple's site where you can register complaints, make suggestions, or gush enthusiastically about GarageBand.

Tip: Don't expect a personal reply from Steve Jobs.

Register GarageBand

This is a link to yet another Apple Web page. Registering GarageBand simply means giving Apple your contact information so you can access Apple's online support documents, receive upgrade notices, get special offers, and so on.

There's no penalty for *not* registering, by the way. Apple just wants to know more about who you are, so that it can offer you exciting new waves of junk mail.

Hide GarageBand, Hide Others, Show All

These aren't GarageBand's commands—they're Mac OS X's.

In any case, they determine which of the various programs running on your Mac are *visible* onscreen at any given moment.

The Hide Others command is probably the most popular of these three. It zaps away the windows of all other programs—including the Finder—so that the GarageBand window is the only one you see.

Tip: If you know this golden Mac OS X trick, you may never need to use the Hide Others command: To switch into GarageBand from another program, hold down the ⌘ and Option keys when clicking the GarageBand icon in the Dock. Doing so simultaneously brings GarageBand to the front *and* hides all other programs you have running, producing an uncluttered, distraction-free view of GarageBand.

Quit GarageBand

This command closes GarageBand. If you've worked on your project since the last time you used the Save command, the program gives you one last chance to save your work.

File Menu

These commands are pretty standard. You see them in word processors, painting programs—and music programs.

New

Creates a new, untitled GarageBand project file. (GarageBand first asks you to save your changes to the outgoing song, if necessary.) *Keyboard shortcut:* ⌘-N.

Open

Presents the Open dialog box, so that you can open an existing GarageBand project file on your hard drive. Once again, you'll be asked whether you want to save the changes to the open file. *Keyboard shortcut:* ⌘-O.

Close

Closes the project file you have open, after first inviting you to save any unsaved changes. At that point, you're technically still in GarageBand, which you can see from the menu bar—but whatever programs were "behind" GarageBand are now shining through the empty space where the window was. Don't be confused.

Save

This command preserves any changes you've made to your project, exactly as in a word processor or any other program. *Keyboard shortcut:* ⌘-S.

Save As

Use this command when you want to create a copy of the current GarageBand project, saved into a different folder location or with a different name. *Keyboard shortcut:* Shift-⌘-S.

Save as Archive

Ordinarily, a GarageBand project file includes only references to whatever loops you've used in the piece. It doesn't include the actual audio or MIDI data, which would make your file very large (they can be several megabytes each).

The trouble is, you may create a GarageBand piece using loops that you've downloaded from the Internet, or installed as part of the GarageBand Jam Pack—loops that other people don't have. This command creates a special version of the GarageBand file that includes *all* of the loops you used. Even though the resulting file takes up a lot of disk space, at least you know that it'll play back properly on anybody else's Mac.

Revert to Saved

GarageBand offers 30 levels of Undo, which lets you retrace your steps if you feel that your creative process has gone off track. But if you've really made a mess of things, you can use this command, which takes the file all the way back to the way it was the last time you used the Save command.

If the Revert to Original command is dimmed out, it's probably because you've just recently saved the document—or have never saved it.

Export to iTunes

As described at length in Chapter 8, this command is the shining portal that awaits at the end of almost every GarageBand workflow process. This is the command that unleashes your song, getting it out of a format that very few people have (GarageBand) and into iTunes, where you can convert it into a format that millions of people have (an MP3 file, a CD, and so on).

Edit Menu

As you would expect, the commands in the Edit menu help you move sections of your piece from one place to another. The standard Cut, Copy, and Paste commands operate on selected notes and regions as normal.

Undo

Where would this world be without Undo? In GarageBand, you even have a *multiple* Undo. Using this command (and its keyboard equivalent, ⌘-Z), you can reverse your last 30 actions, backing out of your bad decisions with no harm done. How nice to know that if you go too heavy on the reverb, delete an important performance, or rearrange your piece into incoherence, there's a quick and easy way out.

Redo

Redo (Shift-⌘-Z) lets you undo what you just undid. In other words, it reapplies the action you just reversed via the Undo command.

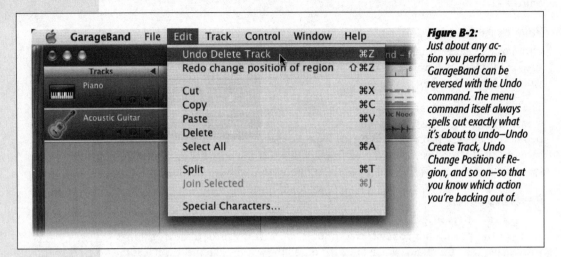

Figure B-2:
Just about any action you perform in GarageBand can be reversed with the Undo command. The menu command itself always spells out exactly what it's about to undo—Undo Create Track, Undo Change Position of Region, and so on—so that you know which action you're backing out of.

Cut, Copy, Paste

These commands work exactly the way they would in a word processor, only now you're editing regions in the timeline, notes in the Track Editor, or selected bits of Real Instrument regions in the Track Editor. You make a selection and then use Cut or Copy to bring it to your invisible Macintosh clipboard. Then you click elsewhere in the timeline and use the Paste command to deposit those notes or pieces of regions in a new location. *Keyboard shortcuts:* ⌘-X for cut, ⌘-C for Copy, ⌘-V for Paste.

Delete

This command removes the selected notes, regions, track, or Track Editor selection from the piece *without* placing it onto the Clipboard. *Keyboard shortcut:* Delete key.

Select All

This command behaves in different ways, depending on when you use it in Garage-Band.

- It selects all regions visible in the timeline, in all tracks.

- In the Track Editor, it selects all regions in the track, or (if only one region is highlighted in the timeline) all notes in the region.

Keyboard shortcut: ⌘-A.

Split

This command chops the selected region or regions in two at the location of the Playhead's vertical line. (Exactly which regions it splits has to do with which ones you selected first, by clicking or Shift-clicking.) *Keyboard shortcut:* ⌘-T, which is the same as the Split command in iMovie.

Join Selected

You can use this command to connect any two green Software Instrument regions, or any two purple Real Instrument regions, into a single unified region. (It doesn't work on blue Apple Loops.)

Join Selected is especially useful because it lets you combine regions into one, making them (it) easier to copy, paste, loop, and so on. *Keyboard shortcut:* ⌘-J.

Special Characters

This little item is a standard member of the Edit menu in many Mac OS X programs. It brings up the Character Palette, a little table of symbols (currency, mathematical, punctuation, and so on) from all of your fonts, making it easy to find and insert a particular symbol.

It has absolutely no relevance or use in GarageBand.

Track Menu

This menu, as you could have guessed, is all about manipulating tracks, those beloved horizontal parallel parking places for musical information.

Show Track Mixer/Hide Track Mixer

The track mixer is a little panel that slides out from the track headers. It contains controls for setting the track volume level and pan position (where the instrument seems to come from in the left-to-right stereo field). It also contains blinking level meters that help you avoid setting the volume level so high that distortion results.

Much more detail on the Track Mixer appears on page 140.

Keyboard shortcut: ⌘-Y.

Show Track Info/Hide Track Info

This command summons or dismisses the Track Info dialog box for the selected track, where you can change the instrument sound, icon, format (stereo/mono), or effects for the track.

Tip: Most of the time, it's easier to open this dialog box just by double-clicking the *track header* (where the track name appears).

Keyboard shortcut: ⌘-I. The same keystroke both opens and closes the dialog box.

New Track

Opens the New Track dialog box, so that you can specify which kind of track you want to create (Real Instrument or Software Instrument), which channels it should "listen to" when you record, whether or not you want the Monitor function on (which

APPENDIX B: GARAGEBAND, MENU BY MENU   **233**

passes the audio of your playing through the Mac speaker), and what icon you want to appear next to its name.

Keyboard shortcut: Option-⌘-N.

Delete Track

Removes the entire track from your project, complete with any music that it contains.

Keyboard shortcut: ⌘-Delete.

Duplicate Track

This command is slightly misleading. It creates a second track just beneath the selected one, containing the same instrument and effects settings—but *without* any of the musical material. (If you want to truly duplicate what was in the first track, you must Option-drag them downward into the new track, or use Copy and Paste.)

Keyboard shortcut: ⌘-D.

New Basic Track

Creates a new Real Instrument track, instantly and without the intrusion of any dialog box, with no effects applied. It's a great command when inspiration strikes, you're ready to record, and you really don't feel like making any choices in some dialog box.

Control Menu

The commands here are the only menu commands related to recording and editing—the meat of your GarageBand time.

Metronome

This command turns the steady clicking of the GarageBand metronome on or off. (Whether it plays only during recording, or during both playback and recording, depends on what you've selected in the GarageBand→Preferences→General dialog box.)

Keyboard shortcut: ⌘-U.

Count In

When a checkmark appears next to this menu command, GarageBand will count you in to a new recording by clicking off one measure (that is, four clicks in 4/4 time) before the recording actually starts to roll. The idea is to get you into the feeling and the tempo of the piece before you start playing. It's the software equivalent of your garage band drummer saying, "And-a one! Two! Three! Four!"

Snap to Grid

An underlying rhythm grid is everywhere in GarageBand, helping you to line up notes and regions with each other to keep the music in sync. You determine the value of this grid using the pop-up menu shown in Figure B-3. And you determine whether or not notes and regions snap into position with the grid lines by using this command. When a checkmark appears here, you'll find it impossible to drag notes or regions horizontally anywhere except aligned with a grid line. (When no checkmark appears, you're free to slide notes or regions horizontally anywhere you like.)

The Track Editor has its own grid pop-up menu, which controls how GarageBand *quantizes* selected notes (page 94), as well as the value of any new notes that you create by ⌘-clicking in the Track Editor.

Keyboard shortcut: ⌘-G.

Figure B-3:
Use this pop-up menu to specify the rhythmic unit of the grid lines that appear in the timeline and the Track Editor. Actually, as you can see here, the timeline and Track Editor each have their own Grid value pop-up menu.

Two Grid pop-up menus: One for the timeline, one for the Track Editor

Show Loop Browser/Hide Loop Browser

This command shows or hides the Loop browser at the bottom of the GarageBand window, the array of buttons or columns that help you find a prerecorded loop for use in your piece. It's the menu-bar equivalent of clicking the little eyeball icon at the lower-left corner of the GarageBand window.

Keyboard shortcut: ⌘-L.

Show Editor/Hide Editor

This command shows or hides the Track Editor at the bottom of the GarageBand window—the special editing window where the individual notes in a green Software Instrument region appear as horizontal bars, and blue or purple Real Instrument regions in a waveform graph. Using this menu bar command is the same as clicking the little pair-of-scissors button at the lower-left corner of the GarageBand window.

Keyboard shortcut: ⌘-E.

Window Menu

The Window menu is filled with all the standard Mac OS X window-manipulating commands.

Minimize

Collapses the GarageBand window into the Dock, in standard Mac OS X fashion. It's just like pressing ⌘-M or clicking the yellow Minimize button in the upper-left corner of any window.

Zoom

Enlarges any GarageBand window to fill your entire screen (although it's kind enough to avoid covering up your Dock). Choosing this command is the same as clicking the green Zoom button in the upper-left corner of the GarageBand window. (You'll probably want to use this feature every time you start up GarageBand, because you'll need all the room you can get.)

If you choose the Zoom command (or click the Zoom button) again, the window shrinks back to its original proportions.

Keyboard

Opens up the beloved GarageBand onscreen keyboard which, in a pinch, you can use to record notes by clicking the little piano keys with your mouse.

Keyboard shortcut: ⌘-K.

Bring All to Front

Every now and then, the windows of two different Mac OS X programs get shuffled together, so that one GarageBand window is sandwiched between, say, two Safari windows. This command brings all your GarageBand windows to the front so they're not being blocked by any other program's windows. (Clicking GarageBand's icon on the Dock does the same thing.)

Help Menu

You know all too well that GarageBand comes with no user manual—that's why you're reading this book! What official Apple documentation you do get appears in this menu.

GarageBand Help

Choosing it (or pressing ⌘-?) opens Apple's Help Viewer program, which provides dozens of many articles documenting the various GarageBand features. It gives you a searchable reference at your disposal if you forget how to do something (or lose this book).

Keyboard Shortcuts

This is really just another link into the GarageBand Help system, but a particularly valuable one. It takes you to a table showing more than 50 keyboard shortcuts in GarageBand. (They're also listed in Appendix C.)

The GarageBand Keyboard Shortcuts

The mouse is for suckers. When there's no time to lose, efficiency fanatics don't waste calories lumbering up to those menus. They memorize the keyboard shortcuts instead—at least for the commands they use a lot.

Navigating GarageBand

Function	Keystroke
Play/Pause	Space bar
Jump to start	Home or Z
Jump to end	End or Option-Z
Jump back one measure	Left arrow
Skip forward one measure	Right arrow
Jump back one screenful	Page up
Skip forward one screenful	Page down
Zoom in	Control-Left arrow
Zoom out	Control-Right arrow

Manipulating Tracks

New track	⌘-Option-N
Delete selected track	Option-Delete
Select previous/next track	Up arrow/Down arrow
Mute/unmute selected track	M
Solo/unsolo selected track	S
Show/hide track-volume track	A

Show/hide master track   ⌘-B
Show/hide Track Info dialog box ⌘-I

Recording

Start/stop recording   R
Cycling on/off   C
Metronome on/off   ⌘-U
Show onscreen keyboard   ⌘-K

Editing and Arranging

Undo   ⌘-Z
Redo   Shift-⌘-Z
Cut   ⌘-X
Copy   ⌘-C
Paste   ⌘-V
Delete   Delete
Select all   ⌘-A
Split region at Playhead   ⌘-T
Join selected (regions)   ⌘-J
Snap to grid (on/off)   ⌘-G
Show/hide track mixer   ⌘-R
Show/hide Track Editor   ⌘-E
Show/hide loop browser   ⌘-L
Master volume up/down   ⌘-up arrow, ⌘-down arrow

File and Window Management

New   ⌘-N
Open   ⌘-O
Close   ⌘-W
Save   ⌘-S
Save as   Shift-⌘-S
GarageBand Preferences   ⌘-comma (,)
Hide GarageBand   ⌘-H
Hide other applications   Option-⌘- H
Quit GarageBand   ⌘-Q
GarageBand Help   ⌘-question mark (?)

Index

Index

GARAGEBAND: THE MISSING MANUAL

Colophon

This book was written and edited in Microsoft Word X on various Macs.

The screenshots were captured with Ambrosia Software's Snapz Pro X *(www. ambrosiasw.com)*. Adobe Photoshop CS and Macromedia Freehand MX *(www.adobe. com)* were called in as required for touching them up.

The book was designed and laid out in Adobe InDesign 3.0 on a PowerBook G3, Power Mac G4, and Power Mac G5. The fonts used include Formata (as the sans-serif family) and Minion (as the serif body face). To provide the and ⌘ symbols, custom fonts were created using Macromedia Fontographer.

The book was then generated as an Adobe Acrobat PDF file for proofreading, indexing, and final transmission to the printing plant.